PERSPECTIVES on EMBODIMENT

The Intersections of Nature and Culture

EDITED BY

GAIL WEISS & HONI FERN HABER

ROUTLEDGE
NEW YORK and LONDON

Published in 1999 by
Routledge
29 West 35th Street
New York, NY 10001

Published in Great Britain by
Routledge
11 New Fetter Lane
London EC4P 4EE

Copyright © 1999 by Routledge
Text Design by Debora Hilu

Printed in the United States of America on acid-free paper.

10 9 8 7 6 5 4 3 2 1

Library of Congress Cataloging-in-Publication Data

Perspectives on embodiment : the intersections of nature and culture / Gail
Weiss and Honi Fern Haber, editors
    p.   cm.
    Papers "inspired by an NEH summer Seminar on Embodiment ... held at
the University of California, Santa Cruz in the summer of 1994"—Introd.
    Includes bibliographical references and index.
    ISBN 0-415-91585-6 (hardcover : alk. paper). — ISBN 0-415-91586-4
(pbk. : alk. paper)
    1. Body image—Congresses. 2. Body schema—Congresses.
I. Weiss, Gail, 1959–   .   II. Haber, Honi Fern, 1958–1995.
BF697.5.B63P47   1999
128'.6—dc21   98–22730
                                                        CIP

CONTENTS

Part 3. Rewriting the History of the Body

For Honi

PREFACE

Honi Fern Haber, the co-editor of this anthology, died of cancer on December 22, 1995. She was thirty-seven years old. Honi was granted tenure in the Philosophy Department at the University of Colorado, Denver the spring before she died, and a library has been established in the Philosophy Department there in her name. This book is the last work to which her name will be attached, and its publication was very important to her. In fact, this anthology was her idea. She conceived the project during the 1994 National Endowment for the Humanities (NEH) Summer Institute we both participated in, entitled, "Embodiment: The Intersection between Nature and Culture" at the University of California, Santa Cruz.

Communication among members of the Institute was greatly facilitated by an embodiment e-mail list that NEH set up for us. Honi and I continued the friendship we had begun at the Institute on e-mail, and she asked me to co-edit the volume with her. It was through the e-mail list that we learned of the death of one of the guest speakers at the Institute, Professor Samuel Todes (Philosophy, Northwestern University), shortly after the summer was over. I remember our surprise over his death; none of us, including Sam himself, had realized that he was already dying of cancer during those wonderful summer days.

Little did we know, Sam's death was itself a harbinger of Honi's own cancer diagnosis a few months later. At first, and for a long time afterwards, there was hope that Honi's cancer was treatable. She underwent chemotherapy for many months and even managed to attend The International Association of Philosophy and Literature (IAPL) Conference at Villanova University in May 1995 where, with John Carvalho's help, we had organized a session for contributors to our volume to present short versions of their papers. When I saw her there, she was her usual buoyant, defiant self, despite the fact that she had lost a substantial amount of weight and was unable to taste the food that she ate. This was because her cancer was located in her throat and neck and her mouth had been scorched by the chemotherapy, leaving her desire for good food intact, but making her unable to enjoy it since everything she ate tasted burnt despite its tantalizing smell. Nonetheless, Honi was jubilant at feeling strong enough to come to a professional conference, and she was hopeful that the chemotherapy had succeeded in eradicating all traces of the cancer.

Two months after IAPL, Honi sent me an e-mail message. Since we were in regular touch with one another about the volume, I was hardly prepared for what it contained. Characteristically, she began by inquiring about me and then about the status of the essays we had solicited for the volume. Only then did she let "the bomb" drop. Her doctors had discovered another tumor, requiring another round of chemotherapy as well as the removal of her jaw. Here is what she said:

> Right now I feel really strong and defiant about all of this. I am going to fucking fight this thing! And I know that working helps me to get through this, so I am hoping that I can still do whatever is necessary for this project. It looks like I would be having chemo starting the week of the 20th [of July] and then I believe it would be 4 weeks until I have the surgery. After that I can't really say what I will be like. And in fact, I don't really know how I will react to chemo, some people get really sick and some people don't. But I will work as long as I can.

Even at this point, Honi was still hoping to write her own essay for the volume, a hope that was cut short by her rapid deterioration after the jaw surgery. This was her intention, in her own words:

> I was planning on revising a paper I have on the politics of cross-dressing for our volume, but now I am thinking that I want to write about this experience. I want to write in a personal and direct tone, which is usually not done in philosophy, but I think it is important, especially when we are talking about embodiment, to talk about real embodied experience. So I am hoping we can accommodate a less "academic" piece, and in fact writing style is an issue which is important to feminist philosophy, and I will talk about that too. Anyway, this is what I am planning to do, but it will need to be written . . . SO maybe this experience will give me the courage to find a new voice . . . SOMETHING positive HAS to come out of it!

I was overwhelmed by this message, by the despair so clearly expressed and dismissed, and by her incredible determination to focus on the future, and what she still hoped to accomplish. I encouraged her to write the paper. Honi, as those who also knew her can attest, never wanted sympathy. Indeed, for a long time she did not want the contributors to the volume to know about her progressively worsening situation. Eventually, however, she decided to send an e-mail message to our embodiment list. The jaw surgery and additional round of chemotherapy had still not succeeded in eradicating the cancer and she was down to her final hope—a radical drug treatment program at Sloan-Kettering Hospital in New York. I think she figured that it was better to take the opportunity to speak in her own words about her condition than to have us all get a message from someone else, as had happened with Sam Todes. This was her message:

> My body, that real, fleshy, oozing body, is very much with me these days. All philosophical dilemmas about it have been resolved in like manner to Berkeley's rock.
>
> Many, but not all of you, know that I have been battling head and neck cancer. This is usually a disease that attacks tobacco chewing, old alcoholics…sounds just like me eh? So there is no reason why this should be happening to me, or why it should be so aggressive. I just underwent another major surgery in August and it is back again…so now I am off to Sloan-Kettering in New York to see about some experimental protocol and I really do not know what the future holds for me.
>
> I did want to let everyone know that despite all that had been happening the embodiment book is proceeding smoothly and the articles are being re-read by readers at Routledge. With the exception of a couple of pieces all the essays are in and they look quite wonderful. I am really excited about this collection! I wanted to state publicly how extraordinary Gail Weiss has been in taking up the slack whenever I had to be dealing with medical issues. This collection really has a fairy godmother, and it is she. Whatever the future holds for me, and whether or not I am able to see this project out, you can all be assured that Gail will see it to the shelves. Don't let her have a breakdown though. Please let her know if any of you could volunteer some time to help her should she need it.
>
> Don't get me wrong, I am not checking out yet (whatever the doctors say), and my grubby fingerprints may in fact be all over the final version of our book! But I did want to tell you, you know what they say about living a healthy life and eating your greens, etc? Well I tell you: Throw the broccoli overboard, light the charcoal and that stogie, and get out those shot glasses!

The end of the message was classic Honi: "Hope this note finds everyone well and productive. And oh, the good news is, I did get that early tenure!"

Re-reading these lines, I am overcome with conflicting emotions: grief that she is no longer here to see that the volume is indeed a reality, that she is no longer able to write and to teach and to spend time with family and friends; amazement at her incredible sense of humor and at how she was able to use this humor as a weapon against the debilitating effects of her illness; and, above all, admiration at her remarkable courage and will to live. When her husband Larry Scott called me to say that she had died, he told me that she looked as beautiful before her death as she had looked the day he married her. "You see, Honi," I wanted to tell her, "you need not have worried about being radically disfigured after your surgery. Your beauty always shone through."

For those of us who cared for her, Honi's boldness and stubborn resistance were an intrinsic part of that beauty, a subversively and startlingly feminine beauty that she exemplified through and through. Roger King, an old friend and colleague, best summed up Honi's distinctive personality in his obituary for her memorial service: "She was a meticulous scholar, yet refused to cloister herself exclusively in the life of the mind. She was passionate, energetic, and wild."

Honi Haber's life, as well as her death, offers a perspective on embodiment that is rarely acknowledged in academia outside of feminist circles. It is my hope that Honi's moving articulation of her own resistance to cancer will help to remind us that embodiment is, above all, a concrete, bodily affair, and that it is an experience that we can and must share together.

Gail Weiss
Summer 1998

ACKNOWLEDGMENTS

All anthologies are collaborative enterprises and this one is no exception. Not only did Honi and I collaborate in selecting the essays that comprise this volume, but all of the contributors played a crucial, ongoing role in determining the final shape of the book itself. Since Honi became seriously ill quite soon after this project commenced, she was unable to participate in many of the decisions that needed to be made in putting this collection together. The solicitude of the contributors that I experienced in this very difficult situation, their patience with the inevitable delays that resulted in the actual publication of the volume, and their continued offers of help in moving the project forward, were all greatly appreciated.

One of the most positive aspects of editing this volume for me has been the number of friendships I have made through the process. Although all of the contributors to the volume were either participants or staff of the 1994 National Endowment of the Humanities Institute on "Embodiment: The Intersection of Nature and Culture" at the University of California, Santa Cruz, I did not have the chance at that time to get to know many of them as well as I did later through our frequent correspondence regarding their essays and the volume itself. I feel incredibly fortunate to have been able to work with such fine scholars and wonderful people. Special thanks go to the two directors of the Institute: to David Hoy whom I frequently consulted when I was experiencing difficulties of one sort or another with the production process, and to Bert Dreyfus who was extremely diligent in responding to my specific queries.

Honi Haber's husband, Larry Scott, deserves special mention for his willingness to read the Preface in advance, and for his dedication to seeing this final publication of Honi's get to press. He and I had a wonderful time in Denver looking over pictures of Honi to pick one for the Preface that would best capture her maverick spirit and we were both happy with the result. I know that Honi would also have thanked her parents, brother, friends, and colleagues for supporting her during her final months battling cancer, and that she was especially appreciative of her department chair, Mitchell Aboulafia's willingness to do whatever he could to lessen her inevitable sense of guilt over not being able to fulfill all of her academic responsibilities as her health declined.

Acknowledgments

I, too, would like to thank my family, friends, and colleagues for supporting my work on this volume. My husband, Sam Brooke, deserves a
medal for seeing me through both this project and the simultaneous completion of *Body Images: Embodiment as Intercorporeality* (Routledge 1999),
and for assuming much of the burden of the care of our five small children
(the last two of whom were born after this project commenced) so that I
could devote myself to making yet another pressing deadline. Working in
such a congenial department has provided me with many colleagues to
turn to when I needed advice or just someone to vent to when I was feeling overwhelmed. Anna Goldstein was enormously helpful in organizing
the contributors' biographical statements and in tracking down missing
information. I thank all of them for providing me with encouragement
and a stimulating intellectual atmosphere which emblematizes the very
best of what the academy has to offer.

On both Honi's and my own behalf, I would like to conclude by thank-
ing Maureen MacGrogan, our initial editor for this project, Gayatri
Patnaik, who proved a wonderful editorial successor, T.J. Mancini, and the
production staff at Routledge for guiding this volume so skillfully through
the publication process. I am also indebted once again to Valerie Hazel for
her expert work on the index. Their confidence in the volume matched our
own, and the book could not have been produced without their arduous
work behind the scenes.

INTRODUCTION

GAIL WEISS AND HONI FERN HABER

Today, the body is, in many ways, more visible than it has ever been. From women's clothing fashions that continually seek new ways to exhibit flesh to a veritable explosion of both popular and academic writing on the body, the body is increasingly being identified as central to our sense of agency as well as a distinctive cultural artifact in its own right. Contemporary critical explorations of the body cut across disciplines and have become occasions for questioning the rigidity of disciplinary boundaries themselves. This current, interdisciplinary discourse on the body is producing its own corporeal effects in both theory and practice.

The present collection was inspired by a National Endowment for the Humanities summer institute on embodiment directed by Professors Hubert Dreyfus and David Hoy held at the University of California, Santa Cruz in 1994. This volume is itself indebted to the rich, interdisciplinary discussions on embodiment that occurred during those eight weeks, not only within the seminar itself, but also in our coffee breaks, afternoon reading groups, and evening get-togethers. The essays included here offer several different perspectives on what it means to be embodied in the late twentieth century. Despite differences in approach, methodology, subject matter, and style, these perspectives are united in their attempt to break down the binary opposition between nature and culture that has all too often been symbolized and reinforced by an association of the body with nature and consciousness with culture.

The tradition of Western metaphysics has been sadly negligent in its treatment of the body, and has tended either to view the body as part of our "animal" nature or, in accordance with a Cartesian approach, has treated it merely as a physical mechanism. Much of the recent work that focuses on the body attempts to undermine this tradition's neglect and devaluation of the body and, at the same time, reveal the consequences of that neglect and devaluation for contemporary understandings of the body. In the process of critiquing philosophy's own negligence regarding the body, the very expression "the body" has become problematized, and is increasingly supplanted by the term "embodiment." The move from one expression to another corresponds directly to a shift from viewing the body as a nongendered, prediscursive phenomenon that plays a central role in perception, cognition, action, and nature to a *way* of living or inhabiting the world through one's acculturated body.

Maurice Merleau-Ponty stands out as a notable exception to the Western tradition's neglect of the body. His understanding of the body as the subject, rather than the object of perception, seeks to overcome the practical and theoretical limitations of a metaphysical mind/body dualism. In their essay, "The Challenge of Merleau-Ponty's Phenomenology of Embodiment for Cognitive Science," Hubert and Stuart Dreyfus explicate two central, but rarely discussed, notions in Merleau-Ponty's *Phenomenology of Perception*, namely, **intentional arc** and **maximum grip**. Dreyfus and Dreyfus argue that if one tries to implement Merleau-Ponty's understanding of skill acquisition in a neural network, one finds that in order to learn to generalize input/output pairs to new situations the way human beings do, a network needs to share crucial aspects of the human-body structure.

Mark Johnson, a philosopher who shares the Dreyfus's conviction that cognitive science must be informed by an embodied perspective, has been instrumental in developing a new approach that he terms "embodied cognitive science." In his essay, "Embodied Reason," Johnson argues that reasoning develops out of everyday, bodily activities and is schematically structured through basic bodily metaphors. Together, these two essays help to chart a course for future research programs in cognitive science.

In "Affordances: An Ecological Approach to First Philosophy," John Sanders employs an embodied perspective to develop what he calls a metaphysics of affordances. More specifically, Sanders argues that psychologist J. J. Gibson's affordance theory, a theory that maintains that what is perceived is deeply a function of the kind of creature I am and the kind of body I have, is compatible with a holistic ecological approach that considers organisms in interaction with their environment. Considered jointly, Sanders claims these perspectives provide a way of talking about the world that harmonizes with human experience, contemporary physics, and contemporary ecological approaches to perceptual and developmental psychology.

Thomas Csordas offers an historical account of the increasing attention paid to embodiment in contemporary anthropological theory. In his essay, "Embodiment and Cultural Phenomenology," he argues that the body often remains implicit in anthropological theories of culture, which historically have utilized the discourse of symbols, meanings, knowledge, practices, customs, or traits. Csordas explores what anthropology can offer to the development of an interdisciplinary cultural phenomenology of embodiment through an examination of current anthropological literature on the expression of emotion, the experience of pain, ritual healing, language, dietary practices, and political violence.

The essays just mentioned comprise part two of this volume, and collectively they reveal the foundational role the phenomenon of embodiment can and must play in the further development of the human sciences. Part one addresses some of the distinctive, corporeal challenges that human beings face on a daily basis, challenges that result from what might be called the intersubjective politics of embodiment. The first essay, David Hoy's "Critical Resistance: Foucault and Bourdieu," traces the body as a site of ethical resistance to social domination through the work of Nietzsche, Foucault, and Bourdieu. Hoy argues that the body can retain a sense of agency, despite its ongoing subjection to what Foucault has called "disciplinary regimes." Indeed, although Nietzsche, Foucault, and Bourdieu all emphasize the power of the hegemonic sociopolitical forces that continually shape our own subjectivity, Hoy shows that these three thinkers nonetheless open up a space for bodily resistance that makes alternative discourses possible.

In "The Soul of America: Whiteness and the Disappearing of Bodies in the Progressive Era," Tracy Fessenden shows how late nineteenth- and early twentieth-century treatises ranging from the explicitly racist literature of the Ku Klux Klan to the socially "progressive" discourses of academicians and social reformers, systematically equated racial bodies with racial souls, white skin with "Anglo-Saxon ideas." Fessenden argues that the "unconscious" racism of an intellectual elite that included a number of ideologically diverse reformers—e.g., Margaret Sanger, Washington Gladden, Charlotte Perkins Gilman, Madison Bell Grant—not only reinforced but provided spiritual justification for the Ku Klux Klan's vision of a physically all-white America. She concludes by raising the issue of whether contemporary discussions of "multiculturalism" may not also harbor hidden racist agendas that have yet to be acknowledged and addressed.

Gail Weiss's essay, "The Abject Borders of the Body Image," and Sean O'Connell's essay, "Claiming One's Identity: A Constructivist/Narrativist Approach," offer two different perspectives on how a sense of self is constructed through simultaneous processes of incorporation and exclusion. The former essay draws upon Kristeva's account of abjection in *Powers of Horror*, tracing the formation of the body image through that which fails to be included within it, namely, those abjected body fluids, parts, and processes that actively shape the body image through the force of their exclusion. Focusing on the "invisible" corporeal effects of racial and gender stereotypes, Weiss argues that the development of a "normal" (nondistorted) body image both requires and legitimates techniques of bodily distortion, a process which forces us to reexamine the criteria that distinguish "normal" from "abnormal" bodies.

O'Connell's concern is to show how it is possible to affirm a given sexual identity (e.g., a gay identity) while at the same time acknowledging that

that identity is socially constructed and open to change. O'Connell develops this position by reading Ricoeur's narrative conception of identity through Butler's description of sex as a regulatory ideal materialized in the body through normatively governed reiterative practices. He appeals to Ricoeur's notion of "attestation" to explain how one might authentically assume a given identity in a manner that does not preclude other identifications.

The final section of this book, *Rewriting the History of the Body*, begins with an essay by historian Martin Jay. In an earlier, major work entitled, *Downcast Eyes: The Denigration of Vision in Twentieth-Century French Thought*, Jay explores how the twentieth-century French critique of ocularcentrism exhibited in the works of Bergson, Bataille, Sartre, Merleau-Ponty, Lacan, Althusser, Foucault, Barthes, Derrida, Irigaray, Levinas, and Lyotard situates contemporary understandings of vision, the visual, the eye, the gaze, blindness, scopic regimes, desires, and linguistic experience. Jay's contribution to this volume, "Returning the Gaze: The American Response to the French Critique of Ocularcentrism," explores the impact of these French theorists on American art criticism in the second half of the twentieth century.

Charles Shepherdson's essay, "The Epoch of the Body: Need and Demand in Kojève and Lacan," examines psychoanalysis's repudiation of both naturalist and historicist accounts of the body and sexual difference. In particular, Shepherdson claims that psychoanalysis offers an account of the Symbolic order that cannot be assessed through either biomedical or sociohistorical models. Through its contestation of both naturalism and historicism, he maintains, Freudian psychoanalysis developed its own theoretical specificity and unique historical position. More specifically, Shepherdson argues that sexuality cannot be understood psychoanalytically in terms of the opposition between a biological sex and historical gender. Addressing the psychoanalytic understanding of sexuality through the "epochal" question of sexual difference helps to clarify why psychoanalysis must be critically interpreted on its own terms. Shepherdson begins this work of interpretation through an analysis of the relationship between need, demand, and the drive in Kojève and Lacan.

Kevin O'Neill's essay, "Disciplining the Dead," explores how memorial photographs (i.e., photographs of the newly dead) reveal the meaning of death and its relation to the work of the living in nineteenth-century America. O'Neill concentrates on the significance of changes in photographic representations of the dead in the period between 1843 and 1890. These representations moved from portraits of the dead to depictions of a scene of mourning which included the dead family member. O'Neill suggests that this transition can be explained in part by the emerging presence of "funerary professionals," who began to control not only the dead, but the ways in which photographers could depict them. Through the establishment of this new disciplinary regime, both life and death were reconceptualized in mutually exclusive terms.

Yet another form of control over bodies is discussed by Thomas Tierney in "The Preservation and Ownership of the Body." Here Tierney examines the relation between the classic liberal notions of self-ownership and self-preservation, and their manifestation in the health institutions and literature of the early modern period. After establishing this historical configuration, he focuses on its recent disruptions by contemporary medical techniques such as gene cloning and organ transplantation. Tierney concludes with a critical examination of recent legal and bioethical debates that throw traditional assumptions about the subject and the importance of self-preservation into doubt and disorder.

Together, these essays indeed offer a variety of perspectives on embodiment. Read side by side, they reveal the endless complexity and richness of our corporeal life. Rather than sum up a given field of study or even delineate its boundaries, the very diversity of this anthology seeks to promote new perspectives on embodiment and new ways of thinking about bodies. To do this, as these essays show, we must look back to previous traditions and normative practices, forward to the future actualization of what are as yet only theoretical possibilities, and, most of all, we must keep our focus on the present, the temporal dimension that alone allows us to incorporate both the lessons we learn from the past and the hopes we have for the future.

PART ONE

Identifying
Bodies
and
Bodily
Identifications

ONE

CRITICAL RESISTANCE: FOUCAULT AND BOURDIEU

DAVID COUZENS HOY

Is the body invariant across history and culture, or is it the product of social constitution? With the exception of Nietzsche, canonical modern philosophers since Descartes usually take the first alternative for granted, if they think about the body at all. In contrast, recent French thinkers like Michel Foucault and Pierre Bourdieu make strong cases for taking the second hypothesis more seriously. Foucault and Bourdieu see subjectivity as extensively constructed by social and historical factors that are below the level of consciousness and thus less transparent to phenomenological introspection. They show to an even greater extent than their phenomenological precursor, Maurice Merleau-Ponty, that much of our comportment is already built into our bodies in ways that we do not and perhaps cannot attend to explicitly.

Foucault is, of course, directly influenced by Nietzsche. Foucault adapts not only the hypothesis that the body is entirely malleable over the course of history, but also Nietzsche's genealogical method for investigating this hypothesis. For both Foucault and Bourdieu the philosophical methods of their time were inadequate for the task of investigating embodied social practices. The phenomenological and structuralist methods were too unhistorical to do justice to the radical historicity of the body, and the dialectical method was too mechanistic and eschatological. Foucault prefers Nietzsche's genealogical method for writing "effective" history precisely because it

> places within a process of development everything considered immortal in humanity. We believe that feelings are immutable, but every sentiment, particularly the noblest and most disinterested, has a history. . . . We believe, in any event, that the body obeys the exclusive laws of physiology and that it escapes the influence of history, but this too is false. The body is molded by a great many distinct regimes; it is broken down by the rhythms of work, rest, and holidays; it is poisoned by food or values, through eating habits or moral laws; it constructs resistances. "Effective"

history differs from traditional history in being without constants. *Nothing in humans—not even their body—is sufficiently stable to serve as the basis for self-recognition or for understanding others.*[1]

So Foucault and Nietzsche are often characterized as holding that the body is, to use a current but problematic phrase that I shall be calling into question, "socially constructed." But this is only part of their view. Both Nietzsche and Foucault also see the body as the basis of our being, a basis that has been covered up by the intellectualist philosophical tradition.

In this critical assessment of the Cartesian tradition they are joined by Bourdieu. As a sociologist Bourdieu is more interested in persistence and continuity, in contrast to Foucault, who emphasizes transience and discontinuity. But even more than Foucault, Bourdieu sees comportment as predominantly configured by the social structures (the "habitus") and bodily orientation (or "hexis") that individuals acquire through their upbringing in a particular culture or class. "Bodily hexis," says Bourdieu both in *Esquisse d'une théorie de la pratique* (1977) and in *Le sens pratique* (1980), "is political mythology realized, *em-bodied*, turned into a permanent disposition, a durable way of standing, speaking, walking, and thereby of feeling and thinking."[2] In the earlier work Bourdieu adds (probably more strongly than he would today), "[t]he principles em-bodied in this way are placed beyond the grasp of consciousness, and hence cannot be touched by voluntary, deliberate transformation, cannot even be made explicit. . . ."[3]

At the same time, however, the recourse to embodiment in Nietzsche, Foucault, and Bourdieu is not a reductionism to the biological. While the term *embodiment* certainly suggests that there is a biological dimension to comportment, it is not a term that refers directly to the biological phenomenon independently of related concepts and of cultural context. "Body" may seem like an essence, or like what philosophers call a natural-kind term (like "water," "heat," or "gold"). But I take these French thinkers to be understanding the body as more akin to "money," or "love," or "power," or "justice." These terms designate social phenomena that are certainly real, but that depend on their concepts and culture and that are not independent natural kinds.[4]

The particular difficulty that I want to address in comparing these theories of embodiment concerns their normative dimension. These are not simply theories of how the body is *formed*, but they also imply critically that the social construction of the body *deforms* it. There are some obvious objections, however, that need to be discussed. If there is nothing natural to the body, then how could one say that it has been deformed? How could any social construction be assessed as better or worse than any other? How could domination even be identified as such? Furthermore, if conscious agents are powerless to change or resist their acculturated understanding of how to comport themselves, of what value is the sociological or genealogical effort to bring this process of bodily construction to light?

These questions show how problematic the hypothesis of the historicity of the body can be. In this essay I will be concerned with the serious ethical and political risks involved in asserting the social and historical malleability of the body. In particular, I will be investigating whether Foucault and Bourdieu can steer safely between the dangers of determinism and voluntarism while also avoiding fatalism and relativism. Given that both theorists are often accused of portraying individual agents as powerless and ineffective in bringing about social transformation, I will be working toward a conclusion about whether their theories of embodiment are internally consistent with their attempts to account for the emancipatory possibility of critical resistance to domination.

FOUCAULT

To set up the problem more carefully, let me first look at Foucault as one way of working out how there could be a history of the body at the same time as the body is asserted to be the basis of our being. Foucault clearly derives his understanding of the critical potential of genealogy from Nietzsche. In "Nietzsche, Genealogy, History" Foucault sees the task of genealogical, critical histories as the double one of exposing both "a body totally imprinted by history and the process of history's destruction of the body" (FR 83). Note that historical forces are said simultaneously not only to shape but also to destroy the body. But if the body is always already *in* history, if there is already a history of the body, was there ever anything the body was *before* history and that is now destroyed? Or is what gets destroyed never natural, but only the destruction of some previous destruction?

Hubert Dreyfus and Paul Rabinow have seen this problem in their book on Foucault. Insofar as the body is the basis to which genealogy ties its interpretations, the body should become the basis for the *critical* thrust of genealogy.[5] They are not convinced, however, that Foucault explains adequately *how* the body functions as the basis of critique and resistance. One of the critical questions about Foucault with which they conclude their book raises the question of whether Foucault has not paid too high a price by abandoning Merleau-Ponty's phenomenological method in favor of Nietzsche's genealogical method.

> Is the main philosophic task to give a content to Merleau-Ponty's analysis of *le corps propre*? Or is such an attempt which finds ahistorical and

cross-cultural structures in the body misdirected? If there are such struc-tures can one appeal to them without returning to naturalism? *Is one of the bases for resistance to bio-power to be found in the body?* Can the body be totally transformed by disciplinary techniques? Merleau-Ponty sees the body as having *a telos* towards rationality and explicitness; if he is correct how is it that power and organizational rationality are so infrequently linked in other cultures? If, on the other hand, power and rationality are not grounded in the body's need to get a maximum grip on the world, what is the relation between the body's capacities and power? (MF 206; emphasis added)

Dreyfus and Rabinow see Foucault as somewhere between Nietzsche and Merleau-Ponty. From Nietzsche, Foucault has learned about the mal-leability of the body, but they find Foucault "elusive" about whether the body is entirely malleable (MF 111). The reason for this elusiveness is, on their interpretation, that Foucault is also drawn to Merleau-Ponty's cross-cultural, ahistorical bodily constants like up-down asymmetry, size and brightness constancy in perception as well as social constancy in response to gestures, facial expression, and sexual signification. But although Foucault has learned from Merleau-Ponty about knowers being embodied, Foucault wants to add the historical and cultural dimensions of the body's situatedness that Merleau-Ponty ignores (MF 166). They then suggest that following Merleau-Ponty would give Foucault the lived body as a position from which to criticize the practices of manipulation and forma-tion that have also conditioned the investigator: "If the lived body is *more* than the result of the disciplinary technologies that have been brought to bear upon it, it would perhaps provide a position from which to criticize these practices, and maybe even a way to account for the tendency towards rationalization and the tendency of this tendency to hide itself" (MF 167; emphasis added). The problem they see is that Foucault never actually specifies this "more" and has "remained silent" about what are the bodily invariants that would be needed to ground this critique (MF 112).

This critique of Foucault's silence about invariants would be devastating if invariants were the only way to fill out the "more" that the body must be for it to supply the point of resistance to the total reshaping of the body through bio-power. I would like to suggest two responses to that critique. The first is a counter-criticism and the second is a more constructive response.

The counter-criticism is simply the negative point that even if there are bodily invariants, they would not be all that is necessary to make an appeal to the body as the basis for critique and resistance. It is not necessary for Foucault to deny that there are invariants. Surely all human beings, what-ever their culture or time, have felt pain. The more interesting question is how they have interpreted the experience of pain. And maybe the experience of pain is so conditioned by the cultural-historical interpretations of it that there is little more that can be said about it than that it is generally aversive. The point is that invariance need not be denied altogether, but the very universality of such invariants may be so thin as to make them uninteresting, or too thin to answer the more interesting critical questions. So even if there are bodily universals, and Foucault need not deny that there are, these universals may be too thin to serve as the basis of the more concrete criticisms and resistances.

Thus, in describing his method of doing the "history of systems of thought," Foucault clarifies what he means by "experience" (which comes close to Merleau-Ponty's lived body but with the historical-cultural dimensions added) and insists that he is not denying that there might be universal structures involved in experiences, even if experiences are always singular:

> Singular forms of experience may perfectly well harbor universal structures; they may well not be independent from the concrete determinations of social existence. However, neither those determinations nor those structures can allow for experiences (that is, for understandings of a certain type, for rules of a certain form, for certain modes of consciousness of oneself and others) except through thought. . . . [T]his thought has a historicity which is proper to it. That it should have this historicity does not mean it is deprived of all universal form, but instead that the putting into play of these universal forms is itself historical (FR 335).

So Foucault is insisting that the universals by themselves do not determine how they are experienced (or interpreted) concretely. Correlatively, they cannot be the exclusive basis of criticism and resistance, since how they are embodied is also crucial, and criticism must also reveal how these embodied experiences are *transformable*:

> There is a third and final principle implied by this enterprise [of Foucault's "history of thought"]: an awareness that criticism—understood as analysis of the historical conditions which bear on the creation of links to truth, to rules, and to the self—does not mark out impassable boundaries or describe closed systems; it brings to light *transformable* singularities. These transformations could not take place except by means of a working of thought upon itself; that is the principle of the history of thought as critical activity (FR 335–36; emphasis added).

Foucault thus construes his own genealogical enterprise as an effective form of critical resistance.

Beyond this defensive line of response, however, lies a second, more constructive line of response. There is another sense in which the body is "more" than any particular way in which it has been "socially constructed."

If the body can be shown to have been lived differently historically (through genealogy), or to be lived differently culturally (through ethnography), then the body can be seen to be "more" than what it now has become, even if this "more" is not claimed to be "universal," or "biological," or "natural." The contrast alone will not make us change, of course, but it will open the possibility of change. We will not be able to go back to the past or to step out of our culture entirely, but we may be able to find the resources in ourselves to save ourselves from the destructive tendencies that the contrast reveals.

To explain this constructive response in more detail would require a lengthy discussion of Foucault's historical studies. Let me gesture briefly toward two well-known examples from Foucault's work that come to mind: (1) his study of the normalization that occurs when "docile bodies" are shaped by disciplinary power (as depicted in *Discipline and Punish*), and (2) his later genealogy of ethics. These examples bring out the point that only when genealogy can show the body to have been *destroyed* by historical forces does genealogy become effective, *critical* history in Nietzsche's sense, but without appeal to a priori principles or universal invariants. As Foucault explains in "What Is Enlightenment?," criticism will take a different form when it adopts the hypothesis of historicity instead of the assumption of invariance:

> [C]riticism is no longer going to be practiced in the search for formal structures with universal value, but rather as a historical investigation into the events that have led us to constitute ourselves and to recognize ourselves as subjects of what we are doing, thinking, saying. . . . And this critique will be genealogical in the sense that it will not deduce from the form of what we are, what it is impossible for us to do and to know; but it will separate out, from the contingency that has made us what we are, the possibility of no longer being, doing, or thinking what we are, do, or think (FR 45–46).

To take the first example, normalization is a crucial feature that is revealed in this history of punishment. Foucault is interested not only in how individuals get programmed by the social institutions in which they find themselves, but also why they accept being programmed. He does not want to ask the question of political theory about where the right to punish comes from, but instead, the reverse question about "how were people made to accept the power to punish, or quite simply, when punished, tolerate being so."[6] Part of the answer concerns the use of "norms" not only in prisons, but in all other institutions (such as schools, hospitals, factories, or armies) such that perhaps the entire society threatens to become "carceral":

The judges of normality are present everywhere. We are in the society of the teacher-judge, the doctor-judge, the educator-judge, the "social worker"-judge; it is on them that the universal reign of the normative is based; and each individual, wherever he may find himself, subjects to it his body, his gestures, his behaviour, his aptitudes, his achievements (DP 304).

Contrary to the way his critics often read him, this passage shows that Foucault does not ignore the role of individual agency in the social construction of subjectivity. Social beings are not zombies who have no awareness and agency in their formation (and Foucault should therefore not be called an advocate of the "social construction" of subjectivity, if that phrase is understood in a mechanistic or deterministic way). The point of Bentham's model prison, the Panopticon, is to train individuals to see themselves as being seen: "He who is subjected to a field of visibility, and who knows it, assumes responsibility for the constraints of power; he makes them play spontaneously upon himself; he inscribes in himself the power relation in which he simultaneously plays both roles; he becomes the principle of his own subjection" (DP 202–203). In general, individuals are complicit in the process of their self-formation and they learn to normalize themselves. Indeed, normalization does not suppress individualization, but produces it. However, what it is to be an individual changes once the disciplinary regime colonizes and supplants the older, juridical regime (DP 192–94).

For present purposes it is important to see that Foucault does not criticize normalization in the name of something universal. That would itself be simply a variant of normalization, of thinking that there is a normal, natural, universal way to exist, and that criticism is possible only of the abnormal, or whatever falls short of the normal as an ideal. The mistake to which Foucault is pointing involves the way the normal is taken as a norm. He is not trying to substitute other norms, but instead is trying to deflate the tendency to think that there can be only one set (presumably, one's own) of normal, socially-normed ways to exist or that everything we do must be measured against such social norms. So the point is not to make a better distinction between the normal and the abnormal, but to challenge the social use of that very distinction.

Disciplinary power is not all bad, however. As Nietzsche says about asceticism, learning to restrain oneself can be productive. Similarly, discipline, and especially self-discipline, has advantages and disadvantages. The critical resistance to normalization stems from the sense that normalization has spread too far in our lives, and is blocking off too many other viable forms of living. This constriction of possibilities is achieved when normalization asserts the norms as necessary, or natural, or universal.

Foucault's history is intended to show that the modern understanding of how to punish was an arbitrary invention that at first seemed to be merely one convenient and efficient means among others, but later became the only possible means, and perhaps even an end in itself. As he says of Bentham's sketch of the model, panoptical prison, "A *real* subjection is born mechanically from a *fictitious* relation" (DP 202; emphasis added). Power can be productive if it opens up new possibilities, but it turns into domination if its function becomes entirely the negative one of shrinking and restricting possibilities. Critical resistance will thus involve using the very mechanisms of power to destabilize and subvert domination.

A second example that makes a similar point in a different way is Foucault's "genealogy of ethics" and his late interest in the ideas of "ethical substance" and *ethos*. Instead of offering a Kantian or Habermasian theory of a priori moral principles and procedures, Foucault follows Nietzsche's call for the more concrete practice of critical *history*, that is, genealogical critiques of false universals embedded in the specific ways in which we have been socialized subliminally. In particular, we need more specific analyses of the concrete ethical practices, of what the Greeks call the ethos and Hegel calls *Sittlichkeit* (in contrast to the abstract moral code, or *Moralität*). Foucault thinks of the ethos as personal, but not as private. An individual's ethos is publicly observable, and it is visibly permeated by social norms and political codes.

The general method for investigating change in the ethos is genealogy. Foucault is not doing a genealogy of morals, since Foucault believes that the moral principles that people espouse are fairly constant throughout history. He is doing a genealogy of *ethics*, which involves describing what people *do* more than what they *say*, with *embodied patterns of action* more than with *conscious principles*. An example of this genealogy of ethics comes from the interview, "On the Genealogy of Ethics: An Overview of Work in Progress," where Foucault suggests that changes in the *ethos* between Greek, early Christian, and modern times imply that we can learn that our present ethical and sexual self-understanding is not universal and eternal. Foucault charts the shift in what he calls "ethical substance"—a central term of Hegel's. The history of ethics will thus be the history of the changes in ethical substance (and other aspects of *Sittlichkeit*, including the mode of subjectivization, or *assujetissement*). The moral code containing the standard precepts or universal principles does not change much, in Foucault's opinion. However, this lack of change is not what gives the code its "binding force." On the contrary, that the code does not change much, even though the meaning of what it is to be ethical (the "ethical substance") changes, suggests that the real ethical "glue" must be found at a more concrete level. At this level Foucault is concerned to show that in the case of the ethics of sexual comportment, there have been major shifts in the understanding of what it is to be a sexual being. If his historical genealogy is correct, "sexuality" is a recent and strictly modern phenomenon that differs significantly from what the Greeks called *aphrodisia* or what the early Christians called the flesh (FR 351–59). Sexuality is thereby shown not to be an invariant feature or a natural-kind term, but a culturally variable and transformable phenomenon.

Leaving further details aside, the point of the example is not to suggest that these earlier self-understandings are viable alternatives for us today, since we cannot now go back to them. But they are also not inferior to ours, as a Kantian or Habermasian evolutionary model would imply. So Foucault's point is rather that seeing that other peoples lived successfully with self-interpretations different from our own should suggest that stultifying aspects of ourselves that we had assumed to be universal and eternal might in fact be arbitrary and contingent features that could potentially be changed. On Foucault's account, then, we are not locked into our present self-interpretation. Just as Nietzsche thinks of the body not as a single unity but as a plurality of (sometimes conflicting) drives, Foucault thinks that we are always more than the one, dominant interpretation of ourselves that we tend to take for granted as both universal and natural. Critical resistance thus flows from the realization that the present's self-interpretation is only one among several others that have been viable, and that it should keep itself open to alternative interpretations.

BOURDIEU

In the spectrum between Merleau-Ponty and Nietzsche, Foucault stands very close to Nietzsche. Pierre Bourdieu, in contrast, resists the relativism that threatens the Nietzschean side of this spectrum and stands in a lineage that is closer to Merleau-Ponty.[7] However, Foucault and Bourdieu can profitably be put on the same spectrum insofar as Bourdieu can be read as deepening Foucault's account of how subjectivity is constructed through power relations by providing a much more detailed sociological theory of this process. The central idea of this theory is Bourdieu's concept of the "habitus." This concept can also be taken as Bourdieu's way of adding the social dimension to Merleau-Ponty's theory of embodiment. But Bourdieu does not follow the earlier phenomenological program entirely, for he does not see the social dimension as a secondary layer on top of the primary layer of perception. I read Bourdieu as maintaining that the perceptual is itself conditioned by the social. Showing this will require some interpretation, however, and will depend on the general issue of how

Bourdieu sees the relation between the biological and the social features of embodiment. Once these issues are clarified, I can then go on to the central issue of this essay and ask whether Bourdieu's approach allows for conscious, critical resistance to oppressive socialization.

To understand Bourdieu's notion of habitus one must recognize the difference between that idea and more standard philosophical notions of habit. Standardly, habit is contrasted with deliberation or decisions of the will. Bourdieu, however, criticizes Pascal's advice to act as if one believed in the expectation that the resulting habits of action would lead to the actuality of belief. Bourdieu is persuaded by Bernard Williams that "one cannot both believe *p* and believe that the belief that *p* stems from a decision to believe *p*" (LP 49). Bourdieu argues that we will fail to explain social action if we try to work from a framework in which actions are caused exclusively either by decisions of reason or by reaction to mechanisms that are external to agents. Instead, he wants an account of action as reasonable even if not the product of reasoned design, or as "intelligible and coherent without springing from an intention of coherence and a deliberate decision" (LP 51).

Bourdieu can thus be read as providing a more detailed version of what Foucauldians call "intentionality without a subject." Indeed, Bourdieu uses as metaphors for the habitus a conductorless orchestra or a train laying its own rails (LP 59, 57). He also gives as an example "the intentionless invention of regulated improvisation" of the virtuoso who finds in his own discourse the triggers for his further discourse: "In other words, being produced by a *modus operandi* which is not consciously mastered, the discourse contains an 'objective intention' . . . which outruns the conscious intentions of its apparent author and constantly offers new pertinent stimuli to the *modus operandi* of which it is the product . . ." (LP 57). So the habitus does not work via rigid mechanical causation, or like an algorithm that allows for only one output. Instead, it has a certain plasticity due to the fuzziness, irregularity, and even incoherencies of a few principles that must be "easy to master and use" (LP 86). This plasticity allows for the generation of improvisations. As such it avoids the mechanistic explanations of objectivistic theories of social construction, as well as the subjectivistic explanations of phenomenological theories (especially Sartre's). Bourdieu intends the habitus to be beyond the usual antinomies of free will and determinism, or conscious and unconscious agency, or even the individual and society (LP 55).

Consciousness can try to achieve the same effects as the habitus does, but it cannot do so in the same way. Anthropologists, he believes, cannot simply bewitch themselves and really live the beliefs in witchcraft or magic (LP 68). As a sense for what is practically required, the habitus has a deeper urgency that "excludes all deliberation" (LP 53). Bourdieu characterizes the habitus as the system of "structured, structuring" or "durable, transposable" *dispositions* (LP 52–53). ("Transposable" means that the habitus is adaptable enough to reproduce itself as circumstances change; "transposable" thus does not imply that the habitus itself can be "transformed.") Is he claiming that the habitus is even deeper than perception is for Merleau-Ponty? It seems so, for the habitus is acquired from early experience and then forgotten; it becomes a "second nature" (LP 56) that is "the basis of the perception and appreciation of all subsequent experiences" (LP 54).

But if the habitus becomes second nature, what came first? Biology? Bourdieu does not deny biology, but he sees the biological as always entwined with the social. Sometimes he seems to imply that the biological can be analytically separated from the social. In his famous early essay on "The Kabyle House or the World Reversed" he finds pairs of universals combined into an ordered set that explains how both the Berber house and the Berber universe are structured: "Thus, the house is organized in accordance with a set of homologous oppositions—high:low :: light:dark :: day:night :: male:female :: *nif:h'urma* :: fertilizing:able to be fertilized" (LP 275). Even in the later *Logic of Practice* he speaks of the "biologically pre-constructed aspect of this [sexual] gymnastics (penetrating or being penetrated, being on top or below, etc.)" (LP 71). In a footnote he mentions the possibility "that specifically biological determinations of sexual identity may help to determine social position (e.g. by favouring dispositions more or less close to the established definition of excellence which, in a class society, are more or less favourable to social mobility)" (LP 293, n. 5). But this footnote follows a sentence claiming that social determinations constitute not only social identity, but "probably also the sexual dispositions themselves" (LP 71). He also cites evidence that awareness of sexual differentiation comes into being simultaneously with perception of social differences, such as those between the differing social roles of the father and the mother (LP 78). So his considered view must be that the habitus is precisely the ability to unify what is socially necessary and what is biologically necessary. This produces:

> a biological (and especially sexual) reading of social properties and a social reading of sexual properties, thus leading to a social re-use of biological properties and a biological re-use of social properties. . . . In a society divided into classes, all the products of a given agent, by an essential overdetermination, speak inseparably and simultaneously of his/her class—or, more precisely, his/her position and rising or falling trajectory within the social structure—and of his/her body—or, more precisely, of all the properties, always socially qualified, of which he/she is the bearer: sexual ones, of course, but also physical properties that are praised, like strength or beauty, or stigmatized (LP 79).

I interpret Bourdieu's method, therefore, as being different from the phenomenological search for a primary perceptual level that is the basis for other levels, including the social. Instead, the body is where the practical belief is instantiated, and the habitus is what one is born into, such that one can never completely know what one is doing, although what one does has more sense than one knows (LP 69). Conscious representation will never capture this practical knowledge, which is built into such things as bodily postures (bowing, etc.) that immediately recall associated thoughts and feelings. Adapting Proust, Bourdieu says that "arms and legs are full of numb imperatives" (LP 69). These imperatives may seem insignificant (e.g., "sit up straight," "don't hold your knife in your left hand") but they amount in the end to a whole system or bodily hexis that seems perfectly "natural" but which Bourdieu shows to be an embodied "political mythology" (LP 69). The bodily hexis and the habitus are thus two sides of the same coin. Are there any actions that are not structured by this bodily hexis and its social habitus? The answer is, apparently not:

> But in fact all the actions performed in a structured space and time are immediately qualified symbolically and function as structural exercises through which practical mastery of the fundamental schemes is constituted. . . . [T]he whole social order imposes itself at the deepest level of the bodily dispositions . . . (LP 75).

Now that I have sketched Bourdieu's account of the habitus, I would like to examine two standard criticisms of it. The first is that individuals have very little free play within the habitus. The second is that Bourdieu insists so strongly on the habitus' ability to *reproduce* itself that there is no room to account for social *transformation*.[8] That is, there appears to be little attention in Bourdieu to the possibility of individual agency, social critique, or historical change.

Bourdieu has several lines of response to these criticisms. On the first point, it could be argued that although the habitus is all-pervasive, it also has a degree of plasticity, and thus does not entirely preclude agency, whether individual or collective. Bourdieu is not a determinist. On the contrary, the notion of the habitus is intended to *explain* agency. It does so better than Sartre's subjectivistic model of radical choice precisely because it recognizes that what must be explained is always choice within a structured situation that individuals do not themselves consciously structure. The habitus is built up from early experiences that are themselves prior to or simultaneous with the emergence of our subjective sense of our individual identities. But the weight of this early experience, according to Bourdieu, leads to self-reinforcement and resistance to change, as protection against crisis (LP 60–61). We tend to prefer the familiar that we have already coped with, and we build up *nonconscious, unwilled* strategies for avoiding the perception of other possibilities. This leads Bourdieu to see the force of the habitus as deeply conservative. What looks to a philosopher like Heidegger as possibilities coming to us from the future are really, for Bourdieu, the result of the *reproduction* of past objective structures. Bourdieu substitutes this presence of the past for Heidegger's anticipation of the future (LP 62).

In sum, the habitus does help to explain how individual agency is possible because it explains how our perceptions of possibilities are narrowed down to a range within which we can comport ourselves with enough play to feel as if we are choosing freely and meaningfully. Bourdieu does not rule out our sense of "personal" style, since this is a social fact that must be recognized. But he does see personal style as "never more than a deviation in relation to the style of a period or class" (LP 60). Individuals are treated as essentially identical if they share the same social habitus (LP 59). This habitus constructs the present world but it also turns the "present of the presumed world" into "the only one [the habitus] can ever know" (LP 64). The habitus explains how we perceive the possibilities for action that we do, but at the same time that it therefore explains agency, its explanation is that social agency tends much more toward reproduction and confirmation rather than transformation: "The habitus is the principle of a selective perception of the indices tending to confirm and reinforce it rather than transform it" (LP 64).

So the thrust of the habitus is conservative. But one must distinguish between the phenomenon of the habitus and the sociological *theory* of the habitus. The question then becomes, is Bourdieu's theory itself incapable of social critique and resistance? Commentators have noticed that he does not address himself to cases of social transformation or historical change. But Bourdieu is himself critical of either social classes (for instance, the petite bourgeoisie) or social phenomena (like officialization and symbolic violence). He sees sociology as reflexive, as a socioanalysis that, like psychoanalysis, can dispel the social myths that perpetuate domination (AIRS 51ff.). He is not a fatalistic functionalist even if he does see such a high degree of necessity in how social behavior is produced. Yet this perception of necessity is precisely the motivation to resist that necessity by a scientific sociology that will unmask the social self-deception or misrecognition that perpetuates the illusion of necessity:

> I am often stunned by the degree to which things are determined: sometimes I think to myself, "This is impossible, people are going to think that you exaggerate." And, believe me, I do not rejoice over this. Indeed,

I think that if I perceive necessity so acutely, it is because I find it particularly unbearable (AIRS 200).

Here he implies that the necessity is never total, and that the socioanalysis that portrays this necessity itself leads to resistance insofar as necessity is abhorrent.

Unfortunately, there is also a "winner loses" dilemma here: the more that necessity is portrayed, the less successful resistance will appear to be able to be. Bourdieu does not seem to feel the full force of this dilemma, for he insists instead, without much argument, that we should opt not for sociologistic resignation, but for a "rational utopianism" that uses "the knowledge of the probable to make the possible come true" (AIRS 197). I infer therefore that he is not really talking about necessity as fatalistic determinism or functionalism, but only as probability. In his own terms, then, we should see the habitus not as a deterministic, causal explanation, but only ever as an interpretation or a model that makes social comportment intelligible.[9] In Bourdieu's own language, we should not confuse the model of reality with the reality of the model.

The example of gender illuminates how Bourdieu's approach could have a critical thrust. In his portrayal of traditional Berber culture he shows the male/female opposition to be so basic that most other binary oppositions reflect it as well. But he is clear that there is a political mythology here: "male order is so deeply grounded as to need no justification: it imposes itself as self-evident, universal. . ." (AIRS 171). The deep necessity thus does not imply that the ordering is justified, but works precisely to veil possibilities that would flow from recognition of the lack of justification: "male *sociodicy* owes its specific efficacy to the fact that it legitimates a relation of domination by inscribing it in a biological which is itself a biologized *social construction*" (AIRS 172; emphasis added). Biology itself, when put to social use, becomes a socially constructed category that can serve to constrict social possibilities.

He also offers a reading of Virginia Woolf's *To the Lighthouse* as portraying "the domination of the dominant by his domination" (AIRS 173). That is, women are portrayed as being able to ignore the *illusio* that leads men to engage in the central games of society. Women can thus escape the normal will-to-dominate. They attain by living through a Bourdieuian socioanalysis to a lucid view of the games that males play in their "desperate and somewhat pathetic effort" to live up to the society's ideal of what it is to be a man.

In sum, clearly Bourdieu's reflexive sociology is intended to be critical, however fatalistic his theory and practice seem. But I will point out that the appearance of determinism and resignation is generated precisely by the extent to which action is theorized as stemming much more from the body and its unconscious practices than from conscious intentions. So the strategy of moving the body from the periphery of our theories to their centers is not without its dangers. The more pervasive and inaccessible the practices of bodily socialization are made out to be, the less criticism and resistance seem possible or worthwhile.

THE SOCIAL ONTOLOGY OF RESISTANCE

Refusing the assumption of transhistorical bodily invariants and hypothesizing instead the historical situatedness of the body thus carries theoretical risks. A major task becomes that of explaining how the social fabric makes resistance possible. Furthermore, if the theorist sees the theory and its empirical application as itself a form of social critique or destabilization, then that methodological possibility also must be consistent with the ontological explanation of both domination and resistance.

There are thus at least two ways to hear the question, how is critical resistance possible? This question could be taken as a request for practical, political guidelines about how to distinguish what is socially evil from what is socially good, and how to overcome the evil. But although both Foucault and Bourdieu have been politically active as private individuals, their theories do not aspire to legislating a priori precepts about the form that criticism and resistance must take in different circumstances. The contingencies of each situation will require *phronesis*, or the practical wisdom to see what the singular situation demands.

But they do not ignore the question altogether, for it can also be understood along the lines of Kant's famous question, how is experience possible? Here the question is less one of practical politics than of social ontology. Of course, Foucault and Bourdieu reject the approach of transcendental philosophy, but they do try to explain the conditions for the possibility of resistance. That is, they offer some account of how social reality can produce a phenomenon like resistance, even if they desist from *prescribing* the forms that it must take in each and every case.

Bourdieu's account, as reconstructed aptly by Loïc Wacquant, starts from the recognition of how problematic resistance is, and how difficult it is to distinguish resistance from submission (AIRS 23–24). What he calls the unresolvable contradiction of resistance is that whereas resistance might seem liberating and submission alienating, in fact resistance is often alienating while submission can be liberating (AIRS 24, cited by Wacquant). Thus, the dominated can resist by trying to efface the signs of difference that have led to their domination. But this strategy has the same effect as assimilation, and thus looks like submission. Or the dominated can instead try to dominate their own domination by accepting and accentuating the characteristics that mark them as dominated. But this too does not look much different from giving in to domination.[10]

Bourdieu thus starts from an honest recognition of the complexity of the phenomenon of the complicity of the dominated in their own domination. On his social ontology, whether this submission is voluntary or involuntary is beside the point, for *"the dispositions which incline them to this complicity are also the effect, embodied, of domination"* (AIRS 24, cited by Wacquant). That is, the dominated are not in a position to judge their dispositions outside of the dominating framework, and they will probably not experience their existence as the result of domination because their own dispositions fit the social field in which they find themselves.

So as Foucault also emphasizes, domination functions more effectively when the arbitrariness of the asymmetrical relations remains invisible. What might help to make the asymmetries visible and thus to call for critical questioning and resistance? As I indicated, Bourdieu's answer is the socioanalysis itself. He thinks that the reflexivity of the sociological insight into how asymmetrically the social situation is structured can neutralize the force of the bodily dispositions. Bourdieu thus believes that to a degree knowledge can be emancipatory. The better we understand the external constraints on our thought and action, the more we will see through them and the less effective they will become.[11] Reflexive sociology is therefore itself understood to be a form of critical resistance. It aspires to objectivity and reason in the sense that it grasps the truth of a social configuration. But it recognizes that its own stance is produced by its own social configuration, so it does not claim insight into transhistorical structures or a priori principles.

The problem with this response is that it is not clearly compatible with Bourdieu's strong statements (especially in earlier writings) about how inaccessible the habitus is to conscious recognition and transformation. Whether Bourdieu has really explained how neutralization and destabilization of the habitus would be possible is a matter of continuing debate. If the reading of Bourdieu that I have sketched is correct, the answer depends on emphasizing the plasticity of the habitus. The habitus structures how the world is intelligible, but this grid of intelligibility does not strictly determine what we do. There is room for the perception of different possibilities, and thus for improvised courses of action. Insofar as this grid of intelligibility functions by narrowing the range of perceived possibilities, becoming more reflexive about the grid itself would in fact seem to widen the range of perceived possibilities and thus to weaken the grip of the compulsions to compliance.

Foucault could say much the same thing for his method of genealogy. Of course, Bourdieu's epistemological claims are stronger than Foucault's, for Bourdieu's stress on scientific explanation implies that a particular socioanalysis must be taken as the one right explanation of the social structure. Foucault does not claim the status of science for genealogy, and would probably settle for the suggestion that a particular genealogical account was one of several possible interpretations. But Foucault could nevertheless say that the account was a valid interpretation. Like Bourdieu, Foucault does not have to believe that knowledge is a matter only of power. On the contrary, he could maintain that the knowledge represented by a successful genealogical unveiling of asymmetries and false universals can itself be an efficacious means of resisting domination. For domination to be resisted effectively it must first be revealed.

But if Foucault could accept this metatheoretical defense, he would not stop there. He also addresses the issue of explaining the conditions for the possibility of resistance. He does so by building resistance into power relations from the start. For Foucault, power is not what would be in effect if determinism were true, and if an individual had only one course of action open. Instead, power implies having more than one option open, and domination occurs when people buy into options that entrap them in asymmetrical relations that blind them to their real range of possibilities.

Foucault thus insists (against his critics) that his theory does not dismiss freedom and individual agency. Instead, he maintains that one could not speak of power unless one could also speak of freedom. Correlatively, where power is found, there resistance will be found as well:

> One must observe also that there cannot be relations of power unless the subjects are free. . . . That means that in the relations of power, there is necessarily the possibility of resistance, for if there were no possibility of resistance—[for instance,] of violent resistance, of escape, of ruse, of strategies that reverse the situation—there would be no relations of power.[12]

So resistance does not come on the scene secondarily, only in response to power. Instead, resistance is found in the social ontology from the start. Without a power network it would not even make sense to speak of either resistance or domination, and patterns of resistance and domination are the signs that a power network exists. Moreover, power needs resistance, and would not be operative without it. Power depends on points of resistance to spread itself more extensively through the social network.[13] Of course, resistance can also interfere with power. In an apparent paradox similar to the one pointed out by Bourdieu, however, resistance does not always only disrupt power. Sometimes resistance serves the ends of domination more than it inhibits them. So Foucault cannot guarantee in advance that the genealogical unveiling of domination will be effective and liberating. But genealogical analysis can at least aim at *minimizing domination*, and that is the professed ideal of Foucault's own philosophical ethos.

The critics of Foucault and Bourdieu probably will not be satisfied with these responses, and they may continue to see functionalism or determinism in either or both of them. But to my mind both the later Foucault and the more recent Bourdieu make a concerted and illuminating effort to test the extent to which a theory of embodiment based on the hypothesis of the body's historicity can explain the conditions for critical resistance to the social forces behind embodiment without having to construct transcendental arguments for a priori principles or universal invariants. Of course, my concern in this essay has been mainly with their metatheoretical efforts to avoid paradox. However, it is really their concrete genealogical and ethnographic work that is the more decisive test for the usefulness and plausibility of the hypothesis of the historicity of the body.

NOTES

1. Michel Foucault, "Nietzsche, Genealogy, History," *The Foucault Reader*, ed. Paul Rabinow (New York: Pantheon, 1984), pp. 87–88; translation modified; emphasis added. Further references to this reader will be cited in the text as FR.
2. Pierre Bourdieu, *The Logic of Practice*, trans. Richard Nice (Stanford: Stanford University Press, 1990), pp. 69–70. Hereafter cited in the text as LP. Compare Bourdieu, *Outline of a Theory of Practice*, trans. Richard Nice (Cambridge: Cambridge University Press, 1977), pp. 93–94.
3. Pierre Bourdieu, *Outline of a Theory of Practice*, p. 94.
4. See Daniel C. Dennett, *Consciousness Explained* (Boston: Little Brown and Company, 1991), p. 24. Taking "body" as a natural kind may be the result of the mistake that Dennett calls armchair naturalism: "the assumption that whatever nature makes is a natural kind" (p. 381).
5. Hubert L. Dreyfus and Paul Rabinow, *Michel Foucault: Beyond Structuralism and Hermeneutics*, 2nd ed. (Chicago: University of Chicago Press, 1983), p. 167. Hereafter cited in the text as MF.
6. Michel Foucault, *Discipline and Punish: The Birth of the Prison*, trans. Alan Sheridan (New York: Vintage, 1979), p. 303. Hereafter cited in the text as DP.
7. Bourdieu resists relativism and defends the objectivity of his own sociological studies by arguing for a different understanding of objectivity than is found in absolutist philosophy or in objectivistic approaches to sociology. See, for instance, Pierre Bourdieu and Loïc Wacquant, *An Invitation to Reflexive Sociology* (Chicago: University of Chicago Press, 1992), pp. 51ff. Cited in the text as AIRS.

8. See Craig Calhoun, "Habitus, Field, and Capital: The Question of Historical Specificity," in *Bourdieu: Critical Perspectives*, eds. Craig Calhoun, Edward LiPuma, & Moishe Postone (Chicago: University of Chicago Press, 1993), p. 72.

9. For an account of Bourdieu that reads him as offering a theory of the intelligibility of action in contrast to a theory of the causal generation of action, see Theodore Richard Schatzki, "Overdue Analysis of Bourdieu's Theory of Practice," *Inquiry*, vol. 30, pp. 113–35.

10. In a similar vein, Elizabeth Grosz in *Volatile Bodies: Toward a Corporeal Feminism* (Bloomington: Indiana University Press, 1994) remarks while addressing Sandra Lee Bartky's well-known essay, "Foucault, Femininity and the Modernization of Patriarchal Power," that the "practices of femininity can readily function, in certain contexts that are difficult to ascertain in advance, as modes of guerrilla subversion of patriarchal codes, although the line between compliance and subversion is always a fine one, difficult to draw with any certainty" (p. 144). Grosz then adds the important point that outside a given power network (or social "field," Bourdieu could say) there is no way to describe an action as either resistance or compliance: "Its enmeshment in disciplinary regimes is the condition of the subject's social effectivity, as either conformist or subversive" (p. 144).

11. See Wacquant, AIRS 49.

12. Michel Foucault, "The Ethics of Care for the Self: An Interview with Michel Foucault on January 20, 1984," *Philosophy and Social Criticism*, vol. 12, p. 123.

13. See Dreyfus & Rabinow, MF 147.

TWO

THE SOUL OF AMERICA: WHITENESS AND THE DISAPPEARING OF BODIES IN THE PROGRESSIVE ERA

TRACY FESSENDEN

The problem with trying to think about whiteness as a racial category, according to film theorist Richard Dyer, is that whiteness, in film as in other forms of cultural representation, "seems not to be there as a subject at all." Part of the difficulty is that whiteness seems to stand for so much else besides race: safety and radiance, for example, as opposed to danger and darkness. Moreover, black is almost always particularizing in the way that white seldom is. Books like *Waverley* or *Wuthering Heights* or *A Moveable Feast* are about Jacobite intrigues or tempestuous lovers or American expatriates before they are about white people; *Equiano's Travels* or *Sula* are about black people before they are about eighteenth-century diarists or midwestern women. Generally, black is clearly marked out as a category, whereas white, because it seems to be nothing in particular, man-ages also to be "everything," coterminous with the entire range of human diversity (44-46). This makes it hard not only to analyze whiteness but hard even to see it, much less to see its meanings as socially produced and secured through Anglo-Saxon domination.

Characteristically, white racism trades on that invisibility. "*My eye, though covered, is all-seeing,*" reads a line from a poem called "The Soul of America," reprinted among the papers read at the first annual meeting of the Grand Dragons Knights of the Ku Klux Klan in July 1923. The poet is named Daisy Douglas Barr; the poem's persona is the Invisible Empire itself:

My heart is heavy, but not relenting;
Sorrowful but not hopeless;
Pure but ever able to master the unclean . . .
I am the Spirit of Righteousness
They call me the Ku Klux Klan.
I am more than the uncouth robe and hood
With which I am clothed.
YEA, I AM THE SOUL OF AMERICA (135).

The Soul of America was also the title chosen by University of Pennsylvania literature professor Arthur Hobson Quinn for his 1932 contribution to a philosophy of United States history. Quinn's interpretation of America, he explained, was a racial one; his project was to rank the "great races of Western Europe" in the order of their "influence on the American soul." Number one on the list that emerges is "the English race," whose "courage, order, self-respect," "respect for law," and "sense of racial integrity," defined, for Quinn, what it meant to be supremely American (3–13).

Placed side by side, these two versions of *The Soul of America* bear witness to the mutual dependence of a crude racism of skin color and a more discriminating racism of character. In the late nineteenth and early twentieth centuries, exchanges between racial bodies and racial souls—between, say, white skin and Anglo-Saxon ideas, or between the conscious racism of Southern bigots and the "unconscious" racism of a Northeastern intellectual elite—figure in the work of a number of ideologically diverse reformers, who made it their project to realize the Ku Klux Klan's physically all-white America in the seemingly more benign form of Arthur Quinn's spiritually all-white America.

Critic Walter Benn Michaels and biologists Richard Lewontin and Stephen Jay Gould have remarked on this transformation as a "rewriting of biology as ideology," a disavowal of "vulgar" racism in favor of an insistence on a set of racial principles—intelligence, self-control, and so on—that transcend visibility.[1] Even the superior "sense of racial integrity" that, for Quinn, distinguishes the genuine American is more or less intangible; writers in the 1920s called it "race consciousness." Race consciousness represents both the essentializing of race and the essentializing of racism, since to rewrite biology as ideology—race as race consciousness—is at once to appeal to allegedly biological differences between races and to appear to reject such appeals by lifting them into a disembodied idiom of "culture" and "citizenship." An exemplary instance of that rewriting, Quinn's *The Soul of America* keeps visible, but only barely visible, the centrality of race to a discourse of culture that even today seems always ready, but is crucially never quite able, to disown it. In this essay I want briefly to trace this reflex of spiritualizing race as it occurs across a number of discourses—eugenics, first-wave feminism, Jim Crow racism, the Social Gospel, multiculturalism—that belong to or have their roots in Progressive Era reforms.

Myra Jehlen suggests that

> [it] is precisely because the concept of America is rooted in the physical finite that it can be infinitely metaphysical. . . . Indeed, in a country whose

historical identity is seen as inherent in its land, theories that locate the roots of personal identity in bodily attributes clearly make pragmatic sense. . . . His self-consciousness rendered cosmic in comparison to the unconscious earth, [American man] was nonetheless reintegrated—his body and soul, himself and the world, made one—through his identification with the physical universe, an identification whose natural priority, moreover, ensured his transcendent primacy (13-14).

In this model by which, as Jehlen puts it, "the Protestant soul acquires a newly powerful body" (9), a divinized, Americanized "nature" furnishes analogies for human perfectibility. In the late nineteenth and early twentieth centuries, these analogies increasingly took the form of social-Darwinian justifications for the amassing of wealth by robber barons. Thus, for example, John D. Rockefeller could defend the Standard Oil monopoly as "merely a survival of the fittest. . . . The American beauty rose can be produced in the splendor and fragrance which bring cheer to the beholder only by sacrificing the early buds which grow up around it. This is *not* an evil tendency in business. It is merely the working out of a law of nature and a law of God" (quoted in Hofstadter, 45). Or again, Calvin Coolidge, who said that "the business of America is business," also said that "advertising ministers to the spiritual side of trade"; it was "a great power . . . which charges [the American businessman] with the high responsibility of inspiring and ennobling the commercial world," a "part of the greater work of the regeneration and redemption of all mankind" (quoted in Berlant, 110).

In the natural theology of American capitalism, salvation is defined as material success, because nature knows no other standard. At the same time, as in these examples, the evolutionary winners within the natural order are by that fact endowed with a vast and impersonal spiritual power. And if capitalism was one way of turning nature to self-transcendence, racial imperialism was another; frequently, in fact, these two blur together in the hazy rhetoric of worldly religious mission. Theologian Josiah Strong, for example, saw behind the gross national product a "race of unequalled energy, with all the majesty of wealth and numbers behind it," a representative "of the largest liberty, the purest Christianity, the highest civilization." The inherited, "peculiarly aggressive traits" of the American "race" were calculated, Strong believed, "to impress its institutions upon mankind," and "spread itself over the earth" (175). For Indiana congressman Albert J. Beveridge, the success of the American businessman was evidence that God had made the American people the "master-organizers of the world" to "administer government among savage and senile peoples" and "establish system where chaos reigned" (quoted in Bowers, 121–22). And according to John Fiske, philosopher, historian, and one-time president of the United States Anti-Immigration Society, the providential transfer of the American continent "into the hands of the dollar-hunters" and "out of the hands of the scalp-hunters" was a signal episode in the evolutionary process, for it offered material confirmation that "the race which gained control of North America must become the dominant race of the world, and . . . prevail in the struggle for life." "Only when it is possible to speak of the United States as stretching from pole to pole," said Fiske, "can the world be said to have become truly Christian" (*American Political Ideas*, 130, 15). For Fiske, global Americanization was a stage, as the successive acquisition of "erect posture and articulate speech" were stages, in a teleological process by which man would one day "put . . . on immortality" ("Life Everlasting," in *The Writings of John Fiske*, 21:415).

Fiske's interpretation of the pivotal "American segment" of cosmic evolution drew heavily on Herbert Spencer, whose writings were made the basis for sweeping educational reforms in the United States at the turn of the century. "Bear constantly in mind," Spencer had written in *Education: Moral, Intellectual, and Physical*, "that the aim of your discipline is to produce a *self-governing being*, not a being *governed by others*" (quoted in R. Elias, 22; emphasis Spencer's). Anglo-Americans prided themselves on the capacity for self-government that a government of, by, and for the people presupposed; as Woodrow Wilson put it in his *History of the American People* (1908), the original settlers were a "self-helping race of Englishmen." Wilson, however, didn't think of himself as an Anglo-American. In his 1880 lectures on the discovery and colonization of America, John Fiske rejected the terms Anglo-American, English-American, and even Anglo-Saxon in favor of the inclusive designation "English race," for the American Revolution, he claimed, had actually given us "two Englands," "alike prepared to work with might and main toward the political regeneration of mankind" (*American Political Ideas*, 180). For "English race," Theodore Roosevelt substituted "American race" (quoted in Gosset, 319), and Wilson fell in with Roosevelt in thus distinguishing "real Americans" from "hyphenated Americans" (Hitchens, 128).

It is with a necessary degree of alarm, then, that Wilson's *History of the American People* records a change in immigration patterns at the turn of the century:

> Throughout the century men of the sturdy stocks of Europe had made up the main strain of foreign blood which was every year added to the vital working force of the country . . . but now there came multitudes of men from the lowest class from the south of Italy and men of the meaner sort out of Hungary and Poland, men out of the ranks where there was neither skill nor energy nor any initiative of quick intelligence; and they came in

numbers which increased from year to year, as if the countries of the south of Europe were disburdening themselves of the more sordid and hapless elements of their population (5.212–13).

In Wilson's *History*, distinctions like these between "sturdy" and "sordid," "vital" and "hapless," work rhetorically to make the capacity to articulate clear boundaries between different kinds of people, and to maintain integral bonds among the same kinds of people, a characteristic of "real Americans," not "hyphenated Americans." The importance of this sort of boundary formation was not lost on the Klan of the Progressive Era. "Take the Japanese Immigration question, or your Jim Crow decisions," wrote the Grand Dragon of Illinois, defending the Klan's selective admissions policy at their 1923 meeting.

> Our Federal Government can properly restrict immigration and exclude certain persons or classes deemed undesirable from its borders. So too, the Invisible Empire can proscribe its membership or citizenship. If this were not so our government would be overrun with undesirables, and instead of being a Nation of the people, by the people, and for the people, become a veritable melting pot for the scum of the earth (34).

The new Klan targeted not just African-Americans but "hyphenated" Americans generally, Asians as well as southern and eastern Europeans, Catholics and Jews, all "exploiters" and "usurpers" who laid fraudulent claim to "America's birthright" (60). As the above passage makes clear, however, Klan-style nativism would have been impossible without the legal underpinnings of Jim Crow. And what is most striking about this invocation of Jim Crow is that what begins as a comparison between the restrictive policies of the Klan and those of the United States ends up as an assertion of one-to-one equivalence: Were it *not* the case that the Klan enjoyed the same, juridically endorsed powers of discrimination that belonged to the federal government, then not only the Invisible Empire but the nation itself would be infiltrated with undesirables.

Under the Wilson administration, Jim Crow was the law of the land;[2] and in this way the success of the new Klan marked its difference from the old Klan. In the antebellum South, white race loyalty had obviously worked *against* national loyalty, and the first white vigilante movements of Reconstruction sprang up in response to what Southern whites saw as the clash between sectional and national interests. But the triumphant nationalism that followed the Spanish-American War accommodated Southern race hatred as well as it did the Anglophilia of the Northeast and the grass-roots antimodernism of the West, and as the South moved to the forefront of the nativist movement, Confederate ardor and American patriotism became increasingly difficult to tell apart. Where the old Klan had repudiated the U.S. Constitution, the new Klan hallowed it as "the greatest constructive government document ever struck off by pen of man. It brought order out of chaos. It developed National cohesiveness and destroyed the power of dissintegration [*sic*]. It softened state pride and magnified love of country. It took thirteen weak, selfish, and quarreling states and amalgamated them into a national unit" (21). The true American patriot, according to a Grand Titan of the Realm of Texas, seeks "the spirit of our fathers," that is, the framers, for only "he who lifts himself above the fog of personal promotion, advancement and aggrandizement, and lives his life in the clear blue air of devotion to his country and its government, is a real citizen" (18).

The Klansman's claim to a pure American identity that was indivisibly racial and spiritual looked somewhat tenuous, however, if it was true, as the Klan also claimed, that "this country of ours is not a nation of Americans, but a conglomerate mass of aliens—alien in thought and act" (59–60). Whereas John Fiske and Josiah Strong had put their faith in the Anglo-Saxon's innate superiority as an evolutionary check on lesser breeds, later observers of migration like Yale economist Francis A. Walker pointed with alarm to "the entrance into our political, social, and industrial life of . . . vast masses of peasantry, degraded below our utmost conceptions," "beaten men from beaten races; representing the worst failures in the struggle for existence" (quoted in Fine, 6). More disquieting still, these evolutionary "failures" were outbreeding the group supposed to have been winners. To these observers, the Great War had been "dysgenic" for real Americans: Writing in 1917, Henry Fairfield Osborn noted with regret that among the departing regiments from California and Oregon "the Anglo-Saxon type was dominant over every other and the purest members of this type largely outnumbered the others"; "the sad thought was continually in my mind," he says, that "this race was passing, that this war will take a very heavy toll of this strain of Anglo-Saxon life which has played so large a part in American history" (Osborn in the "Preface" to Grant, xi–xiii).

Four years later, Seth K. Humphrey pointed out that more than five million American men "of the forward races" had indeed been killed in the war, leaving five million white women, by his own argument, actually or effectively widowed, and so casting "the astounding fertility of our labor immigrants" in vivid relief against "the infertility of the effective American stocks" (249, 50). "Astounding fertility" evidenced a lack of self-mastery that made these new waves of immigrants impervious to Fiske's or anyone else's schemes for total assimilation. Where Theodore Roosevelt had argued for the thorough "Americanization" of arriving foreigners in speech, culture, and politics, now Madison Grant warned that "democratic ideals among a homogenous population of Nordic blood, as in England or America, is one thing, but it is quite another for the white man to share his blood with, *or intrust his ideals to*, brown, yellow, black, or red men. This is suicide pure and simple" (Grant in the "Introduction" to Stoddard, xxxii; my emphasis). By the "white man's ideals," Grant evidently meant something close to what Quinn meant by the soul of America.

Quinn, Stoddard, Grant, and the Klan were no doubt responding, in part, to the perception of there being too *many* bodies in America that were *not* representative of what Quinn called the "great races of Western Europe." But their writings also suggest a more troubled response to the fact of the body itself. The rewriting of "race" as "soul" in these texts points to the insufficiency of a principle of identity conceived of either as wholly independent of the body (otherwise "soul" needn't be grounded in "race"), or as precisely identical with it (otherwise "race" needn't be taken up into the airier regions of "soul"). It points, as Walter Michaels puts it in another context, to a condition of nonidentity with either body or soul, to a self that consists neither in simply *having* a body nor in *being* a body but rather in being embodied (*The Gold Standard and the Logic of Naturalism*, 21–22). And the project of Western "civilization," a project to which Stoddard and company were clearly devoted, is one in which the condition of embodiment is felt as successively more problematic.

This, by my reading, is the argument of Norbert Elias's magisterial, now-classic analysis of *The Civilizing Process*, which compellingly depicts Western "progress" as a far-ranging series of shifts in the direction of bodily abstraction, of abstraction from things. Moving through a several-century sequence of writings on manners, Elias traces the advancing pressure-toward-disembodiment across several registers of successive admonition: first that eating be done with the right hand only and then that utensils be introduced to eliminate the necessity of contact; first that the carver of meat "not bring dishonor" through the undignified display of bodily effort and then that the carving be done out of sight; first that bodily functions be hidden from view and then that they not even be mentioned. "Civilization," Elias suggests, is the frame through which the national consciousness of Western nation-states is expressed, in that it sums up everything in which contemporary Western societies feel themselves superior to "developing" countries or to earlier societies: a detachment from tendencies that, once moved away from, emerge retrospectively as "instinctual," a refinement of feelings of delicacy, a radical contraposition of "nature" and "culture." ("Let others paint lions, eagles, and other creatures on their coats of arms," Erasmus of Rotterdam instructs in his *De civilitate morum puerilium*, a sixteenth-century manual on deportment for young boys. "More true nobility is possessed by those who can inscribe on their shields all that they have achieved through the cultivation of the arts and sciences" [quoted in N. Elias, 74].)

In *Distinction: A Social Critique of the Judgement of Taste*, Pierre Bourdieu follows Elias in suggesting that the ethos of elective distance from the natural world, reproduced by the "cultivated" in their choices and values, is also the condition for those choices and values. The "high" aesthetic of disinterest and autonomy, the pure gaze of Kantian detachment, emerges, in this reading, as the symbolic counterpart of what the dominant sector of society enjoys as an active distance from economic necessity and practical urgency. There can be no question, in this view, of separating aesthetics from politics, since the same material and conceptual shifts that make "detachment"—the valorization of the spiritual over the sensual, manner over matter—either possible or desirable also give rise to the earliest and enduring form of the state as the guardian of behavior denoted as civilized.

But words like "distance" and "detachment" tell only half of this story, because the pressure-toward-disembodiment that defines the civilizing process is accompanied, even underwritten, by an advancing sense of the physical world's inevitability, by increasing sensitivity to the bodily and the material as that which will not, finally, be put by.[3] Thus, for example, widespread interest in spiritualism emerges among Western elites in the nineteenth century not (or not only) as the attempt to transcend the physical world but as the fervent hope that even the disembodied realm of the dead might be made accessible in material terms. Sir William Crookes, president in the 1890s of *both* the British Association for the Advancement of Science and the British Society for Psychical Research, allowed his findings on x-rays, radio waves, and other vibrations to suggest that if the ear were only sensitive enough we could hear the voices of the dead speaking to us on some as-yet uncharted frequency, just as, if the ear were attuned to the vibrations of light waves, we might indeed "hear" colors (Stark, 216–17). In an 1890 essay on "What Psychical Research Has Accomplished," William James granted the plausibility of F. W. Myers's theory that "ordinary consciousness" could be likened to "the visible part of the solar spectrum" while "the total consciousness is like that spectrum prolonged by the inclusion of the ultra-red and ultra-violet rays. In the psychic spectrum the 'ultra' parts may embrace a far wider range, both of physiological and of psychical activity than is open to our ordinary consciousness and memory" (38–39; quoted in Stark, 217–18).

The subtlest reaches of consciousness, in this reading, belong to that part of the psychic spectrum tuned into our ancestral voices, here figured as (invisible) color. "We all know it instinctively," said Senator Henry Cabot Lodge, speaking before the 54th U.S. Congress in 1896, "although it is so impalpable that we can scarcely define it, and yet so deeply marked that not even the physiological differences between the [races] are more persistent or more obvious. When we speak of a race, then, we . . . mean the moral and intellectual character[istic]s which in their association *make the soul of the race*, and which represent the product of all its past . . . an unconscious inheritance from their ancestors, *upon which argument has no effect*" (quoted in Lofgren, 98–99; my emphasis).

These evolving understandings of race as fundamentally spiritual made skin color something more than skin-deep; thus Justice Henry Billings Brown could uphold the Louisiana statute providing separate accommodations for black railway passengers even when no "mixture of colored blood was . . . discernible" (538) in their skins, as none was in Homer Plessy's. Writing for the Court in *Plessy v. Ferguson* (1896), Brown affirmed that "legislation is powerless to eradicate racial instincts or to abolish distinctions based on physical differences" (551), implying that "distinctions based on physical differences" may well be "instinctual," hence belonging to the (invisible) realm of feeling, disposition, or latency.[4] Just how precarious was this liberation of race from its biological markers at the turn of the century, however, can be gauged from responses to the African-American writer William Hannibal Thomas's 1901 polemic *The American Negro*. Thomas infuriated black readers by describing the negro as "pompous," "arrogant," "bestial," "servile," "craven," "negligent," "coarse," and "vulgar." More tellingly, he infuriated whites by his suggestion that being a "negro" was a matter of character and not of color: "Any man, of whatever hue, who exhibits the characteristic traits I shall hereafter describe is a negro; otherwise he is not" (quoted in Luker, 294). Having made the point that race is a matter of traits and temperaments, not just skin color, Progressive racism could tether those intangibles ever more securely to race, insisting that what transcended biology remained hereditary. Or as Lothrop Stoddard put it, "Civilization is the body, the race is the soul. Let the soul vanish, and the body moulders into the inanimate dust from which it came" (300; quoted in Michaels, "Souls," 201).

That "race" was the "soul" was the message not only of racists who borrowed the vocabulary of Christian theology, but also of a number of liberal theologians who talked about race. "[T]he races themselves are radically unlike" wrote the Social Gospel theologian George Harris; to be Anglo-Saxon, Chinese, Latin, or Negro "is to have certain characteristics which are part of one's constitution, and which one cannot change any easier than the leopard can change his spots, or the Chinaman or negro his coloring" (18). Another American theologian of race, Edgar Gardner Murphy, argued that "the deepest thing about any man—next to his humanity itself—is his race," and that "the negro is no exception": The "persisting and persuasive individuality of race is the ground and basis of his essential culture." In this "deeper sense," Murphy insisted, "no negro can escape, or ought to escape, the Africa of his past"; "I beg [the negro] to follow, not those who would turn him into a white man, but those who would turn him into the worthier . . . possibilities of his own nature." Murphy's appreciation of diversity was also his argument for segregation: White and Negro cultures could be brought together, he argued, only on "terms of tragic loss" for whites. "No negro ought to escape the Africa of his past," Murphy asserted, yet he also insisted that "Africa itself, in any of the intelligible terms of social experience or institutional achievement, has never spoken . . . The race is undiscovered and its soul unfound" (quoted in Luker, 285–86).

For these writers, African and European Americans, belonging to distinct races, may lay claim to distinct cultures, but only the Europeans count as "culture" in the elevating and improving sense. "[W]e have only one race," the feminist reformer Charlotte Perkins Gilman told the Pasadena Nationalist Club in the late 1890s, "that will so much as allow a man to speak his mind as to our unnecessary evils" ("Human Nature," *A Nonfiction Reader*, 49). As Edward Said has pointed out, this Arnoldian idea of culture as inherently ennobling "entails not only venerating one's own culture but also thinking of it as somehow divorced from, because transcending, the everyday world" (xiii). Thus "culture" in the anti-miscegenationist utopia of Gilman's 1915 novel *Herland* is defined as "real soul culture" (78): To have a culture means to be "at work, slowly and carefully, developing in [one's] whole people . . . stronger and clearer minds, sweeter dispositions, higher capacities" (106)—this, says the novel's sociologist narrator, is truly "education for citizenship" (108).

The setting of *Herland*, where parthenogenesis becomes the special talent of Aryan "New Women" (56) after their husbands die in a battle with darker-skinned "natives," strikingly mirrors racist scenarios of the dysgenic aftermath of the First World War. By way of a eugenically happy solution to the problem of the five million American women "of the forward races" whom the war had left without prospective reproductive partners, Seth K. Humphrey alluded delicately to the recent perfection of "scientific methods for the transference of the essence of life," thanks to which it was now possible "to gain a distinguished father for one's children as impersonally as one would take inspiration from his books, or his lectures, or any of his distant acts" (249, 251).

For racial purists, then, biological reproduction could proceed as "impersonally" as bookish inspiration. And if reading and reproduction were not quite the same thing, neither were they finally to be separated. The best program for "keeping America American," wrote the reformer Charles Conant Josey in a 1923 book called *Race and National Solidarity*, would be a "spiritual revival" of "art, science, philosophy, and religion"; for "in this revival the ties of race and the heritage of a glorious past will be stressed, and we may expect that our group will act more and more as a unit, for it will feel itself more and more a single whole" (250).

Josey doesn't say it here, but for many racist writers of the 1920s, the cultivation of *esprit de corps* among white Americans necessitated, beyond a commitment to the Great Books, a certain sympathy to the claims of the (white) women's suffrage movement.[5] Distressed by the inclusion of African-American men and "ignorant foreigners" in the franchise, Elizabeth Cady Stanton in 1895 declared that the "remedy" for the domination of one sex over another was the "education of the higher, more tender sentiments of humanity, the mother-thought omnipresent in every department of life. Her ideal must be represented in the state, the church, and the home" (2). Or as Charles Gould put it in a 1920 anti-immigration tract titled *America: A Family Matter*, American traditions "cannot be taught" but must instead "come to us with mother's milk" (163). This is the alternative pedagogy at work in the all-female utopia of *Herland*, which is governed by the principle of "mother-love," described in the novel not as "instinct" but "religion," something at once "National, Racial, Human" (68–69).

This new, spiritual understanding of citizenship, with its sentimental underpinnings of maternal nurture, subtly reinforced a racial understanding of citizenship. The development of a notion of citizenship as a "family matter," a question of birth—in 1924 the Johnson-Reed Immigration Act, for example, vastly restricted new immigration by assigning quotas keyed to the demographic composition of America a generation before—is paralleled by the increasing stringency of miscegenation statutes in the American states. In the same year that the Coolidge administration passed the Johnson-Reed Act, the state of Virginia passed a "Bill to Preserve the Integrity of the White Race," which revoked the state's relatively liberal antebellum policy of defining as black persons of one-eighth or more African "blood," and said that henceforth a man or woman with "*any* Negro blood shall be deemed and taken to be a colored person and forbidden by law to marry a white person" (U.S. Supreme Court, *Records and Briefs* in the case of *Loving v. Virginia*, 3ff.).

This strand of racism made the African-American—even the visibly "white" African-American—the model for the alien who was unassimilable. In a 1908 essay titled "A Suggestion on the Negro Problem," Gilman wrote: "We have to consider the unavoidable presence of a large body of aliens . . . widely dissimilar and in many respects inferior, whose present status is to us a social injury." The solution she proposes situates her between the assimilationism of global Americanization and the anti-assimilationism of 100 percent Americanism—put another way, between the conviction of a common scale of human value with Anglo-Saxons at the top (call this humanism) and the conviction of incommensurable *differences* between races (call this pluralism). In a humanist key, Gilman assigns races "A" and "B" to "evolutionary status" 10 and 4, respectively, in order to pose the question of how Race A "can best and most quickly promote the status of race B." The answer, a compulsory labor corps from which exemplary Negroes might be released "on probation, as it were," requires a shift to the pluralist key: a consideration of "the social, economic, political, and religious conditions" in America to which the Negro is "by heredity" a stranger, and the "fullest understanding of the special characteristics of the negro," among them his penchant for particular forms of "light and color, rhythm and music" (*Nonfiction Reader*, 176–78, 181–83). In this model, the "social injury" of the Negro's present status is ameliorated by a celebration of ineluctable *difference*: Between the Negro's favored cultural forms and the American Anglo-Saxon's, Gilman insists, runs the iron law of "heredity." Here she rests her case, finally, on an assimilationist argument: "From the foreigner of every sort the American is made by sharing with him the advantages of our institutions—even by compelling him to partake of that advantage" (179). In fifteen years, however, Gilman would lament that the nation was now "full half of varied Unamericans," the result of "our recent feeble efforts to digest the indigestible and assimilate the unassimilable" ("Is America Too Hospitable?" *Nonfiction Reader*, 294).

Writing her autobiography in 1923, Gilman cited as "the most marked change which has been wrought by a lifetime's experience" her increasing awareness of "the deep, wide, lasting vital difference between races" (*The Living of Charlotte Perkins Gilman*, 329). Increasingly, these deep and lasting racial differences were imagined in Progressive thought as stages of democracy. As a character in one of Gilman's novels puts it, "the human race is in different stages of development, and only some of the races . . . have reached the democratic stage" (*With Her in Ourland*, 155). This understanding of democracy as the highest of evolutionary stages enabled white Protestant Americans, men and women, to read their privileged status as their more highly developed willingness to extend "equality" to others. "After [an anti-immigration] speech of mine in Cooper Union," Gilman wrote in 1923, a "scornful" immigrant "demanded from the floor: 'What is an American?' A good answer which I did not think of then would have been: 'An American is the sort of person who builds a place like this for you to enjoy'" (*Living*, 316).

The superiority of Anglo-Saxon democratic ideas had frequently been invoked as an argument for white women's suffrage and against the Fourteenth and Fifteenth Amendments; the same rhetoric survived, dis-linked from but not unsupportive of the cause of women's rights, well into the twentieth century. In *America: A Family Matter*, Gould argued that "it is all very well for savages to give themselves a name which, being translated, signifies 'men' or 'the man' and which implies that all the surrounding tribes are inferior beings and not to be considered as men. But for enlightened and civilized people to look down upon other races as altogether and in every respect inferior, evinces the narrow-mindedness of the savage rather than the broadminded view of educated intelligence" (16). Gould continued with impassioned celebrations of *difference* ("In each case we find varying characteristics, any of which are extremely valuable, and each valuable characteristic should be prized and nurtured by its possessors ..." [17]) that anticipate with remarkable acuity the tendency to see the American academy's touted hospitality to multiculturalism as proof of Euro-Americans' admirable broadmindedness and largesse. A typescript I have of an introductory lecture in a 1992–93 European history course at Harvard University concludes by suggesting that "it is surely no accident that we who today live in societies shaped by European cultures, ideas, and values are the ones most sensitive to the differences among people and the need to understand and embrace them all" (Ozment, 16).[6]

This model of multiculturalism as the connoisseurship of cultural difference has sound Progressivist roots. We find it, for example, at the "University of Man" at the 1904 St. Louis Exposition, where native peoples from three continents were exhibited in all their alluring exoticism,[7] or Buffalo Bill Cody's Wild West Show, which toured the United States and Europe at the turn of the century with an "educational" message about the defeat of the Plains Indians' noble way of life.[8] These instances of the controlled display of racial otherness, under democratic auspices, bring into focus another dimension of the Progressive spiritualization of race, the terms of its extension of "brotherhood" to other members of what was increasingly figured during this period as the Family of Man. What they suggest is that only after having been defeated as rival social formations, "subtracted" from democratic social space,[9] sometimes literally "disappeared," could the embodied "differences among people," as the Harvard lecture benignly puts it, be brought forward and "embraced" by the privileged subject schooled in "sensitivity" and "understanding."

In her *Reconstructing Womanhood: The Emergence of the Afro-American Woman Novelist*, Hazel Carby has warned us against a too facile insistence on feminism's historical commitment to racial equality among women. As Carby puts it, "the search to establish that these bonds of sisterhood have always existed has led to a feminist historiography and criticism which denies the hierarchical structuring of the relations between black and white women and often takes the concerns of articulate, middle-class white women as the norm" (17). I would also suggest, however, that what we have been able to recover of the history of Progressive reform movements of the late nineteenth and early twentieth centuries, including the American women's movement, should warn us against equally facile celebrations of the racial differences these movements call into visibility, for it is clear that for many white reformers, these differences were championed for their tacit support of the hierarchies they embed. It is also clear that the eager embrace of human diversity by American elites in the early twentieth century, what Daniel Lerner in 1958 called "the spread of empathy around the world" (52),[10] was intimately bound up in the American extension of power over "alien" populations at home and abroad.

It may not be too soon to begin historicizing multiculturalism, in the same way that Carby, among many others, has begun the task of historicizing feminism, in order to challenge its representation as a monolith, to uncover and to work to redress its complicities with injustice, and to avoid having to defend it in the very terms by which it is most frequently attacked. In the representations of the academy offered today by both the right and the left, the aims of multiculturalism and of other emancipatory discourses (e.g., Marxist, feminist, queer) are given as being much the same. But the assumption that they are the same, I suggest, may make it difficult to see where demands for equality, or for the revaluing of currently devalued differences, do or do not line up with the history that figures the enlightened appreciation of diversity as a racial or national trait, another of the spiritual hallmarks of whiteness.

NOTES

1. The phrase "rewriting of biology as ideology" is Michaels's, "The Souls of White Folk," 191. This discussion is particularly indebted to Michaels's essay and to Elaine Scarry's "Introduction" in *Literature and the Body*, vii–xxvii. In particular, I take the notion, and the importance, of the spiritualization of race from Michaels, who develops it in *Our America: Nativism, Modernism, and Pluralism*.
2. See Rogin, 94–99.
3. Elaine Scarry has written brilliantly of the elusive-yet-entrenched quality of embodied political identity:

   The extent to which . . . the nation-state resides unnoticed in the intricate recesses of personhood, penetrates the deepest layers of consciousness, and manifests itself in the body itself is hard to assess; for it seems at any given moment "hardly" there, yet seems at many moments, however hardly, *there* . . . in the learned postures, gestures, gait, the ease or reluctance with which it breaks into a smile; *there* in the regional accent . . . The political identity of the body is usually learned unconsciously, effortlessly, and very early—it is said that within a few months of life British infants have learned to hold their eyebrows in a raised position . . . To the extent that the body is political, it tends to be unalterably political and thus acquires an apparent *apolitical* character precisely by being unsusceptible to, beyond the reach of, any *new* political imposition (*The Body in Pain*, 108–110).

4. I take this discussion of the Plessy case from Lofgren, 95ff; Michaels, "Souls of White Folk," 188–92; Sundquist.

5. For a fascinating discussion of the racial ideologies of the American woman's suffrage movement, see Newman. I am indebted to Newman for this quote from Stanton as well as for my understanding of the connection between the woman's movement and the discourses of civilization.

6. Ozment, 16. In this lecture, Ozment stresses the "multicultural" character of premodern Europe, warning against representations of Europe or the West as a racist monolith. My question is why a history of racial, ethnic, and religious contact and conflict—which, as it happens, characterizes other continents besides the European—should particularly suit Europeans above all others for the work of cultural appreciation. I am grateful to William H. Chrisman for making this typescript available to me.

7. For a compelling account of one human subject exhibited at the "University of Man," see Bradford and Blume.

8. For a poignant reading of mainstream "revivals" of decimated Native American cultures, see Wexler.

9. I take the notion of "democratic social space" from Fisher, while reading it somewhat less benignly than he.

10. Lerner's monograph became the unlikely inspiration for Stephen Greenblatt's chapter "The Improvisation of Power," in *Renaissance Self-Fashioning*. Making the point that "what Lerner calls empathy Shakespeare calls Iago," Greenblatt suggests that "Lerner misleads only by insisting . . . that it is an act of imaginative generosity, a sympathetic appreciation of the situation of the other fellow. For when he speaks confidently of the 'spread of empathy around the world,' we must understand that he is speaking of the exercise of Western power, power that is creative as well as destructive, but that is scarcely ever wholly disinterested or benign" (228).

REFERENCES

Berlant, Lauren. 1991. "National Bodies/National Brands: Imitation of Life." In *Comparative American Identities: Race, Sex, and Nationality in the Modern Text*. Ed. Hortense J. Spillers. New York: Routledge. 110–140.

Bourdieu, Pierre. 1984. *Distinction: A Social Critique of the Judgement of Taste.* Translated by Richard Nice. Cambridge, MA: Harvard University Press.

Bowers, Claude G. 1932. *Beveridge and the Progressive Era.* Cambridge, MA: The Riverside Press.

Bradford, Phillips Verner and Harvey Blume. 1992. *Ota Benga: The Pygmy in the Zoo.* New York: Delta.

Carby, Hazel. 1987. *Reconstructing Womanhood: The Emergence of the Afro-American Woman Novelist.* New York: Oxford University Press.

Daniels, George H. 1971. *Science in American Society.* New York: Knopf.

Dyer, Richard. 1988. "White." *Screen* 29.4 (Autumn): 44–65.

Elias, Norbert. 1978. *The Civilizing Process.* Translated by Edmund Jephcott. New York: Urizen Books.

Elias, Robert H. 1977. *"Entangling Alliances with None": An Essay on the Individual in the American Twenties.* New York: Norton.

Fine, David M. 1977. *The City, the Immigrant, and American Fiction, 1880–1920.* Metchen, N.J.: Scarecrow Press.

Fisher, Philip. 1988. "Democratic Social Space: Whitman, Melville, and the Promise of American Transparency." *Representations* 24 (Fall): 60–101.

Fiske, John. 1885. *American Political Ideas Viewed from the Standpoint of Universal History.* New York.

———. 1902. *The Writings of John Fiske.* 24 vols. Cambridge, MA: Riverside Press.

Gilman, Charlotte Perkins. 1916. "With Her in Ourland," in *Forerunner* 7 (June).

———. 1935. *The Living of Charlotte Perkins Gilman, An Autobiography.* New York: D. Appleton-Century.

———. 1979. *Herland.* New York: Pantheon.

———. 1991. *A Non-Fiction Reader.* Ed. Larry Ceplair. New York: Columbia University Press.

Gossett, Thomas F. 1964. *Race: The History of an Idea in America.* Dallas: Southern Methodist University Press.

Gould, Charles W. 1920. *America: A Family Matter.* New York: Charles Scribner's Sons.

Gould, Stephen Jay. 1981. *The Mismeasure of Man.* New York: Norton.

Grand Dragons Knights of the Ku Klux Klan. 1977. *Papers Read at the Meeting of Grand Dragons Knights of the Ku Klux Klan At Their First Annual Meeting.* 1923. Repr. New York: Arno Press.

Grant, Madison Bell. 1970. *The Passing of the Great Race.* 1918. Repr. New York: Arno Press.

Greenblatt, Stephen. 1980. *Renaissance Self-Fashioning.* Chicago: University of Chicago Press.

Harris, George. 1897. *Inequality and Progress.* Boston.

Hitchens, Christopher. 1990. *Blood, Class, and Nostalgia: Anglo-American Ironies.* New York: Farrar, Strauss & Giroux.

Hofstadter, Richard. 1959. *Social Darwinism in American Thought*. New York: George Braziller.

Humphrey, Seth K. 1920. *The Racial Prospect*. New York: Charles Scribner's Sons.

James, William. 1961. *William James on Psychical Research*. Eds. Gardner Murphy and Robert O. Ballou. London: Chatto and Windus.

Jehlen, Myra. 1986. *American Incarnation: The Individual, the Nation, and the Continent*. Cambridge, MA: Harvard University Press.

Josey, Charles Conant. 1923. *Race and National Solidarity*. New York: Charles Scribner's Sons.

Lerner, Daniel. 1958. *The Passing of Traditional Society*. Glencoe, Illinois: The Free Press.

Lewontin, Richard C., Steven Rose, and Leon Kaminer. 1984. *Not in Our Genes: Biology, Ideology, and Human Nature*. New York: Pantheon.

Lofgren, Charles A. 1987. *The Plessy Case: A Legal-Historical Interpretation*. New York: Oxford University Press.

Luker, Ralph E. 1987. *The Social Gospel in Black and White: American Racial Reform 1885–1912*. Chapel Hill: University of North Carolina Press.

Michaels, Walter Benn. 1987. *The Gold Standard and the Logic of Naturalism: American Literature at the Turn of the Century*. Berkeley and Los Angeles: University of California Press.

———. 1988. "The Souls of White Folk." In *Literature and the Body*. Ed. Elaine Scarry. Baltimore: Johns Hopkins University Press. 185–206.

_____. 1995. *Our America: Nativism, Modernism, and Pluralism*. Durham: Duke University Press.

Newman, Louise. 1992. *Laying Claim to Difference: Ideologies of Race and Gender in the United States Woman's Movement, 1870–1920*. Ph.D. Dissertation, Brown University.

Ozment, Steve. *Europe Before 1700: The Importance of the Premodern Past*. Typescript, n.d.

Plessy v. Ferguson 163 U.S. 538–552 (1896).

Quinn, Arthur Hobson. 1932. *The Soul of America, Yesterday and Today*. Philadelphia: University of Pennsylvania Press.

Rogin, Michael Paul. 1987. *Ronald Reagan, the Movie, and Other Episodes in Political Demonology*. Berkeley and Los Angeles: University of California Press.

Said, Edward. 1992. *Culture and Imperialism*. New York: Knopf.

Scarry, Elaine. 1985. *The Body in Pain: The Making and Unmaking of the World*. New York: Oxford University Press.

_____. 1988. "Introduction." In *Literature and the Body*. Baltimore: Johns Hopkins University Press.

Stanton, Elizabeth Cady. 1895. "Educated Suffrage." *Independent* (February 14), 2.

Stark, Cruce. 1983. "The Color of 'The Damned Thing': The Occult as Suprasensational." In *The Haunted Dusk: American Supernatural Fiction,*

1820–1920. Ed. Howard Kerr, John W. Crowley, and Charles L. Crow. Athens: The University of Georgia Press. 209–228.

Stoddard, Lothrop. 1920. *The Rising Tide of Color Against White World-Supremacy*. New York: Charles Scribner's Sons.

Strong, Josiah. 1885. *Our Country: Its Possible Future and Its Present Crisis*. New York.

Sundquist, Eric J. 1988. "Mark Twain and Homer Plessy." *Representations* 24 (Fall): 102–28.

Virginia Code SS 1–14; in U.S. Supreme Court, *Records and Briefs* in the case of *Loving v. Virginia* 388 U.S. 1 (1967).

Wexler, Laura. 1992. "Tender Violence: Literary Eavesdropping, Domestic Fiction, and Educational Reform." In *The Culture of Sentiment: Race, Gender, and Sentimentality in Nineteenth Century America*. Ed. Shirley Samuels. New York: Oxford University Press. 9–38.

Wilson, Woodrow. 1931. *A History of the American People*. 5 vols. New York: Wm. H. Wise & Co.

THREE

THE ABJECT BORDERS OF THE BODY IMAGE

GAIL WEISS

> On the days when I am not tortured by hunger, the dread of becoming fat
> again moves to the center. Two things, then, torture me: First, hunger.
> Second, the dread of getting fatter. I find no way out of this noose. . . .
> Horrible feeling of emptiness. Horrible fear of this feeling. I have nothing
> that can dull this feeling.
>
> —Ludwig Binswanger (1958: 253)

> In the medical model, the body of the subject is the passive tablet on
> which disorder is inscribed. Deciphering that inscription is usually seen
> as a matter of determining the "cause" of the disorder; sometimes (as with
> psychoanalysis) *interpretation* of symptoms will be involved. But always
> the process requires a trained—that is to say, highly specialized—profes-
> sional whose expertise alone can unlock the secrets of the disordered
> body. For the feminist analyst, by contrast, the disordered body, like all
> bodies, is engaged in a process of making meaning, of "labor on the body."
> From this perspective, anorexia (for example) is never *merely* regressive,
> never *merely* a fall into illness and chaos. Nor is it facilitated simply by
> bedazzlement by cultural images, "indoctrination" by what happens, arbi-
> trarily, to be in fashion at this time. Rather, the "relentless pursuit of
> excessive thinness" is an attempt to embody certain values, to create a
> body that will speak for the self in a meaningful and powerful way.
>
> —Susan Bordo (1993: 67)

In his famous essay on the "mirror stage," Jacques Lacan argues that as the
young child comes to identify with her specular image in the mirror, the
"form of its totality" that is acquired obscures a certain constitutive loss, or,
more accurately, series of losses that make the coherence of the body image
possible. According to Judith Butler:

> The mirror stage is not a *developmental* account of how the idea of one's
> own body comes into being. It does suggest, however, that the capacity to
> project a *morphe*, a shape, onto a surface is part of the psychic (and phan-
> tasmatic) elaboration, centering, and containment of one's own bodily

contours. This process of psychic projection or elaboration implies as well that the sense of one's own body is not (only) achieved through differentiating from another (the maternal body), but that any sense of bodily contour, as projected, is articulated through a necessary self-division and self-estrangement (Butler 1993: 71).

While Lacan devotes much attention to the (alienating) identity that arises out of the child's identification with her specular image, both Butler and Julia Kristeva concentrate on what fails to be subsumed within that identity, on what is left out of the totalizing process that transforms momentary and diverse bodily sensations into a unified body image.[1] For Kristeva, that which is "lost" or which resists incorporation into the body image is also precisely what makes the coherent body image possible because it marks the boundary between the body image and what it is not. There is a permanent danger that this boundary will be dissolved, however, since the boundary is only reinforced on one side, the Symbolic side. The "other side" is the unnameable, abject domain that continually threatens to overrun its carefully established borders. The fragility of the border in turn undermines the stability and coherence of the body image; as Kristeva notes:

> The more or less beautiful image in which I behold or recognize myself rests upon an abjection that sunders it as soon as repression, the constant watchman, is relaxed (Kristeva 1982: 13).

This abject specter, which continually haunts the ego and seeks to disrupt the continuity of the body image, is all the more terrifying because it is a ghost incarnated in flesh, blood, spit, mucus, faeces, vomit, urine, pus, and other bodily fluids. Hence, the boundary between the body image and what it is not is not (merely) a symbolic one; rather, it must also be understood as a corporeal refusal of corporeality. As Elizabeth Grosz observes:

> Abjection involves the paradoxically necessary but impossible desire to transcend corporeality. It is a refusal of the defiling, impure, uncontrollable materiality of the subject's embodied existence. It is a response to the various bodily cycles of incorporation, absorption, depletion, expulsion, the cycles of material rejuvenation and consumption necessary to sustain itself yet incapable of social recognition and representation. It is an effect of the child's corporeal boundaries being set through the circulation of (socially unacceptable) drive energies and the rhythms of incorporation and evacuation necessary for existence (Grosz 1989: 72; Gross 1990: 88).

Abjection is necessary because some aspects of our corporeal experience must be excluded to enable the coherent construction of both the ego and the body image, but it is also impossible because, as Grosz, Butler, and

Kristeva all suggest, that which is excluded is not eliminated altogether but continually "erupts" and therefore disrupts the privileged sites of inclusion.

In this essay I would like to explore the role that this abject domain plays in the constitution of what we might call "distorted" body images, that is, body images that refuse or resist normalization in a Foucauldian sense. These aberrant body images which are at odds with societal attitudes, individual and social expectations, and which often present self-imposed barriers on an individual's physical capacities are paradigmatically exemplified in the case of "Gertrude," a seventeen-year-old female anorexic patient cited by Dr. Hilde Bruch, who worries while she is undergoing a "re-feeding" program that has brought her weight to just over ninety pounds, that she might be gaining too much weight, that is, getting fat (Bruch 1978: 16).

Although the starving anorexic who is convinced she is overweight serves as a striking example of an individual with a distorted body image, it is evident that distorted body images can be found in a much larger population, including schizophrenics, individuals with multiple personality disorders (who may have several incompatible body images), individuals who have sustained severe nerve damage and/or neurological disturbances, and individuals whose bodies have been labelled "abnormal" by society such as dwarves, giants, and those all too numerous others whom society designates as "freaks."[2]

To begin to discuss the problem of distorted body images, we must first address the rather tricky issue of what the distortion deviates *from* since the very notion of distortion, like the notion of "the Other" that de Beauvoir discusses in *The Second Sex*, suggests some kind of deviation from a norm, a standard that is itself identifiable as such. Locating the Archimidean point against which the distortion can be measured does not seem a viable way to proceed, however, because the body image is itself continually changing in response to physiological changes in the body, as well as in response to the physical and social demands that we face, as individuals, from one moment to the next in our daily lives.

In his classic study of the body image, *The Image and Appearance of the Human Body*, Paul Schilder claims that each of us has, not one, but an infinite number of body images. Distortion, then, cannot be attributed to the presence of a multiplicity of body images, since this multiplicity itself characterizes the "normal" case. And, if we take seriously Butler's claim that "[i]dentifications are multiple and contestatory" then, I would argue, it seems to make sense that multiple, contestatory body images will accompany them (Butler 1993: 99). Susan Bordo challenges the viability of the normal/pathological distinction from yet another perspective, arguing that, with respect to the distorted body images produced by eating disorders, "the anorectic does not 'misperceive' her body; rather, she has learned all too well the dominant cultural standards of *how* to perceive" (Bordo 1993: 57).

Rather than attempting the impossible task of providing a single explanation or "diagnosis" of the phenomenon of body image distortion, I would like to focus instead on the relationship between body image distortion and abjection to see if shedding more light on the latter can lead to a greater understanding of not only distortion, but also the construction of body images that are taken to be "normal." Focusing on corporeal processes of boundary construction and destruction is especially crucial, for, I will argue, it is through the setting up and breaking down of boundaries that both distorted and nondistorted body images come to play a normative role in identity formation.

While Kristeva is especially interested in the question, "Where then lies the border, the initial phantasmatic limit that establishes the clean and proper self of the speaking and/or social being?" (Kristeva 1982: 85), and posits the origin of abjection in the child's simultaneous longing for and horror of its pre-individuated connection with the maternal body, I am interested not in the ultimate source of the abject (indeed, unlike Kristeva, I do not think that the domain of the abject can be traced to a single corporeal relationship or site), but in the process of abjection itself, a process described by Kristeva as an act of expulsion, a self-purging whereby with the food I vomit, I also "expel *myself*, I spit *myself* out, I abject *myself* within the same motion through which 'I' claim to establish myself" (Kristeva 1982: 3). Expelling (parts of) myself to establish myself as a member of the Symbolic order, I create corporeal boundaries between myself and what is not myself, and, in so doing, actively constitute myself as an idiosyncratic entity. On this account, abjection is necessary to create the boundaries that will individuate the self, but to recognize the need to create these boundaries is also to recognize the fragility of the self that is so constituted, and so not only the abject, but the very process of abjection must also be buried, repressed, denied.[3] According to Grosz:

> Abjection is the underside of the symbolic. It is what the symbolic must reject, cover over and contain. The symbolic requires that a border separate or protect the subject from this abyss which beckons and haunts it: the abject entices and attracts the subject ever closer to its edge. It is an insistence on the subject's necessary relation to death, to animality, and to materiality, being the subject's recognition and refusal of its corporeality. The abject demonstrates the impossibility of clear-cut borders, lines of demarcation, divisions between the clean and the unclean, the proper and the improper, order and disorder (Grosz 1990: 89).

For Grosz, Butler, and Kristeva, the attempt to establish corporeal borders will inevitably fail, not only because of (imperialistic) desires to see (and perhaps conquer) what lies beyond the "borderlands," or because of the seductive force of the abject itself, but because of the phantasmatic status of the "I" that simultaneously requires and disavows the need for borders to assure itself of its own autonomy and discreteness. In *Unbearable Weight: Feminism, Western Culture, and the Body*, Susan Bordo emphasizes that the very project of demarcating the "I" from what it is not relies upon a dualistic metaphysics, a metaphysics that devalues the corporeality of the body by contrasting its alleged passivity and "brute" materiality with the transcendent, mental activity associated with the "I," activity that has traditionally been associated with human reason, will, vitality, and spirit. And, Bordo reminds us: "This duality of active spirit/passive body is also gendered, and it has been one of the most historically powerful of the dualities that inform Western ideologies of gender" (Bordo 1993: 11).

While it is crucial to recognize the repudiation of one's own corporeality that accompanies these psychic processes of boundary construction constitutive of the subject as such, Butler points out that the ongoing attempt to establish these borders, once and for all, also functions to demarcate those who "count" as subjects from those who do not:

> This exclusionary matrix by which subjects are formed thus requires the simultaneous production of a domain of abject beings, those who are not yet "subjects," but who form the constitutive outside to the domain of the subject. The abject designates here precisely those "unlivable" and "uninhabitable" zones of social life which are nevertheless densely populated by those who do not enjoy the status of the subject, but whose living under the sign of the "unlivable" is required to circumscribe the domain of the subject. This zone of uninhabitability will constitute the defining limit of the subject's domain; it will constitute that site of dreaded identification against which—and by virtue of which—the domain of the subject will circumscribe its own claim to autonomy and to life. In this sense, then, the subject is constituted through the force of exclusion and abjection, one which produces a constitutive outside to the subject, an abjected outside, which is, after all, "inside" the subject as its own founding repudiation (Butler 1993: 3).

How are we to understand this "force of exclusion and abjection," much less the precipitating role it plays in the formation of the subject and its body images? In a 1980 interview, Kristeva offers a poignant description of abjection as

> an extremely strong feeling which is at once somatic and symbolic, and which is above all a revolt of the person against an external menace from

which one wants to keep oneself at a distance, but of which one has the impression that it is not only an external menace but that it may menace us from the inside. So it is a desire for separation, for becoming autonomous and also the feeling of an impossibility of doing so—whence the element of crisis which the notion of abjection carries within it. Taken to its logical consequences, it is an impossible assemblage of elements, with a connotation of a "fragile limit" (Kristeva 1988: 135–136).

If (the process of) abjection is necessary for the development of a coherent body image, the repudiation of what lies beyond the "fragile limit" that marks the border between the "I" and the "not-I" will give rise to its own body image distortions as certain bodily fluids, bodily activities, and body parts are disavowed and refused a legitimate place in the construction of a corporeal identity. For Kristeva, as well as for Grosz (but for strikingly different reasons), the price of such delegitimization is far too high. Kristeva stresses the creative "juices" that flow from this abjected domain, in the form of 1) the revolutionary possibilities of poetic language and 2) the maternal reenactment of (what Kristeva takes to be) the "original narcissistic crisis" through pregnancy and childbirth. As Kelly Oliver observes in her discussion of the subversive significance of maternity and poetic language for Kristeva: "Like poetic language, pregnancy is a case where identity contains alterity as a heterogeneous other without completely losing its integrity" (Oliver 1993: 183). And yet, there is a darker side to these attempts somehow to come to terms with the abject, for, as Butler observes, they may end up reinforcing the hegemony of the Symbolic order that they are supposed to belie.

In her essay entitled, "The Body Politics of Julia Kristeva," Butler describes Kristeva's celebration of poetic language and pregnancy as follows:

> for Kristeva, poetry and maternity represent privileged practices within paternally sanctioned culture which permit a nonpsychotic experience of that heterogeneity and dependency characteristic of the maternal terrain. These acts of *poesis* reveal an instinctual heterogeneity that subsequently exposes the repressed ground of the Symbolic, challenges the mastery of the univocal signifier, and diffuses the autonomy of the subject who postures as their necessary ground. The heterogeneity of drives operates culturally as a subversive strategy of displacement, one which dislodges the hegemony of the paternal law by releasing the repressed multiplicity interior to language itself (Butler 1989: 85–86).

Butler goes on to offer a powerful critique not only of Kristeva's reification of poetry and maternity as successful subversive strategies but, more fundamentally, of Kristeva's understanding of the abject as founding rather than being found or constructed within the Symbolic order. Butler argues that Kristeva focuses exclusively on the prohibitive effects of repression (of the abject), and does not acknowledge, as does Foucault, the generative effects of repression that can include the very production of "the object that it comes to deny." Privileging the maternal body as a means of celebrating the (abject) corporeal heterogeneity that, for Kristeva, both precedes and is disavowed by the Symbolic order, results, Butler claims, in Kristeva's failing to see that

> The female body that is freed from the shackles of the paternal law may well prove to be yet another incarnation of that law, posing as subversive but operating in the service of that law's self-amplification and proliferation (Butler 1990b: 93).

In her essay, "Ours to Jew or Die," Kristeva herself recognizes the danger of positing "an object of hatred and desire, of threat and aggressivity, of envy and abomination" (all terms which at various times have been used to describe the maternal body by Kristeva as well as by others), an abject object, in this case the Jew, which "gives thought a focus where all contradictions are explained and satisfied" (Kristeva 1982: 178). The anti-Semite, according to Kristeva, by projecting this abject object outside the Symbolic law, ensures that the Jew is not protected by it; moreover, not content with the punishment meted out by the Symbolic order to those who transgress it, the anti-Semite seeks to destroy the Symbolic law in order to construct a new Law, beyond the Symbolic, a Law purged of the threats the abject other continually poses to the Symbolic order. This new Law, unlike the "constraining and frustrating symbolic one . . . would be absolute, full, and reassuring" (Kristeva 1982: 178). This desire to move beyond all limits, for Kristeva, self-destructs on its own limits, namely, its reliance on what she calls "the deadliest of fantasies" (Kristeva 1982: 180). This deadly fantasy is, indeed, a fantasy of death—the death of the abject other that is viewed as necessary to maintain the corporeal integrity of the self. As an external projection of one's own abjected corporeality, the expulsion of the abject other from the Symbolic order seeks to purge the self so that it may be reborn without the taint of defilement. For Kristeva, such a desire itself reinforces, rather than denies, the power the abject wields *within* the Symbolic order's own carefully defined boundaries. "The abject," she claims,

> is perverse because it neither gives up nor assumes a prohibition, a rule, or a law; but turns them aside, misleads, corrupts; uses them, takes advantage of them, the better to deny them. It kills in the name of life— a progressive despot; it lives at the behest of death . . . (Kristeva 1982: 15).

Regardless, then, of whether one seeks the origin of abjection within or outside of the Symbolic order, it is clear that the abject is a force that must constantly be reckoned with from within the Symbolic domain. For Kristeva,

> abjection is coextensive with social and symbolic order, on the individual as well as on the collective level. By virtue of this, abjection, just like *prohibition of incest*, is a universal phenomenon; one encounters it as soon as the symbolic and/or social dimension of man is constituted, and this throughout the course of civilization. But abjection assumes specific shapes and different codings according to the various "symbolic systems" (Kristeva 1982: 68).

In *Bodies that Matter*, Butler explores some of the diverse shapes and codings abjection takes on in order to reveal the constitutive role the processes of abjection and exclusion play in the formation of the subject. Naming the abject other, compelling the abject other to exist as "the abject," excluding the abject other from certain privileges, regions, and social practices, are strategies we employ to distance ourselves from the recognition of our own self-alienation and self-repudiation. Through these forces of abjection and exclusion, the abject is provided with a concrete identity and occupies a place, whether that place be a prison, a refugee center, a ghetto, a concentration camp, or another yet to be constructed "zone of uninhabitability," a place where society can dispose of its "excrement."

In her essay entitled, "What Does Cannibalism Speak? Jean de Léry and the Tupinamba Lesson," Sara Castro-Klaren furthers our understanding of how the abject other is projected "outside" the subject through the abjection of its own unresolved physical and psychical "horrors." Specifically, Castro-Klaren explores "how anthropophagy and the orgies observed among the Caribs and the Tupi speak, as they construct the 'savage,' of the dark night of the soul of the subject" (Castro-Klaren 1993: 26). She appeals to Kristeva's notion of the abject to interpret the fascination/horror of the "civilized" European (e.g., Columbus, Léry, and their audiences) for the cannibalistic practices of these "savages," practices that were rarely witnessed firsthand but whose recountings were compelled by expectant ethnographers who eagerly interrogated those natives willing to "confess" them. According to Castro-Klaren, Léry's own, highly respected and widely influential ethnographic study of the Tupi, reveals more about Léry and sixteenth-century French Christianity than it does about the Tupi:

> Three months of precarious exile (October 1557–January 1558) among the Tupi, away from the inimical French Catholic settlers in the bay of Guanabara, arrested and traversed by twenty years in a France bled and

scorched by religious wars, are transformed into a text that surreptitiously and yet obviously deals with the hottest issue of the day: the transubstantiation of bread and wine into the flesh and blood of the only son of God. Anthropophagy among the Tupi is the substitute construct for theophagy among the Christians. The representation of the Tupi as orgiastic cannibals enables Léry, the survivor of at least three major famines . . . in which civilized men were allowed to eat human flesh, to collect his thoughts on the great prohibitions. He collects them, here inscribes them as memory of the journey to "over there" and projects upon them the business of the other "over here". The unspeakable status of incest, offerings of the flesh of the firstborn, sex outside a guilt complex, cannot and do not therefore fall within the realm of the subject. As Kristeva puts it, abjection transforms the "anxiety of the borderline subject into the site of the Other" (Castro-Klaren 1993: 34–35).

If, as Kristeva, Grosz, Butler, and Castro-Klaren all suggest, the construction of the abject other ultimately represents our (unsuccessful) attempts to repudiate our own abjection, what effects do these attempts and the existence of this abject other have upon our own body images and upon our own understanding of the phenomenon of distortion? Grosz's own somatic reading of abjection provides us with some important clues. "Abjection," she observes,

> is the body's acknowledgement that the boundaries and limits imposed on it are really social projections—effects of desire, not nature. It testifies to the precarious grasp of the subject on its own identity, an assertion that the subject may slide back into the impure chaos out of which it was formed (Grosz 1990: 90).

Despite their productive analyses of the phenomenon of abjection and the role both the abject other and abjection play in the processes of identity formation, Kristeva, Butler, and Grosz all seem to leave us with an "unlivable" dilemma that we nonetheless continue to live out from one moment to the next. We cannot dispense with the abject without dispensing with our own identities, since the latter are founded upon the former. On the other hand, we can hardly "embrace" the abject without its ceasing to be the abject, a process which will, inevitably it seems, force the creation of a new abject object to take the place of the old one.[4] The refusal of identity is not an option either, since the refusal of identity is itself the taking up of an identity position, and, in either case, we will always find identities (and abject objects) projected upon us regardless of our wishes, needs, or desires.

To the extent that our own body fluids and body parts are implicated in these processes of abjection and exclusion, the coherence of the body images we develop can, as Lacan first noted, only be a precarious fantasy, one that we maintain with difficulty. If certain bodily functions, desires, and practices are, by social (and physical) necessity, expelled from participation in the construction of the body image, then, to return to our original question, on what basis are we to distinguish distorted body images from body images that are not distorted? It would seem that the normalized body image, one that complies with the imperatives of the Symbolic order, can only arise on the basis of bodily distortions (and perhaps contortions), performative exclusions that mark the threshold of the abject. And yet, insofar as that which has been abjected continually overruns its carefully circumscribed borders, it appears that these abject sites of our corporeality continue to seep into our own body images, threatening their coherence, and disrupting our attempts to contain our bodily excesses and deficiencies.

To distinguish distorted body images from nondistorted body images is, then, a much more difficult task than one may at first suppose. Perhaps what is needed is a new vocabulary for those body images that resist normalization, body images that refuse to cohere, or that somehow do manage to cohere in what looks, from an outsider's perspective, to be an impossible configuration. What does seem to be clear is that when bodies are at odds with their own body images, when that which is needed to sustain the body (e.g. relationships with other people, food, drink, clothing, shelter) becomes the abject other, distortion may turn out to be the only viable strategy for survival, and, paradoxically, an affirmation predicated on a negation of life.

Susan Bordo, in particular, emphasizes the moral connotations that accompany this repudiation of (aspects of) embodied existence, arguing that "food refusal, weight loss, commitment to exercise, and ability to tolerate bodily pain and exhaustion have become cultural metaphors for self-determination, will, and moral fortitude" (Bordo 1993: 68). In such a cultural climate, she maintains, it is hardly surprising that eating disorders are on the rise, especially among young women, nor is it surprising to find that self-starvation itself has deep spiritual dimensions that are in turn nourished by the traditional mind/body dualism that associates the mind with transcendence and the body with immanence. "Within such a framework," Bordo asserts,

> interpreting anorexia requires, not technical or professional expertise, but awareness of the many layers of cultural signification that are crystallized in the disorder (Bordo 1993: 67).

Chief among these "layers of cultural signification," for Bordo, is what she calls an "amazingly durable and flexible strategy of social control," namely, "the discipline and normalization of the female body." Indeed, Bordo goes on to claim that this is "perhaps the only gender oppression that exercises itself, although to different degrees and in different forms, across age, race, class, and sexual orientation" (Bordo 1993: 166). The predominant techniques through which this discipline and normalization are accomplished, she suggests, are "diet, makeup, and dress—central organizing principles of time and space in the day of many women" (Bordo 1993: 166).

A danger of Bordo's account as well as the account of Morag MacSween who also offers a feminist social constructionist perspective on anorexia is that in attempting to draw our attention to the limitations of medical models that tend either to ignore or minimize the substantial, motivating role that cultural norms and expectations regarding the "perfect" female body play in eating disorders, they lose sight of the fact that it is medicine and not culture to which we must look to treat these eating disorders and the body image distortions associated with them.[5] That is to say, while Bordo and MacSween are correct in arguing that as long as doctors refuse to acknowledge the cultural forces that encourage women to starve themselves in the pursuit of an elusive, ascetic body ideal, they will fail to understand why these disorders are so prevalent as well as how to eradicate them; it is nonetheless extremely problematic to claim, as Bordo does, that interpreting anorexia does not require "technical or professional expertise."

If, as Bordo suggests, anorexia nervosa is indeed a psychopathology only to the extent that psychopathology is itself the "crystallization of culture," it is nonetheless the case that it is not culture that is killing anorexic women and men, but their agonistic relationships with their own bodies. While Bordo would certainly recognize the validity of this point, her argument is that "[o]ur bodies, not less than anything else that is human, are constituted by culture" (Bordo 1993: 142). Moreover, she also maintains that "female bodies have historically been significantly more vulnerable than male bodies to extremes in . . . cultural manipulation of the body" (Bordo 1993: 143). Working from a feminist social constructionist perspective, Bordo traces this female corporeal vulnerability not to anatomical differences between males and females, but to cultural forces themselves, forces that have defined women (and, more specifically, thin women) as the object of masculine desire. MacSween reinforces this point when she claims that "[i]t is not the body itself which makes women 'passive vessels,' but how that body is *socially constructed*" (MacSween 1993: 50).[6]

The question thus becomes, why has slenderness become the aesthetic ideal for women (as well as for men, as Bordo repeatedly acknowledges)? Why is slenderness what our patriarchal culture has come to associate with its body image ideal? These are indeed important questions, questions that Bordo addresses creatively and incisively in her work, but her answers, while complicated and historically nuanced, tend to be generated out of only one of the multi-dimensions she originally argues for, namely culture itself. While a feminist cultural analysis can certainly aid us in addressing these questions, it is woefully inadequate when it comes to resolving the issues themselves, that is, treating the diverse corporeal effects of these multi-faceted symptoms. Even setting the issue of treatment aside, it is clear that one cannot even begin to interpret the lived, bodily dimensions of anorexia unless one has either direct (either as a doctor, nurse, therapist or social worker) or indirect access to information obtained in clinical work with anorexics.

By abjecting the "fat" body from the culturally constructed aesthetic domain, people and not just body parts are designated as the abject other, doomed to exist in those uninhabitable, unlivable regions that Butler reminds us are, in point of fact, densely populated. Indeed, these regions are not just inhabited by those who are considered or consider themselves to be overweight. In fact, I would argue, they are currently in danger of being overpopulated insofar as none of us can forever live up to what Audre Lorde calls the "mythical norm." And for women, by definition, it is impossible even to try. This is because this mythical norm consists of those who are "white, thin, male, young, heterosexual, Christian, and financially secure" (Lorde 1990: 282). Despite the fact that this norm is also impossible for men of color, homosexual men, poor men, old men, and non-Christian men to achieve as well, in America and in much of Europe, this mythical norm indeed serves to define a cultural body image ideal. And, to the extent that this mythical norm functions as an imaginary, identificatory pole that regulates our satisfaction/dissatisfaction with our own specular images, it is clear that the elaboration of a coherent body image is itself an arduous task.

Returning to a question which I raised earlier in this essay, namely, how do we account for "distorted" body images, such as that of the anorexic, it is clear that the answer cannot be reduced to the contradictions between her own body image and the perceptions of others (i.e., her view of herself as overweight, and others' view of her as emaciated), since such an explanation only takes us back to the Sartrian tension between being-for-others and being-for-itself, a tension that characterizes not only the anorexic's existence but everyone who is nonanorexic as well.[7] Nor do I think it can be answered by appealing to the enormous social pressure (real as it is) that the hegemonic cultural body ideal of the tall, thin body, places upon us.[8] Paradoxically, I would argue, the deadly distortions in the anorexic's body image stem from its excessive *coherence*, a coherence that can only be maintained through her disidentification with and repudiation of her own multiple body images.

To develop this point further, what I am claiming is that although there are very real contradictions in the anorexic's body image (and, although they take different forms, they are also present in other individuals' body images that are viewed as pathologically distorted), the contradictions themselves should not be viewed as the cause of the distortions. This is because, as I have tried to show throughout this essay, we all have contradictions in our body images, contradictions that on a Lacanian analysis stem from the irresolvable gap between our own diverse and fluid bodily sensations on the one hand, and our identification with the unified, integrated specular image that subjectivates us. While Lacan does not acknowledge the (nonpsychotic) possibility of an individual's possessing multiple body images, he does recognize that the gestalt that arises out of the identification of the subject with the specular image, attains its coherence at the expense of our lived corporeality:

> The fact is that the total form of the body by which the subject anticipates in a mirage the maturation of his power is given to him only as *Gestalt*, that is to say, in an exteriority in which this form is certainly more constituent than constituted, but in which it appears to him above all in a constrasting size (*un relief de stature*) that fixes it and in a symmetry that inverts it, in contrast with the turbulent movements that the subject feels are animating him. Thus, this Gestalt—whose pregnancy should be regarded as bound up with the species, though its motor style remains scarcely recognizable—by these two aspects of its appearance, symbolizes the mental permanence of the *I*, at the same time as it prefigures its alienating destination; it is still pregnant with the correspondences that unite the *I* with the statue in which man projects himself, with the phantoms that dominate him, or with the automaton in which, in an ambiguous relation, the world of his own making tends to find completion (Lacan 1977: 2–3).

This strange pregnancy, which is not distinctive to women, but is characteristic of "the species" as a whole, itself symbolizes the crucial disjunction between the corporeality of the subject and the specular image through which that subject is constituted. More simply, Lacan's metaphorical use of pregnancy as a characteristic of the species (and not of women in particular) further dissociates this Gestalt from the actual bodies of women (and men). By identifying the specular image with a statue, with "phantoms that dominate" and with an automaton in which "the world of his own making tends to find completion," Lacan points simultaneously to the enabling and the oppressive potentialities that accompany the gestation of the subject.

The turbulence that characterizes our lived bodily experience, a turbulence which, for Lacan, is psychically rejected in favor of a projected (imaginary) identification with the specular image, can, as he well recognized, never be denied altogether. Indeed, I would maintain that this turbulence is expressed and even accentuated in the transitions we continually make between one body image and another. For the nonpathological subject, I would argue, it is the very multiplicity of these body images that guarantees that we cannot invest too heavily in any one of them, and these multiple body images themselves offer points of resistance to the development of too strong an identification with a singularly alienating specular (or even cultural) image. That is, these multiple body images serve to destabilize the hegemony of any particular body image ideal, and are precisely what allows us to maintain a sense of corporeal fluidity.

By contrast, I am claiming that it is precisely the lack of *destabilization* in the anorexic's body image that is the source of its deadly destructiveness. Thus, rather than view the anorexic as an incoherent or contradictory subject, I am claiming that she is *too* coherent, psychically and corporeally dominated by what "Ellen West," the pseudonymous anorexic subject of Ludwig Binswanger's famous case study, repeatedly identified as her *idée fixée*, namely, the "dread of getting fat." Indeed, the "mocking" phantoms that accompany her desire to be an ethereal or "fleshless" body, phantoms that remind her that she can never realize her ideal, do not destabilize the dominance of this idea but actually reinforce its hegemony. The power of their ghostly presence is incarnated in Ellen's poem "The Evil Thoughts," a poem that does not succeed in exorcising these "demons," but which only seems to strengthen their force and ubiquity:

> One time we were your thinking,
> Your hoping pure and proud!
> Where now are all your projects,
> The dreams that used to crowd?
>
> Now all of them lie buried,
> Scattered in wind and storm,
> And you've become a nothing,
> A timid earthy worm.
>
> So then we had to leave you,
> To dark night we must flee;
> The curse which fell upon you
> Has made us black to see.
>
> If you seek peace and quiet,
> Then we'll come creeping nigh
> And we'll take vengeance on you
> With our derisive cry.
>
> If you seek joy and gladness,
> We'll hurry to your side;

Accusing you and jeering
We'll e'er with you abide!
(Binswanger 1958: 244)

The dread of getting fat, in Ellen's life, continually wins out over a competing "wish for harmless eating," and, designated as untreatable by her doctors, she returns home to die. The final day of her life shows the futility of protest against these phantoms, who cannot be nourished by any earthly sustenance:

> On the third day of being home she is as if transformed. At breakfast she eats butter and sugar, at noon she eats so much that—for the first time in thirteen years!—she is satisfied by her food and gets really full. At afternoon coffee she eats chocolate creams and Easter eggs. She takes a walk with her husband, reads poems by Rilke, Storm, Goethe, and Tennyson, is amused by the first chapter of Mark Twain's "Christian Science," is in a positively festive mood, and all heaviness seems to have fallen away from her. She writes letters, the last one to a fellow patient here to whom she had become so attached. In the evening she takes a lethal dose of poison, and on the following morning she is dead. "She looked as she had never looked in life—calm and happy and peaceful" (Binswanger 1958: 267).

Ellen's idée fixée, an obsession that can only be vanquished through the annihilation of the body itself, is a perfect example, both literal and symbolic, of a corporeal reduction of an anorexic's universe, a reduction that is facilitated by a singularly oppressive body image. This lack of fluidity and/or multiplicity, indeed the hegemonic nature of this particular body image, offers no way to live the corporeal contradictions that haunt Ellen West. The failure of Ellen's physicians to treat her disease, stems from their inability to teach her more about these contradictions than she already knows. Indeed, Ellen's eloquent and clear-sighted appraisal of her "impossible" existence makes it clear that neither medical, cognitive, nor cultural explanations can begin to do justice to the surprising coherence that marks the distortions of an anorexic's experience.

To arrive at an "embodied understanding" of anorexia and other eating disorders, as Bordo seeks to do, requires beginning with their lived, bodily dimensions rather than with a medical, cognitive, or even cultural diagnosis of them. And, I am arguing, this involves focusing less on the cultural and bodily contradictions that appear in this particular disease, contradictions that are all too apparent not only to outsiders but often to the anorexic herself, but on the need to respond *corporeally* to these contradictions through the creation of multiple body images, body images that will inevitably be in tension with one another, but which, in communicating with one another through the "body image intercourse" discussed by Schilder, allow us to productively negotiate the turbulence of our corporeal existence, a turbulence that cannot and should not be abjected from our body images, since it is precisely what enables us to meet the vicissitudes of our bodily life. Of course, the effectiveness of this process will also depend upon a medical, cultural, and philosophical commitment to multiply our aesthetic body ideals beyond the hegemony of the anticorporeal, fat-free body, an image that continues, in many contemporary societies, both to define and regulate the abject borders of our body images.

NOTES

Gail Weiss's essay, "The Abject Borders of the Body Image" is reprinted from *Body Images: Embodiment as Intercorporeality*, Routledge (1999).

1. It is important to note, however, that Butler and Kristeva differ markedly in their characterization of this abject domain; indeed, Butler explicitly critiques Kristeva's view of the abject/semiotic as inextricably associated with the maternal body and as pre-Symbolic (Butler 1990: 79–93).
2. There are numerous examples of individuals with distorted body images that fall into each of these categories in the clinical, philosophical, and popular literature on the body image. Maurice Merleau-Ponty focuses on the case of Schneider, a World War I veteran who suffered a shrapnel wound to his head and whose peculiar physiological and psychological deficiencies created intense interest among the neurologists who treated him, as well as the Gestalt psychologists who provided their own diagnosis of his unique case. In *Volatile Bodies*, Elizabeth Grosz discusses the phenomenon of multiple personality syndrome,

> in which one of the many personalities inhabiting an individual body has different abilities and defects than another. One personality may require glasses to correct faults in the optical apparatus while another personality has perfect vision; one personality is left-handed, the other right, one personality has certain allergies or disorders missing in the other.

Grosz goes on to note that

> [t]hese are not simply transformations at the level of our ideas of or representations of the body. Our ideas and attitudes seep into the functioning of the body itself, making up the realm of its possibilities or impossibilities (Grosz 1994: 190).

In *Beauty Secrets: Women and the Politics of Appearance*, Wendy Chapkis includes the autobiographical perspective of "Ann," a woman with diastrophic dwarfism who reflects retrospectively on her own distorted body image as an adolescent and young adult. "Ann" traces the cause of this distortion to an inability to "integrate what I really look like with who I am." The difficulty of doing this is encapsulated in her next statement: "You don't want to be confronted with your physical difference all the time. But the shock is enough to kill you if you keep hiding from it" (Chapkis 1986: 20).

All of these examples reveal the complexity of the phenomenon of distortion and also belie the notion that there may be a single cause of the distortion or a single solution to the process of developing a nondistorted body image. As Susan Bordo argues in relation to anorexia and the body image distortions it produces, the phenomenon is overdetermined and therefore multidimensional; this means that it must be approached on a variety of levels (e.g., cultural, familial, physiological, etc.) and from a variety of disciplines in order to be adequately understood, much less treated (Bordo 1993).

3. For present purposes, I am distinguishing abjection from the abject as follows: abjection refers to a process of expulsion, whereby that which has been designated as abject (this can include other people, food, vermin, body fluids, rodents and an infinite number of phenomena) is rejected and, at the same time, the rejection itself is disavowed. The generic term, "the abject object," is used to cover all of the possible sites of abjection.

4. And yet, Kristeva seems to be advocating that we embrace the abject precisely because of its subversive potential to disrupt the hegemony of the Symbolic order (See Kristeva 1982). This perverse utopian vision, however, is questioned by Butler, who argues in *Bodies that Matter* (1993) that the process of identity formation will always involve moments of exclusion, which in turn lead to the designation of an abject domain that consists of all that I-am-not. Butler, unlike Kristeva, sees no way out of this untenable, uninhabitable position, which is *our* position as members of the Symbolic order. Her own political strategy involves becoming aware of the exclusions we are performing in order to be sure that we know what is at stake in basing our identity upon them.

5. See MacSween 1993. I wholeheartedly agree with MacSween that "in anorexia women transform the social meanings and practices through which the feminine body is constructed" (8), a process that makes anorexia and anorexic symptoms meaningful in their own right, rather than, as the predominant medical models suggest, meaningful only insofar as they point to more fundamental conflicts in the anorexic's psychic development (e.g. resulting from early childhood, familial experiences). I also agree with her subsequent claim that "'scientific' psychiatric analyses contain an unquestioned and unanalysed set of 'common-sense' assumptions about 'normality'—that, in short, being 'normal' or 'sane' means being able to function appropriately in a bourgeois patriarchal culture" (25), a task, as MacSween goes on to show, that is much more difficult for women than for men to do successfully especially since the criteria that mark success are quite different for each gender. However, I am less convinced by her argument that anorexia is above all a way of contending

with the conflicting demands placed upon contemporary middle-class women to simultaneously assert their individuality and their femininity. For, if this was indeed so, it seems that many more women would be anorexics than currently are. Ultimately, my reservations regarding both MacSween's and Bordo's analyses of anorexia have to do with their adhering too strictly to a social constructionist perspective since I think that the latter position fails to do justice to aspects of embodied experience that fail to achieve cultural expression, as well as those that exceed or even resist cultural analysis.

6. One difficulty with this latter claim is that it sets up a problematic distinction between the "body itself" and "how that body is socially constructed" as if these were two separable phenomena. Since, from a social constructionist perspective, one cannot "get at" the body itself, all one is left with is its social construction. Although the body is undeniably socially constructed, I do not think that this is the only way in which the body is constructed. As Judith Butler observes in the Introduction to *Bodies that Matter* (1993: 10), "To claim that discourse is formative is not to claim that it originates, causes, or exhaustively composes that which it concedes. . . ."

7. Bordo cites studies that show that most women think they are overweight even when many are not only not overweight, but actually underweight (See Bordo 1993). While this is itself a very disturbing phenomenon, it should also be pointed out that others often see women as being overweight when they are not. Men, in particular, often urge their female partners to lose a few more pounds so that they can more closely embody this homogeneous, culturally-established bodily aesthetic.

8. The cultural bias towards tallness is rarely articulated explicitly but almost always goes hand-in-hand with thinness. "Tall and thin" is a body ideal not only for women but also for men. It is a well-known fact that female models need to be close to six feet tall to have successful modeling careers. While it is seen as a liability for a woman to be "too" tall, and while short, thin women can still be viewed as "cute" or "petite" (expressions that are themselves infantilizing and demeaning), the appellation "beautiful" tends to be reserved for the regal, svelte figure, epitomized by the late Princess Diana.

Popular expressions such as the "short man complex" aptly express both the negative stigma to being a shorter than average male, as well as the cultural assumption that short men mind being short, that is, that they view their height as a defect that they must compensate for by being overly competitive, aggressive, etc.

REFERENCES

Beauvoir, Simone de. 1989. *The Second Sex*. Translated by H.M. Parshley. New York: Vintage Books.

Binswanger, Ludwig. 1958. "The Case of Ellen West." *Existence: A New Dimension in Psychiatry and Psychology*. Eds. Rollo May, Ernest Angel, and Henri F. Ellenberger. Trans. Werner M. Mendel and Joseph Lyons. New York: Basic Books.

Bordo, Susan. 1993. *Unbearable Weight: Feminism, Western Culture, and the Body*. Berkeley: University of California Press.

Bruch, Hilde M.D. 1978. *The Golden Cage: The Enigma of Anorexia Nervosa*. Cambridge: Harvard University Press.

Butler, Judith. 1989. "The Body Politics of Julia Kristeva." *Hypatia* 3(3): 104–117.

———. 1990. *Gender Trouble: Feminism and the Subversion of Identity*. New York: Routledge.

———. 1993. *Bodies that Matter: On the Discursive Limits of "Sex"*. New York: Routledge.

Castro-Klaren, Sara. 1993. "What Does Cannibalism Speak? Jean de Léry and the Tupinamba Lesson." *Carnal Knowledge: Essays on the Flesh, Sex and Sexuality in Hispanic Letters and Film*. Ed. Pamela Bacarisse. Pittsburgh: University of Pittsburgh Press.

Chapkis, Wendy. 1986. *Beauty Secrets: Women and the Politics of Appearance*. Boston: South End Press.

Grosz, Elizabeth. 1989. *Sexual Subversions: Three French Feminists*. Sydney, Australia: Allen and Unwin.

———. 1990. "The Body of Signification." *Abjection, Melancholia and Love: The Work of Julia Kristeva*. Eds. John Fletcher and Andrew Benjamin. New York: Routledge.

———. 1994. *Volatile Bodies: Toward a Corporeal Feminism*. Bloomington: Indiana University Press.

Kristeva, Julia. 1982. *Powers of Horror: An Essay on Abjection*. Trans. Leon S. Roudiez. New York: Columbia University Press.

———. 1988. "Interview." *Women Analyze Women in France, England, and the U.S.* Eds. Elaine Hoffman Bruch and Lucienne J. Serrano. New York: New York University Press.

Lacan, Jacques. 1977. *Écrits: A Selection*. Trans. Alan Sheridan. London: Tavistock Publications.

Lorde, Audre. 1990. "Age, Race, Class, and Sex: Women Redefining Difference." In *Out There: Marginalization and Contemporary Cultures*. Eds. Russell Ferguson, M. Gever, T.T. Minh-ha, and C. West. Cambridge: MIT Press.

MacSween, Morag. 1993. *Anorexic Bodies: A Feminist and Sociological Perspective on Anorexia Nervosa*. London: Routledge.

Oliver, Kelly. 1993. *Reading Kristeva: Unraveling the Double-Bind*. Bloomington: Indiana University Press.

Schilder, Paul. 1950. *The Image and Appearance of the Human Body: Studies in the Constructive Energies of the Psyche*. New York: International Universities Press, Inc.

FOUR

Claiming One's Identity:
A Constructivist/Narrativist Approach

Sean P. O'Connell

The question of whether sexual orientation is a choice has taken multiple forms and has been endlessly debated in modern popular culture. At its most facile level, the issue has been considered important because on it is supposed to hinge the question of how people espousing a same-sex orientation should be treated. The old saw goes that if sexual orientation is not chosen, then those who claim to be homosexual should not be blamed for their condition; it is not "their fault." But ironically, those attempting to use such an approach in order to support gay and lesbian rights now face some serious consequences of their strategy. If sexual orientation is somehow culturally determined, then the project could become changing the environment. Conversely, if it is biologically determined, then the project could become biological manipulation. Realizing these dangers has served as an occasion for gender theorists to recognize that the whole discussion serves merely to reinscribe the privileging of heterosexuality, ultimately to the detriment of any liberatory praxis.[1] Whether nature or nurture is "to blame," the issue is inevitably cure, and the "homosexual" who is to be cured must wonder whether elimination by cure is preferable to those more severe, though in a certain ironic sense, more honest forms employed in the past, such as genocide or lobotomy. All of these end in destroying the person that one is.

A promising path to depriveleging heterosexuality is by thematizing the constructed character of sexuality and the artificiality of making sexual identity and orientation the pivotal axis for determining personal identity. But taking this path poses a number of challenges, which is not to say, however, that following it is not worthwhile. My strategy will be to introduce what appears initially as a superficial challenge, but one whose dimensions will prove to be significant, in order to show how following this path can actually lead in a certain way to the kind of affirmation of identity that can sustain liberatory praxis. What I propose is neither to challenge the wisdom of dropping the question of choice, nor to deny the legitimacy of surrendering essentialism. Instead, I want to explore a particular sense in which it is right to claim that, while sexual orientation and identity are constructed, they are nonetheless real, and that recognizing this particular sense carries with it important implications for approaching life in community.

The challenge that I should like to pose comes from the direction of those who, perhaps after struggle, explicitly identify themselves as lesbian, gay, queer, bisexual, heterosexual, etc. At least on the surface, one might suppose that people attesting to their sexual identity, especially those claiming that their sexual identity is integral to who they *are*, must resist claims that sexuality and sexual identity are constructed. It is worth noting the precise sense in which this is so. Take the person who tells the story of how she came to realize that she *is* a lesbian. Clearly, the story she tells could have gone another way. One might hold with thinkers like John D'Emilio and Michel Foucault that gays and lesbians did not always exist, but are made possible in modern Western culture, and that had this person been born at another time, she simply would have assumed an identity along a different set of matrices.[2] But this is not what is essential to many people who have undergone such an experience. What they want to say is that their identification of themselves as lesbian or gay constitutes a response to something about themselves that they had to integrate into their identity if they were to be true to themselves.[3] The question is whether the claim that sexuality and sexual identity are constructed provides a space for honoring such an attestation on its own terms, or better yet, provides a context for deepening rather than just dismissing it. Unless an affirmative answer can be given, one has to wonder whether those who own such identities as bisexual, gay, lesbian, would be willing to explore this avenue for moving beyond the nature/nurture debate, and whether any opening could be had for engaging American society generally. I should like to signal the possibility of such an answer by considering the work of two thinkers operating in two very different milieus, Paul Ricoeur and Judith Butler.

Ricoeur's initial contribution to this discussion will be to offer a description of cultural language that supports the view that articulations of sexuality and sexual identity, while culturally informed, can nonetheless have disclosive power, though as we shall see, the sense in which this is so must be carefully nuanced to avoid essentialist claims or the privileging of any sexual identity formations. Butler's work will be used to lend support to Ricoeur's position because it arrives at a similar conclusion by a different route, but deepens the discussion by explicitly looking at sexual identity formation, and by addressing the peculiar dangers attaching to all articulations of sexual identity. Engaging Butler's discussion of the latter will make clear that dismissing professions of sexual identity as misguided or mistaken because such identities are "mere constructions" constitutes a form of violence against those who claim them, while refusing to problematize those very identities leads to still other forms of violence. It is in this context that Ricoeur will make a second contribution to the discussion. Ricoeur's account of personal identity as a narrative formation will afford a way of thinking about claims to sexual identity which honors Butler's concerns by making it possible to think about attestations of sexual identity as at once legitimate and subject to the sort of contestation essential to liberatory praxis. In so doing, he will enable us to move the discussion of sexual identity beyond the nature/nurture debate to a richer understanding of the possible meanings of claims to sexual identity and what is at stake in them.

In *Ideology and Utopia*, Ricoeur makes the following case:

> The very flexibility of our biological existence makes necessary another kind of informational system, the cultural system. Because we have no genetic system of information for human behavior, we need a cultural system. No culture exists without such a system. The hypothesis, therefore, is that where human beings exist, a nonsymbolic mode of existence, and even less, a nonsymbolic kind of action, can no longer obtain. Action is immediately ruled by cultural patterns which provide templates or blueprints for the organization of social and psychological processes, perhaps just as genetic codes—I am not certain—provide such templates for the organization of organic processes. In the same way that our experience of the natural world requires a mapping, a mapping is also necessary for our experience of social reality.[4]

Ricoeur goes on to argue that such mappings can perform integrative, legitimizing, and distorting functions. Importantly, he suggests that they have disclosive power. To understand these claims, it is helpful to think of them in the context of Marx's discussion of ideology. According to Ricoeur, symbol and myth, which are understood in Marxist terms as "ideological," function first to integrate the community by giving it a common vision of life, a common language, a common set of practices. It is on the basis of this integrative function that symbol and myth can be used to legitimate a given set of power relations. Here, the distortive potential of ideology, which is one of the central insights of Marxism, comes into play. On Ricoeur's view, this potential for distortion arises because the claims to authority that the rulers in a community make require a level of belief on the part of the ruled that can never be rationally warranted.[5] Ideology can serve to fill the gap between claim and belief, and it is precisely here that ideology becomes distortive. It is important, however, to recognize the specific character of this distortion as Ricoeur interprets it, for here, he is very far from Marx. A typical Marxist would argue that ideologies are distortive when they provide accounts of reality, in particular, accounts of social relations, which are untrue to what really is the case, and which perpetuate the social relations which in fact obtain. Ricoeur would have reservations about such claims insofar as they suggest that there could be real social relations, or accounts of real social relations, which were not symbolically and mythologically mediated. More pointedly, Ricoeur would deny the claim that there is some bedrock "reality" with which symbols and myths more or less agree. Rather, he understands ideology to function distortively when it is put in service to the claim that there is one and only one legitimate form of social relations and corresponding vision of life.

But according to Ricoeur, the possibility of ideological distortion presumes a more primary capacity of myths and symbols to reveal or to disclose.[6] This disclosive power does not lie in their ability to reveal a preestablished, given reality, any more than they distort such a reality. How, then, are we to understand myths and symbols as disclosive? A first step is to dissociate the notion of disclosure with a correspondence theory of truth, one holding that truth is the agreement of a proposition to a state of affairs. As Martin Heidegger would say, such an account relies upon a more primordial experience of truth as aletheia, as the disclosure of a possible way of being in the world that carries with it the foreclosure of other possibilities.[7] Ricoeur sees symbols and myths as operating on the borders between disclosure and foreclosure. They disclose not what is, but what is possible. At the same time, their disclosure operates as a founding, a realizing of the possibilities to which they refer, insofar as they inform the life of a community. It is important to note that Ricoeur sees in symbols and myths both referential and creative dimensions. They act to establish what they articulate, but that articulation is not an arbitrary construction. It is born of insight into possibilities for being. Correlatively, it is important to recognize that such insight is realized at the price of other possibilities that remain closed, and hence that the adoption or rejection of a mythic vision cannot operate on the plane of the sort of correspondence theory of truth popularly assumed by those captivated by a modern scientific ideology.

If we adopt Ricoeur's account of the various possibilities of myths and symbols for disclosure, integration, legitimation, and distortion, it becomes possible to conceive of gender identity as constructed and as making claims to truth, and perhaps even . . . to legitimacy? As we shall see, Ricoeur's turn to narrative identity formation in his more recent works affords a way of thinking identity, including gender identity and sexual orientation, as constructed and as speaking the truth of the subject, even as it makes room for the limits and dangers of any such articulation. But, as previously noted, the contribution that Ricoeur can make to the discussion benefits through an encounter with Judith Butler's work, for Butler provides a nuanced account of the constructed character of gender identity which fleshes out the tension between the necessity of rejecting the very possibility of certain identities if others are to be realized, and the violences that just such rejections can incur, violences resulting in particular from the refusal to recognize the contingency of particular identity formations and their accompanying foreclosures.

In *Bodies that Matter*, Butler adopts the position that sex is not a biological given on which gender is built, but rather is itself a regulatory ideal materialized in the body through normatively governed reiterative practices. Further, she maintains that it is only by virtue of assuming a sex that one becomes a subject. Her distinctive development of this position weaves together an articulation and defense of the following claims: (1) the materialization of sex in the body is never fully realized, and it is therefore possible to contest regulatory ideals of sex which underlie gender identity;[8] (2) nonetheless, to claim that the sexed body is a construct does not allow for the conclusion that we can do without a construction, for it may well be that constructions are necessary conditions for thinking, living, and making sense;[9] (3) simultaneous with the construction of possible sexual identities is the foreclosure of other identities, and this dialectic of the permissible and the abject determines who counts as subjects and what bodies matter; (4) finally, while Butler does not claim to offer a program for feminist/bisexual/queer/lesbian/gay practice or theory, she is clearly interested in exploring the possibilities for disturbing the boundaries of the thinkable and the unthinkable, livable and abject identities, and believes that this ought to be done.

The first claim attributed to Butler attests to the constructed character of sex and gender identity and is consistent with her earlier work.[10] But the second marks a shift in emphasis that occurs in *Bodies that Matter*. As early as the Introduction, Butler seeks to distance herself from a constructivist position that would illegitimately have to suppose a subject "doing" the construction, or a position that would have to see the constituted subject as the product of a deterministic process. Instead, she suggests that recognizing that there are conditions for the emergence of a subject neither requires a "subject" before the constitution of a subject, nor the foreclosure of agency by making the subject the product and puppet of sociocultural processes.[11] This is important because Butler hereby distances herself from positions that would discount the constructed subject as either an artificial construct "hiding" the "real" subject lying underneath, or those that would discount the constructed subject as a genuine agent. Butler marks the reality of the subject, but the subject as made possible through certain processes and continuously constituted through citationality.

This leads us to the third claim cited above. Butler follows Lacan in recognizing that for a subject to emerge requires a delimiting of what might metaphorically be called an unlimited, indeterminate flow that constitutes the domain of the unsayable, which Lacan nonetheless speaks through his designation of it as the "Real." At the stage of the imaginary, this delimitation begins through the constitution of a unified ego, but this occurs at the price of imposing an image which, in Richard Boothby's words, "fulfills its function of unity only by imposing an intrinsic limitation—only, in effect, by leaving something out. A quantity of energy is pressed into the service of the drive, but there is always an excluded and un-imaged remainder."[12] In other words, in the imaginary, a single, unified ego is formed through an image with which one identifies. But this at the same time entails an alienation of desire. Through the interference of the linguistic community, this identification with the image is broken, and one is introduced into the realm of the symbolic. By taking up the language of the community, it becomes possible to question imaginary identifications, and to raise the question, Who am I? However, this does not involve an unmediated return or rehabilitation of the Real, as if the Real were to be understood as some determinate thing essential to the self to be reincorporated into one's identity.[13] Rather, by entry into the symbolic, it becomes possible to name one's desire as that which is unnamable, and to come to terms with oneself as an incomplete being desiring a completeness, a self-realization that one can never have. This requires, however, assuming a place in language. It is in the symbolic realm that the sexed subject emerges through the injunction to be a given sex and to thereby assume an identity through which to express the lack of that which would bring completeness. That is, in linguistic communities, sexed positions emerge which take on meaning by announcing what identities are possible, and importantly, thereby establishing a realm of the unsayable, unlivable, and unnarratable. Sexed positions constitute the terms in which a subject can be realized through the performance of the sexed identity. What is important about Lacan's account, especially as taken up by Butler, is that it suggests how it is possible to assert that the claim that sexuality is constructed implies neither that such construction is somehow the "free" construction of a preexistent subject, and hence arbitrary, nor that it is determined and immutably fixed. Rather, normative constraints determine the very possibility for the process of performativity that enables the subject to emerge.[14] At the same time, it is vitally important to recognize that precisely because the subject is constituted through the injunction to assume a sex, the subject cannot purely and simply be identified with the sexed identity; there is an instability at the heart of gender identity that refuses to surrender the possibility of contestation. This last point is one which Butler emphasizes in marked contrast to Lacan.[15]

In the story of sexual development that Lacan offers, the child experiences an initial identification with its mother which is disturbed during the Oedipal phase when the child realizes that union with the mother is impossible because of the presence of the father. Sexually, it is the father that is the privileged object of the mother's desire. This recognition takes the form of a prohibition of access to the mother, which in Lacanian terms is designated as the law of the father, and which is constituted as fear of castration. The phallus comes to represent the authority and privilege of the father. It thereby becomes the mark of access to the lost wholeness or completeness that the child seeks to regain. The phallus, then, signifies that which one must have in order to be complete. The fear of castration is an expression of the anxiety that one feels when the imaginary identification with the mother breaks down, and libidinal drives which cannot be accommodated surface. This threat of castration points to the fact that the seemingly original wholeness that has been disrupted was, in fact, illusory.

The phallus promises a retrieval of desire that cannot be realized. Given this account, assuming a sexual identity in a linguistic community through obedience to the law of the father, to the fear of castration, can occur as an attempt to surmount the loss of wholeness signified by the phallus. Sexual identities as such can operate as political signifiers, that is, as identities constituted in the linguistic community which actually produce what they signify, those who do and who do not count as whole subjects capable of political action. But because the phallus cannot deliver on its promises, and because sexual identity is only realized through continual performance of that identity, disidentifications with sexual identities become possible.[16] In Butler's view, this opens a space for disturbing reified sexual identities and for debate regarding such issues as heterosexual privilege.[17]

Further, given the failure of the phallus as a signifier to fulfill its promises, Butler questions the supposition that political action requires the sorts of identifications which political signifiers attempt to realize. That is, she questions whether such identifications as gay, which can function to unify a group, must operate in this way. Why, Butler asks, might disidentification not also be a ground for political praxis?[18] In other words, might we at once identify and disidentify with such identity formations as lesbian, and might this interplay itself be individually and socially transforming? The challenge that Butler poses is formidable and intriguing. On the one hand, she is careful to note that the demand to overcome radically the constitutive constraints by which cultural viability is achieved would be its own form of violence.[19] It would be literally to deny the reality of the subject simply because that reality is constructed, and therefore contingent. It would be to deny the force of the recognition of oneself as gay. On the other hand, the refusal to problematize those constraints promotes two other sorts of violence, violence against the subject by refusing a fundamental condition of subjectivity, potential for transformation, and violence against society by refusing its potential for transformation by turning a blind eye to the partiality of identity categories that claim to be all-inclusive.[20]

I should like to turn now to consider what contribution Ricoeur's narrative approach to identity formation can make for navigating between these various threats of violence. A rich contribution should address three questions: (1) How to respect the claims of subjects regarding their gender identity? (2) How at the same time challenge those very claims when they fail to recognize their own contingency, their status as conditioned possibilities? (3) How to exploit the contingency of gender identity formation for liberatory praxis?

To appreciate Ricoeur's account of human identity as narratively configured, it is necessary to turn to his treatment of the narrative structure of human time in *Time and Narrative*. His thesis is that "time becomes human to the extent that it is articulated through a narrative mode, and narrative attains its full meaning when it becomes a condition of temporal existence."[21] Borrowing from Aristotle's account of plot as the mimesis of action, Ricoeur distinguishes three moments of mimesis in order to describe the way in which temporal experience becomes meaningful. By mimesis 1, Ricoeur denotes a preunderstanding of the world and of life and action.[22] By mimesis 2, he distinguishes the construction of a narrative plot. Drawing upon mimesis 1, creative imagination selects from experience and arranges it into a coherent whole with beginning, middle, and end. By mimesis 3, Ricoeur understands the reception of the text by a reader. This reception can become the occasion for at once reinterpreting and actually refiguring the world of one's life and action.[23] To appreciate Ricoeur's narrative account of time, it is necessary to approach it in the context of the aporia between the scientific conception of time as a sequence of moments in which one moment follows another and every moment is identical to any other, and the human experience of time as a relationship between past, present, and future that constitutes a coherent whole. While we are familiar with the scientific account of time as clock time, every second being equal to every other, to consider imaginatively what it would be like to live as if each moment were the same brings with it a sense of incoherence, and ultimately, meaninglessness. What provides a context for meaningful human action and constitutes the fabric of a coherent life is the interrelation of past, present, and future such that one's characterization of the present conditions one's intending of the future, and these taken together mark the significance that one assigns to the past. Ricoeur's account of a threefold process of mimesis is meant to capture two insights: (1) that meaningful human life is structured narratively; (2) that the construction of a meaningful narrative underpinning human life and action is a creative process that cannot be reduced to a simple recounting of life as lived.[24]

If we turn for a moment to consider life as lived, we note that there are thinkers like Hayden White who argue that life simply is not lived narratively. The narrative structure, he and others argue, is "added on" through reflection.[25] Ricoeur, in his discussion of mimesis 1, on the other hand, provides ground for thinking that narrative coherence guides the living of a human life. He grants that there is good reason for claiming that life as lived does not have the well-rounded, coherent unity of a single, all-encompassing narrative. As lived, there is an open-endedness to life; there are a plethora of events and experiences that resist unification into one coherent narrative; there is the real possibility of being engaged in a number of distinct narratives running concurrently which refuse integration into one another. On the other hand, Ricoeur insists that it would be a mistake to think of anything that could be called human life taking on the purely homogeneous character of clock time.[26] The barriers to a well-rounded narrative are not sufficient to undermine the claim that the domain of human action contains within itself at least an "inchoate narrativity."[27] As Alisdair MacIntyre notes in his exploration of the intentional character of human action, what distinguishes an action from an occurrence is precisely that an action is intentionally undertaken. For this to happen requires that one recognize oneself as operating within a certain set of circumstances in which a given action is appropriate. But this is just to locate oneself in a narrative whole with beginning, middle, and end.[28] Ricoeur's account of the movement from mimesis 1 to mimesis 3 traces a movement from an engagement in life and action informed by the sense of a narrative, or narratives, to a reflective engagement of life conditioned by the intention to comprehend one's life as a unified narrative whole. One suspects that, at its outer limits, such an intention might lead one to take up the construction of social and cosmic narratives as well.

At the end of Volume III of *Time and Narrative*, and in *Oneself as Another*, Ricoeur shifts his attention from exploring the potential of the narrative construction of human time for bridging the aporia between scientific and phenomenological conceptions of time to treating the aporias pertaining to human identity. Specifically, he is interested in showing how an account of narrative identity can avoid either an essentialist account of personal identity that entails holding the subject to be self-identical even when passing through different states, or a view of the subject as ". . . nothing more than a substantialist illusion, whose elimination merely brings to light a pure manifold of cognitions, emotions, and volitions."[29] Such an account would go a long way towards meeting the concerns of this essay, for it would preclude employing categories such as gay, lesbian, straight as if they were unproblematic, or at worst, incomplete, articulations of the identities of subjects that are irremediably "fixed," or conversely, reading all professions of personal identity as arbitrary and misguided constructs.

According to Ricoeur, much of the difficulty that we have with the notion of personal identity results from a conflation of identity with sameness. When one looks back at oneself as a child, one wants to claim that one is the same person. Yet, at the same time, there is clearly a sense in which one is not the same. The tendency to favor one or the other of these valences results in a rigid identification of the self as the same, or in the denial of identity itself based on the fact that one is not the same. To counter this, Ricoeur argues for a replacement of the conception of identity as being the same (idem) with a conception of oneself as self-same (ipse).[30] This latter conception arises by applying the narrative account of human time to personal identity:

> The thesis supported here will be that the identity of the character is comprehensible through the transfer to the character of the operation of emplotment, first applied to the action recounted: characters, we will say, are themselves plots.[31]

The process of emplotment constitutive of a narrative consists in drawing together the heterogeneous elements of a story into a unified whole. In the configuration of a narrative, differences are not simply abolished. In particular, there is a dispersal of episodes that are nonetheless interrelated with one another to form a unified whole.[32] With respect to characters in a narrative, their identities are secured through the coherence of the narrative. But what Ricoeur is suggesting is that we can apply the notion of narrative configuration to an understanding of personal identity itself. Personal identity is realized by drawing together into a unified temporal whole the life of the person.[33] Following Hannah Arendt, Ricoeur maintains, in short, that to tell who someone is means to tell the story of that person's life.[34] In this telling, the individual events and occurrences making up the life of the person, including transformations in modes of thinking and self-conception, at once contribute to the constitution of the self, and pose a challenge to the realization of unified coherence.

With this account of the narrative construction of identity in hand, we can now turn to an admittedly incomplete, but perhaps suggestive, consideration of the three questions with which we began this discussion of Ricoeur. Firstly, how respect the claims of the subject regarding her or his own gender identity? It is possible to approach this question from two different directions. In *Oneself as Another*, Ricoeur notes that the tendency to equate identity with sameness finds support in the recognition of character understood as those distinctive marks of individuals that enable one to identify them as the same through time. Ricoeur maintains that it is in fact character which comes closest to marking a person's identity as the same. However, even character carries with it a temporal dimension, for character is realized through acquired dispositions. Firstly, there are habits. Habits are acquired, but become so determinative of the self that their acquisition is covered over. This gives to the self a permanence in time tantamount to identity as sameness. The second sort of dispositions constituting character are the norms, values, models, etc., inculcated into the person through socialization. This is the entrance of the other into the self actually contributing to the constitution of the self, but again, in a way that covers over or annuls its own contribution.[35] In light of such an account of character formation, it becomes possible to recognize the legitimacy of a claim to a given gender identity without bowing to essentialism or dismissing the person's testimony as misguided. This is indeed who the person has become.

But this first approach, while key to contributing to a nonessentialist account of identity as nonetheless real, only takes us so far, for it ultimately operates as the sort of causal explanation that cannot sufficiently account for agency or for personal determination. Ricoeur affords a way of supplementing this approach that accommodates agency by opening a second avenue for respecting claims of gender identity without bowing to essentialism through his claim that characters are themselves plots. When one *attests* to being gay, this does not amount merely to acknowledging a sedimented character formation. Rather, it entails taking up a vision of reality understood at the very least as the articulation of a possible way of being-in-the-world, and adopting it as the framework for writing a personal narrative, and by extension, a social and cosmic narrative. The issue of authorship in narrative theory is a complex one. Ricoeur would not claim that we author ourselves. He would agree that it is only in and through the other that becoming a person is possible. We always already find ourselves enmeshed in relations with an identity, and as identified. As Butler notes, as early as infancy, we are assigned an identity as male or female through which we become socially recognized as human.[36] An identity is assigned that we do not determine, but with which we cannot fail to be concerned. On the other hand, Ricoeur recognizes, with Heidegger, that who we are is an issue for us. We are not handed the book of our lives as a completed, well-rounded, definitive story. Still, it might be appropriate to say that we are given what could metaphorically be called a gift. Though it would be unwarranted to posit some independent subject as gift-giver, residing in the idea of gift can be the idea of otherness as a source of possible meanings and significance outside the control of the one on whom the gift is bestowed, the idea that one is beholden to that which is other than oneself for one's possibilities for being-in-the-world in such a way that calls for response and at times exerts authority. Heidegger gives us an inkling of this in *The Origin of the Work of Art* through his description of the origin of the work of art as Art. The origin of art is not the self, not even the artist. Rather, according to Heidegger, artworks are born of the struggle between earth and world. They set up a world and set forth the earth, thereby revealing even as they conceal, possibilities for being-in-the-world which call forth and constitute those who enter into them as preservers.[37] In short, human beings do not give themselves their possibilities for being-in-the-world, but stand in need of a disclosure of those possibilities, a gift.

Gifts, of course, can be equivocal in a variety of ways: they can disclose and mask; they can liberate and enslave; they can enliven and oppress. It is precisely because of this ambiguity that we can figure our past as a gift given to which our account of ourselves is a response opening us to the future as affording determinate possibilities and projects. Because we are uniquely positioned with respect to our own lives, uniquely situated with respect to our ownmost possibilities, it is possible to understand our respective accounts of our personal identities as operating on the plane of what Ricoeur calls attestation. Our account of ourselves is a response to the past that we have been given projected into the future. When I testify to who I am, I am at the same time testifying to what I believe in based upon the person that I have become and the possibilities that I can imagine. This by no means implies a simple taking up of the identities afforded by the community in which one finds oneself. Though employing a very different vocabulary, Butler in *Excitable Speech* provides insight into the ambiguity of what I have called "gift," and the multiple possibilities for response. Drawing upon the idea that one comes to "exist," to be recognized and recognizable, to be a subject, through the address of the Other,[38] Butler raises a series of provocative and disturbing questions:

> Could language injure us if we were not, in some sense, linguistic beings, beings who require language in order to be? Is our vulnerability to language a consequence of our being constituted within its terms? If we are formed in language, then that formative power precedes and conditions any decision we might make about it, insulting us from the start, as it were, by its prior power.[39]

Our relation to our own past, to our language, to our communities, to the names that we have been given, is deeply ambiguous. We do not choose our identities, but neither is the choice made for us. We respond to what we have been given, thereby testifying to and transforming who we are. "We're here, We're queer, get used to it." This slogan, reiterated at virtually every gay pride parade, invites an embrace of an identity traditionally marked as abject, the impossible identity of a nonsubject. This identity is not chosen, nor is it essential; it is the mark placed on one through which one constitutes one's identity as a response. One testifies to this identity, and in so doing, calls others to a possibility for being-in-the-world.

Such testimony does not operate at the level of episteme understood as self-founding knowledge. But this does not mean that it does not command a hearing. The power of testimony lies in the belief that one has in the one who testifies. Such belief may be only in the sincerity of the one testifying. But this need not be the case. Might it be that the compelling character of the testimony of someone testifying to her or his identity lies in the very narrative that he or she constructs? If we turn again to the question of respect for the claims of the subject regarding gender identity, we might conclude that there is reason for seriously entertaining such claims if we regard the fragility of our own claims about who we are and the world in which we live, claims themselves which are rooted in no more than the gift of being-here affords.

But perhaps it is at this point that we should take up our second question, the question of how to challenge those very claims to gender identity when they fail to recognize their own contingency, their status as conditioned possibilities. Ricoeur makes the following interesting suggestions about the sort of challenge appropriate to attestation:

> the fragmentation that follows from the polysemy of the question "who?". . . gives to attestation its own special fragility, to which is added the vulnerability of a discourse aware of its own lack of foundation. This vulnerability will be expressed in the permanent threat of suspicion, if we allow that suspicion is the specific contrary of attestation. The kinship between attestation and testimony is verified here: there is no "true" testimony without "false" testimony. But there is no recourse against false testimony than another that is more credible; and there is no recourse against suspicion but a more reliable attestation.[40]

We have spoken of the reality of a constructed gender identity. We might go so far as to signal such a reality as a necessary contingency. In other words, while one's history may be contingent, in constituting oneself, one must of necessity come to terms with who one has become by virtue of it. But there are at least two dangers which arise here. Firstly, one might mistakenly suppose that there is only one possible story that can be told out of one's past projecting one into the future. Secondly, one might suppose that what it takes to count as a subject is necessary and fixed. However, when confronting the claim of others to be telling the whole truth, the only possible truth, about themselves and by extension about everyone else, can we not turn once again to the fragility of our own claims to find testimony to mount a significant challenge? Can there be any more solid ground for impinging such testimony offered by the Other? For people who have struggled with the question of whether to assume a lesbian or gay identity, the decision to adopt such an articulation is almost always accompanied by feelings of ambivalence. The experience of owning such identities is liberatory to the extent that it frees one from the determination by others of what counts as a good and meaningful life, preempts the derogatory power of such labels to police action, and provides one a language in which to articulate who one has become. At the same time, because these identity terms carry with them layers of meaning, and in particular insist upon the conflation of sexual identity with identity, their adoption can be experienced as constraining, inhibiting. It is the experience of wrestling with just such difficulties that makes possible challenging those who would presume the unproblematic privileging of the heterosexual matrix in determining identity.

This leads us to our third question: How to exploit the contingency of gender identity formation for liberatory praxis? As we ask who we are and who we are to become, we recognize in the question itself that no one answer is necessary. If it were, there would be no question; decision is born of the recognition that things could be otherwise. On the other hand, there would be no decision if there were nothing about which to decide. Decision is based on something, presumably on the orientation afforded us in the world which I have called gift, keeping in mind that this gift has an ambiguous status, for we must not forget that whatever gifts we have were given us through the constitutive exclusions to which Butler has called our attention. Further, our decisions are not made in isolation, but in social contexts which constitute the conditions of their possibility. Recognition of the contingency, not only of gender identity, but of individual and social identity in general, provides a context and impetus for dialogue aimed at taking seriously the various testimonies that we have to offer regarding the possibilities for living well with and for one another.[41] What this implies is that liberatory praxis cannot operate within the limits of promoting some normative ideal, or even of evaluating possible candidates for social action, such as the realization of social justice. Rather, it must expand its parameters to engage critically the stories informing peoples lives, stories that likewise inform the social ideals pursued. For such critical engagement to occur, it must promote strategies that encourage vulnerability to the stories of others, for one cannot engage critically what one does not take seriously. Finally, it must engage in enabling those who have no voice and who have no language that can do justice to the stories that they might tell to gain voice and to appropriate language, which in turn means enabling the speakers in society to hear the silence required for listening and the development of an attunement to the disruptive power of poetry at work in transformative stories.

NOTES

1. An excellent discussion of the dangers presented by presuming that sexual orientation is either culturally or biologically determined, lending strength to Foucault's claim that all positions are dangerous, is offered by Eve Kosovsky Sedgwick, *Epistemology of the Closet* (Berkeley: University of California Press, 1990), pp. 40–44. [For Foucault's claim, see Michel Foucault, "The Subject and Power," afterword to Hubert Dreyfus and Paul Rabinow, *Michel Foucault: Beyond Structuralism and Hermeneutics* (University of Chicago Press, 1983), p. 232.]

2. John D'Emilio, "Capitalism and Gay Identity," in Laurel Richardson and Verta Taylor, eds., *Feminist Frontiers II* (New York: Random House, 1989), p. 184.

3. This is not to suggest that everyone uses sexual identity labels in relation to themselves in this way, but that this is a claim that is common to many gays and lesbians, as found in the coming out stories that they tell. For further discussion of this, see Judith Roof, *come as you are: sexuality and narrative.* (New York: Columbia University Press, 1996), pp. 104–105.

4. Paul Ricoeur, *Ideology and Utopia*, George H. Taylor, ed. (New York: Columbia University Press, 1986), pp. 11–12.

5. Ibid., pp. 13–14; 257–59.

6. The corpus of Ricoeur's work is marked by a hermeneutic turn that occurs in the third volume of *Freedom and Nature, The Symbolism of Evil*, a turn that can be characterized in terms of Ricoeur's attempt to explore the disclosive power of symbols and myths [Paul Ricoeur, *The Symbolism of Evil*, Emerson Buchanan, trans. (Boston: Beacon Press,1967)], of metaphor [Paul Ricoeur, *The Rule of Metaphor*, Robert Czerny, Kathleen McLaughlin, and John Costello, trans. (Toronto: The University of Toronto Press, 1975)], of narrative [Paul Ricoeur, *Time and Narrative*, Vols. I, II, III, Kathleen McLaughlin and David Pellauer, trans. (Chicago: The University of Chicago Press, 1984, 1985, 1988).] The germ of Ricoeur's fundamental insights regarding the disclosive power of symbol and myth can be found in the concluding chapter of *The Symbolism of Evil*, "The Symbol Gives Rise to Thought" [Paul Ricoeur, *The Symbolism of Evil*, Emerson Buchanan, trans. (New York: Harper and Row, 1969), pp. 347–57.]

7. In this claim, Ricoeur is close to Heidegger's insight in "The Origin of the Work of Art," when he distinguishes between truth as correctness and truth as aletheia. Truth as correctness may be understood in terms of the correspondence theory of truth, while truth as aletheia depends on a more primordial disclosure which Heidegger describes as the "unconcealedness of beings." [Martin Heidegger, "The Origin of the Work of Art," in Martin Heidegger, *Poetry, Language, Thought*, Albert Hofstadter, trans. (New York: Harper and Row, 1971), p. 52.]

8. Butler makes a strong case for this when she agrees with Slavoj Žižek and Jacques Lacan that socially intelligible sexed positions are realized through identity formations relying upon the foreclosure of certain possibilities, but that, contrary to Žižek's view, these constitutive foreclosures are historically,

culturally, socially contingent. [Judith Butler, *Bodies that Matter* (New York: Routledge, 1993), pp. 206–207.]

9. This is a central theme that Butler plays and develops in a variety of contexts in *Bodies that Matter*. See, in particular, *Bodies that Matter*, p. 6; chapters 3 and 7.

10. In *Gender Trouble*, Butler not only argues for the constructed character of gender identity realized in the body through normatively governed reiterative practices, but further maintains that attempts on the part of some feminist theorists to employ essentialist accounts of gender in counterhegemonic ways end by reinstituting "ideal orders" that set up new relations of domination and oppression. See, Judith Butler, *Gender Trouble* (New York: Routledge, 1990), p. 20.

11. Ibid., pp. 6–7.

12. Richard Boothby, *Death and Desire* (New York: Routledge, 1991), p. 58. In his discussion of the Imaginary, Lacan makes the point that the emergence of the ego occurs through the incorporation of certain desires and the exclusion of others. See Jacques Lacan, *The Seminar of Jacques Lacan, Book I: Freud's Papers on Technique, 1953–1954*, Jacques-Alain Miller, ed., John Forrester, trans. (New York: W.W. Norton, 1988).

13. In his discussion of the symbolic in Lacan, Boothby highlights the fact that the function of the Symbolic is to give voice to desire that was excluded in the formation of the ego. (*Death and Desire*, pp. 109–110) But the Symbolic never gives comprehensive voice to the Real, nor is its approach to the Real direct. (*Death and Desire*, p. 113) Butler does not foreground this disruptive potential of the Symbolic, but instead focuses on its productive potential, suggesting that while the Symbolic carries within it the seeds of its own disruption, it nonetheless tends to support the congealing of social identities through citation and performance.

14. *Bodies that Matter*, pp. 187–88; 94. See also, Jacques Lacan, "The function and field of speech and language," in *Écrits: A Selection*, Alan Sheridan, trans. (New York: W.W. Norton, 1977), p. 68.

15. Lacan is less sanguine regarding this possibility for contestation, as seen if one considers the primacy he gives to the name of the father as support for the symbolic function in "The function and field of speech and language in psychoanalysis," in *Écrits*, pp. 65–67.

16. The idea of sexual identities as political signifiers operating as performatives is treated by Butler in her discussion of Slavoj Žižek's use of the notion of "political signifier" in *Bodies that Matter*, ch. 7.

17. Note that Butler distances herself from Lacanians such as Slavoj Žižek who claim that the feminine must occupy the cite of the Real, the unthinkable, unsymbolizable, the foreclosed identity which is the "outside", making the "inside" of the socially intelligible possible, and who place the masculine within discourse and the symbolic. See *Bodies that Matter*, pp. 206–207; pp. 73–74.

18. Ibid, pp. 219–22.

19. Ibid., pp. 117–18.

20. Butler articulates both possibilities in *Bodies that Matter*, p. 115.

21. Paul Ricoeur, *Time and Narrative*, Vol. I, p. 52.

22. Ibid., p. 46.

23. In "Ethics and Narrativity," Peter Kemp offers a cogent account of the three

stages of mimesis, together with the suggestion that mimesis 1 should be understood as narratively configured, consisting of a number of "little stories," a suggestion which extends narrative to a domain that Ricoeur describes as containing within itself an "inchoate narrativity." [Peter Kemp, "Ethics and Narrativity," in *The Philosophy of Paul Ricoeur*, Lewis Dewin Hahn, ed. (Chicago: Open Court, 1995), pp. 373, 377.] Interestingly, David Carr develops a critique of Ricoeur's claim that life contains an "inchoate narrativity," arguing instead that life is lived narratively. [David Carr, *Time, Narrative and History* (Bloomington: Indiana University Press, 1991), p. 15.]

24. Indeed, in *Time and Narrative*, a central aspect of the project is to address the aporia between phenomenological and scientific conceptions of time. Ricoeur turns to the mimetic activity of narrative in order to develop a third conception of time that spans the gap opened by this aporia. [See Paul Ricoeur, *Time and Narrative, Vol. III*, p. 245.]

25. Hayden White, "The Value of Narrativity in the Representation of Reality," in *On Narrative*, W.J.T. Mitchell, ed. (Chicago: University of Chicago Press, 1981), p. 10.

26. *Time and Narrative*, Vol. I, p. 54.

27. "Ethics and Narrativity," p. 373.

28. Alisdair MacIntyre, *After Virtue* (South Bend, IN: University of Notre Dame Press, 1981), pp. 191–93.

29. *Time and Narrative*, Vol. III, p. 246.

30. Paul Ricoeur, *Oneself as Another*, Kathleen Blamey, trans. (Chicago: University of Chicago Press, 1992). See also, *Time and Narrative*, Vol. III, p. 246.

31. Paul Ricoeur, *Oneself as Another*, p. 143.

32. Ibid., pp. 141–42.

33. Ibid., p. 148.

34. *Time and Narrative*, p. 246.

35. *Oneself as Another*, pp. 121–22.

36. *Bodies that Matter*, pp. 7–8.
    In her latest work on hate speech, Butler further insists that it is impossible for human subjects ever to escape being socially constituted as such through naming. [See Judith Butler, *Excitable Speech*, (New York: Routledge, 1997), pp. 4–5.] At the same time, she insists that this by no means precludes contesting and attempting a transformation of the names through which one is constituted as a subject. (See *Excitable Speech*, pp. 33–34.)

37. Martin Heidegger, "The Origin of the Work of Art," pp. 66–68.
    Note that Heidegger develops the notion of gift more explicitly in *On Time and Being* by attempting to think Being and Time in terms of "It gives," the giving of a gift, the gift of presence (where "presence" is distinguished from "the now"), which nonetheless remains concealed in the giving. [See Martin Heidegger, *On Time and Being*, trans. Joan Stambaugh (New York: Harper and Row, 1972), pp. 8–9.]

38. *Excitable Speech*, p. 5.

39. Ibid., pp. 1–2.

40. *Oneself as Another*, p. 22.

41. It is important to emphasize that such recognition serves merely as a propaedeutic to dialogue. The politics and logic of such dialogue are extremely large questions, each of which deserve separate treatment.

Embodied Mind: Phenomenological Approaches to Cognitive Science, Psychology, and Anthropology

FIVE

Embodied Reason

Mark L. Johnson

Human beings are creatures of the flesh. What we can experience and how we make sense of what we experience depend on the kinds of bodies we have and on the ways we interact with the various environments we inhabit. It is through our embodied interactions that we inhabit a world, and it is through our bodies that we are able to understand and act within this world with varying degrees of success.

All of this meaningful, and occasionally thoughtful, interaction begins for us at birth, or even earlier, and so it comes to us prior to our learning any language. It depends, therefore, not primarily on propositions and words, but rather on forms of understanding and reasoning that are rooted in the patterns of our bodily activity.

I shall argue that our conceptualization and reasoning are grounded in our embodiment, that is, in our bodily orientations, manipulations, and movements as we act in our world. No matter how sophisticated our abstractions become, if they are to be meaningful to us, they must retain their intimate ties to our embodied modes of conceptualization and reasoning. We can only experience what our embodiment allows us to experience. We can only conceptualize using conceptual systems grounded in our bodily experience. And we can only reason by means of our embodied, imaginative rationality.

My task, therefore, is to show how there could be a connection between structures of our bodily activity and what we think of as our "higher" cognitive operations. I need to show how patterns of bodily experience work their way up into our understanding and reasoning about our more abstract concepts.

To begin this explanation, we first need to clarify what is to count as "the bodily," as that term is used in the phrase, "the bodily basis of conceptualization and reasoning." A full treatment of the bodily basis of meaning, understanding, and reasoning would have to consider at least the following three levels of embodiment:

(1) **Neurophysiological**—Our experience, conceptualization, and thought are realized neurally. In this sense, they are embodied in neural assemblies and their interactions. However, an adequate explanation of the bodily basis of meaning and reasoning at this level can never consist of neural network models alone. Our neural nets develop as they do only through our interactions within the environments we encounter. Therefore, even at this seemingly basic level of structure, we must avoid thinking of neural assemblies as independent units that simply take input and generate output. We must see those neural assemblies in relation to the entire bodily organism as it operates within concrete situations. Constraints on meaning come both from our bodies (from our perceptual, cognitive, and motor mechanisms) and from the environments in which all our experience and action take place. These environments are at once physical, social, moral, political, and religious.[1]

(2) **Cognitive Unconscious**—The vast majority of our concepts, syntactic mechanisms, and other cognitive structures operate for us automatically and unreflectively. We can, of course, consciously reflect on and frame generalizations about these structures of thought and language, which is what we do in the cognitive sciences. But, for the most part, our conceptual systems operate, as they must, beneath the level of consciousness. The body is crucial at this level, because all of our cognitive mechanisms and structures are grounded in patterns of bodily experience and activity, such as our spatial and temporal orientations, the patterns of our bodily movements, and the ways we manipulate objects. Mental images, image schemas, metaphors, metonymies, concepts, and inference patterns are all tied, directly or indirectly, to these bodily structures of our sensorimotor activities.[2]

(3) **Phenomenological**—The third level of explanation concerns the felt quality of our experience. Description at this level seeks to bring us to awareness of how our experience "feels" to us and how our world reveals itself. An important task in such description is to recover the ordinarily submerged presence of our bodies in what we experience, feel, and think. The goal is to uncover the tacit, background dimension of experience that is mediated by our embodiment and without which we would have no meaningful thought or symbolic expression of any kind.

Ideally, descriptions and explanations at all three of these levels will eventually converge and co-evolve. At present, however, nobody has clearly and comprehensively worked out the relations among accounts at each of these levels, and we have no adequate synthetic picture of how they hang together.[3]

In this paper I focus primarily on the role of embodiment at the cognitive unconscious level, although I make limited reference to our phenomenological experience of embodiment and to neural accounts. I discuss some representative examples of the ways in which our embodiment determines the character of our conceptual systems and the reasoning we do with them.[4]

I. THE MARGINALIZED BODY

The crucial role of human embodiment in all our experience, conceptual structure, and reasoning has only recently been rediscovered, after decades of almost total neglect by Anglo-American analytic philosophy. Within this analytic tradition, philosophy was defined as rigorous logical analysis of our fundamental philosophical concepts. Analytic philosophy was originally founded on the Fregean assumption that concepts, propositions, logical forms, functions, and all of the basic structures of thought have virtually nothing to do with the nature of our bodies. Consequently, this dominant philosophical tradition simply ignored the body.[5]

The idea that our embodiment has no significant role in determining the nature of our conceptual structure has its roots in a widely accepted commonsense view that has been elaborated in various philosophical theories. The commonsense view is this: Things in the world come in kinds—tulips, tigers, tables, toasters. Each particular thing is the kind of thing it is because of the properties it has and that it shares with other things of the same kind.

A number of theories add to this commonsense view the idea that such categories of the world are represented in our minds by signs and that we reason by manipulating those signs. In generative linguistics, formal logic, and certain traditions in artificial intelligence and cognitive science, a "logical form" or "knowledge structure" is seen as a structure of signs (such as sequences of letters) that are meaningless in themselves and have to be interpreted to be meaningful. This interpretation is done by associating a sign with a thing or a category in the world (or within a set theoretical model of the world).

Such a fitting of signs to things in the world, or to a mathematical model of the world, is both disembodied and "literal." It is disembodied in that the body has no constitutive role in characterizing the nature of meaning. It is literal, in that it is not mediated by any imaginative mechanisms, such as mental images, metaphors, prototypes, etc.

To give a simplified example of how this classical view works, consider the sentence, "The chair is green." In classical theories of meaning there would be a concept CHAIR, defined by a list of properties—necessary and sufficient conditions for something to be a chair. Each of these categories is supposedly defined solely in terms of properties of objects existing in the world, which is assumed to be structured as it is independent of any human perception.

The concept GREEN would, likewise, be part of a system of color concepts, with contrasting members such as GREEN-BLUE-RED-YELLOW and special cases like AVOCADO and AQUAMARINE. Again, this system would be only a structured collection of signs, meaningless in themselves, which are made meaningful by being associated with color categories in the world. It is not the body that gives meaning to colors in these theories, but rather the structure of signs and the connection of the system of signs to the external world.

Thus, given the disembodied theory of concepts, a sentence like "The chair is green" should be true just in case the specified member of the category of chairs (which is in the world) is a member of the category of green things (which is in the world). Such a picture of meaning as the relationship between signs and things in the world has long been taken by logicians and philosophers of language as defining meaning and setting out the subject matter of semantics. It was precisely this picture of meaning that was presupposed by early cognitive scientists who spoke of "internal representations of external reality."

II. RECOVERING THE BODY IN MEANING AND THOUGHT

As late as the mid-1970s, this disembodied view of meaning dominated analytic philosophy and was the basis of what I shall call "first-generation cognitive science." First-generation cognitive science was defined mostly by artificial intelligence, functionalism, model theory, and information-processing psychology. It regarded the mind as disembodied and took reason to be logic-like and literal. It defined reasoning as the manipulation of propositional structures. It was founded on the metaphor of the Mind As Computer Program, and it had no role for human embodiment in the structure of concepts and reasoning.

It is not surprising, therefore, that hardly anyone has looked to the cognitive sciences for an understanding of the importance of human embodiment. Instead, they turned for a recovery of the body to phenomenology and to various postmodern movements. However, neither of these approaches has produced an adequate account of the role of the body in conceptualization and reasoning. Phenomenology, by definition, focuses exclusively on the phenomenological level of description and analysis, giving scant attention to both the neurophysiological and cognitive unconscious levels.[6] It has had very little to say about the body's relation to language and thought. And, although postmodern sociology and literary theory emphasize the body as having been marginalized and suppressed in our cultural experience, they tend to regard the body as a socially and culturally constructed "text," downplaying the idea that there are bodily constraints on what we can experience, conceptualize, and reason about.

Since it was scientistic philosophy (in the form of logical empiricism, model theory, and artificial intelligence) that seemed to expunge embodiment from knowledge, concepts, and truth, hardly anyone in philosophy has deemed it appropriate to look to science for a rediscovery of the body in human thought.[7] But this is exactly what I am proposing. What most philosophers have overlooked is a newly developing "second-generation cognitive science" that gives us a wealth of converging evidence from various empirical disciplines that shows how our conceptual systems and the reasoning we do with them are grounded in patterns of bodily activity. This new cognitive science of the embodied mind pays special attention to neurobiology, since it sees reason as defined by the structure of the brain and the body together in their interactions with the environment and other people.

In the embodied mind, abstract reason is not separate from the sensorimotor system, but rather builds on it. Sensorimotor experience is schematized—as in image schemas (e.g., containers, paths, contact, balance, centrality) and motor schemas (grasping, pushing, pulling, moving) that have "logics" that are regular consequences of perception and action. Our more abstract concepts are developed via metaphorical extensions of these basic sensorimotor structures, and our abstract reasoning involves inferences that are basically structure-preserving projections of sensorimotor inferences.[8]

One major consequence of this research is that it provides a major critique of any view that treats meaning and conceptual structure as radically ungrounded and arbitrary. This critique applies equally to deconstructivist views of meaning and to what might be called "neural holism." The former, deconstructivist views regard concepts as defined by their oppositional relations to other concepts, but without any account of how conceptual structure is experientially grounded. Neural holism defines neural networks with virtually no attention to the "external" constraints on those networks that come from the ways our bodies can interact with their environments. Both of these orientations miss the way in which the embodiment of meaning entails constraints on what can be meaningful to us and how we can reason about it. There is considerable flexibility in the ways we can extend and elaborate concepts, but there are always at least some minimal constraints on this process.[9]

The most I can accomplish in this essay is to give simplified examples of some of the ways in which human conceptual structure and reason are grounded in the body. In particular, I want to show how one might go about fleshing out and defending my central claim that our abstract concepts and reasoning "work their way up" out of our embodied experience. Reason does not drop down from above like a transcendent dove; rather, it emerges from the "corporeal" logic and inference structure of our bodily, sensorimotor experience.

III. THE BODILY BASIS OF CONCEPTS

The classical way of accounting for the meaning of sentences like "The chair is green" was shown to be inadequate by the mid-1970s, when cognitive scientists gained a deeper understanding of concepts like GREEN and CHAIR. The problem was that neither of these concepts could be adequately characterized as internal representations of a corresponding external reality. It was discovered that concepts for colors and basic objects could not be characterized adequately without taking into account the contribution of our bodily makeup, experiences, and actions.

Color

In the case of color, it was made clear in the study of the neurophysiology of color vision that there is not, and cannot be, a set of green things in the world taken as independent of the minds, brains, and bodies of speakers.[10] Wavelengths of light and reflectances of surfaces may be aspects of the external world, but color *categories* with all of their structure are not. Color categories are computed by the eye and the brain. We have three kinds of color cones in our retinas. These are connected to neural assemblies in such a way as to produce three fundamental opponent color pairs: red-green, yellow-blue, white-black. The red-green and yellow-blue pairs characterize chromatic colors, while the black-white pairs characterize brightness. Other chromatic colors are computed by the brain from combinations of fundamental chromatic colors.

The result is a *highly structured* set of color categories, and the structure of those categories is reflected linguistically in the kinds of linguistic modifiers that can combine with color terms to designate subcategories. Take, for example, "pure green," "pale green," "deep green," "dark green," "light green," "bluish green," and "yellowish green." These are all subcategories of the category green. These subcategories are determined by the structure of the category green, which is in turn a function of neural structure and light reflectances of surfaces. Thus, "pure green" occurs when there is no contribution made by the cell assemblies for yellow or blue. "Yellowish green" occurs when the firing rate of the cell assemblies for yellow is significant but less than that of the cell assemblies for green. All of these greens are parts of the category green.

In short, a color category like green has a very complex structure. That structure is not part of the external world (i.e., light reflected off surfaces) alone. Rather, it is a function of the interaction of the cell assemblies that define the pure hue green and the way they interact with other color cell assemblies. Note that the nonexistence of a "reddish-green" or a "greenish-red" is a consequence of the fact that green and red are opponent colors, as characterized by neural assemblies.

Thus, no category for green exists in the world external to bodies and brains. There are two reasons for this. First, color exists for us only by virtue of light reflectances, the color cones in our retinas, and the appropriate neural assemblies in our brains. Second, the internal structure of the color categories exists only by virtue of the interactions of those neural assemblies.

In other words, color categories are a product of (1) our bodies and brains and (2) the reflectances of objects in the world. It is the interaction of these two factors that produces color categories with all their structure. Color categories are thus grounded in our bodies (the color cones in our retinas) and brains. It is impossible to specify the meaning of color words simply by the relation of color terms to some objective world independent of the way we perceive and conceptualize it via our bodies and brains.

Phenomenologically, we do perceive and understand the world as if color were out there as part of the world in itself. But the phenomenology of color is a product of our bodies and brains, as well as the world. We need to revise the traditional account of meaning to be able to speak of the world-as-experienced-and-understood-via-our-bodies. We need what Thompson, Palacios, and Varela call an "enactive" theory of color.[11] In short, our embodiment is a creative part of what constitutes reality for us. The color cones and neural assemblies do not just allow us to perceive passively categories of color "out there" independently in the world. Instead, they are an active part of what creates color categories with all their structure.

The way in which colors are embodied explains many of the remarkable results discovered by Brent Berlin, Paul Kay, and their coworkers.[12] The number of basic color terms in the world's languages varies radically from language to language—between two and eleven. If one looks only at the boundaries of the categories, they seem arbitrary. But if speakers of various languages are asked to pick out the best examples of the basic color categories of their language, speakers across languages will pick out the same hues as being central—or best examples—no matter what the language or how many basic color terms it has. The hues that they pick out as being central are determined by the neurophysiology of color vision. That is, the color cones and neural circuitry characterize not just what we perceive, but the meanings of color terms. Not surprisingly, if concepts are fundamentally embodied, then the language for expressing those concepts reflects that embodiment.

Basic-level Categories

The fact that our color categories are "embodied" may seem obvious—a fact that some will say we have known since at least the days of John Locke, who saw color as a "secondary" property that exists only relative to perceivers. Yet this fact is devastating for the traditional theory that concepts get their meanings by standing in objective relations to mind-independent states of affairs in the world. Further evidence that we cannot account for the structure of our concepts and categories merely by reference to "external" states of affairs comes from recent work on basic-level categorization.[13]

On the classical objectivist view of meaning, the meaning of a word like "chair" is given by relating that word to the set of chairs in the world—the world again is seen as independent of any human mind, brain, or body. On this account, the set of chairs in the world is characterized by a collection of necessary and sufficient conditions for something to be a chair. CHAIR would be in a hierarchy of concepts: FURNITURE-CHAIR-ROCKING CHAIR. Within the category FURNITURE, there would be a set of oppositions, such as CHAIR-TABLE-BED-DRESSER. Each concept in the hierarchy would also be defined by a list of properties. Thus, there would be a list of properties defining FURNITURE, and CHAIR would have all of those properties, plus some additional properties that distinguish chairs from other types of furniture, such as beds and tables. And ROCKING CHAIR would have all the properties of CHAIR, but some additional ones to distinguish rocking chairs from desk chairs, barber chairs, and electric chairs.

On the traditional view, the concept CHAIR is in the middle of a hierarchy of concepts, each defined by a list of objective properties. The fact that CHAIR falls into the middle level of the hierarchy is regarded as being simply a result of the objective fact that chairs are types of furniture (i.e., CHAIR has all the properties of FURNITURE) and rocking chairs have additional properties not shared by all chairs. These are alleged to be facts about the nature of things in the world, having no relation to our embodiment.

Within cognitive science this classical picture was overthrown by Brent Berlin, Eleanor Rosch, and their coworkers in the mid-1970s.[14]

They discovered that certain cognitive categories in the middle of such taxonomic hierarchies—what Rosch called "basic-level categories"—have special properties that cannot be explained by the traditional view. These properties can only be explained relative to the nature of human embodiment.

What they discovered was that basic-level categories (such as CHAIR, TREE, CAR) are distinguished from superordinate categories (such as FURNITURE, PLANT, VEHICLE) and from subordinate categories (such as ROCKING CHAIR, OAK TREE, SPORTS CAR) by aspects of our bodies, brains, and minds: mental images, gestalt perception, motor programs, and knowledge structures. The basic level is:

(1) The highest level at which category members have similarly perceived overall shapes. For example, you can recognize a chair or a car by its overall shape. But there is no overall shape that you can assign to a generalized piece of furniture or a vehicle so that you could recognize the category from the shape.

(2) The highest level at which a single mental image can represent the entire category. You can form a mental image of a chair. You can get mental images of opposing categories at this level, such as, tables and beds. But you cannot get a mental image of a general piece of furniture that is not some particular kind of furniture, such as a table or bed.

(3) The highest level at which a person uses similar motor actions for interacting with category members. People have motor programs for interacting with objects at the basic level—interacting with chairs, tables, and beds. There are no motor programs for interacting with generalized pieces of furniture.

(4) The level at which most of our knowledge is organized. Think of all that you know about cars versus what you know about vehicles. You know a handful of things about vehicles, but a huge number of things about cars. It is at the basic level that most of our useful information and knowledge is organized.

As a result of these characteristics of basic-level category structure, the basic level has other priorities over the superordinate and subordinate levels: it is named and understood earlier by children, enters a language earlier, has the shortest primary lexemes, is identified faster by subjects, and is used in neutral contexts. From the perspective of overall theory of the human mind, these are important properties of concepts that cannot be ignored.

The key point in all of this is that the basic level is that level at which people interact optimally with their environments, given the kinds of bodies and brains they have and the kinds of environments they inhabit. Such characteristics of basic-level categories can only be explained relative to the nature of human embodiment. They cannot be explained by the classical theory, because it makes no reference to our bodies, our brains, or our functional interactions. These special properties of basic-level categories do not follow from, and indeed are inconsistent with, the traditional objectivist account of cognitive categories (described above) as being internal representations of an external reality that is taken as independent of human minds and bodies.

IV. THE BODILY BASIS OF REASON

It is one thing to claim that conceptual structure is tied to human embodiment. In itself, that is a striking enough fact, and it is one that undermines the classical view of concepts as disembodied. However, it is a far stronger claim to assert that reason itself is somehow grounded in the nature of our bodies. Following Frege, most philosophers insist that thought and reason must transcend the embodiment of any beings who think and reason.

The strongest evidence for the embodiment of reason comes, again, from second-generation cognitive science. This evidence concerns the image-schematic structure of concepts and reason. The basic idea is that reason is grounded in spatial relations concepts, which are characterized in terms of schematic mental images ("image schemas").[15] These image schemas are common patterns of our bodily orientations, movements, and interactions. Each image schema has its own internal structure that defines its "spatial" or "corporeal" logic. Spatial logics characterize sensorimotor inference and are imaginatively developed to structure our abstract inferences.

In order to see how reason might be grounded in the body in this way, it is useful to consider what psychologists are learning about the role of the infant's bodily experience in the way she understands and makes sense of her world.

The Infant's Corporeal Logic

In what follows, I want to sketch a picture of reason as prefigured in, and developing out of, structures of our embodied activities, such as perception, manipulation of objects, bodily spatial orientation, and movement of our bodies through space. This kind of sensorimotor activity begins before birth, and it is the means by which even the tiniest newborn begins to develop structures of understanding and a sense of self. In *The Interpersonal World of the Infant*,[16] Daniel Stern presents an account of the sense of an emergent self that develops from as early as two weeks up to two years and beyond. Stern argues that from birth (and perhaps earlier) the infant can experience a sense of the structured *processes* of emerging self-organization, even though it probably does not experience a fixed self as a product of these processes. He cites extensive experimental evidence from the past two decades indicating that the infant's subjective experience consists primarily of various bodily rhythms, temporal and emotional changes, pulses, and *patterns of organization*:

> The first such organization concerns the body: its coherence, its actions, its inner feeling states, and the memory of all these. That is the experiential organization with which the sense of a core self is concerned. . . . The sense of an emergent self thus concerns the process and product of forming organization. It concerns the learning about the relations between the infant's sensory experience.[17]

In other words, from the very beginning, the prelinguistic infant starts to have a meaningfully structured world that grows and develops along with its emerging sense of self-identity. That identity consists primarily in the process and structure of the baby's experience, rather than in any sense of a substantial ego. Stern describes three major types of experiences of organization out of which the infant's sense of a self emerges:

(1) **Amodal Perception**: Several studies show that babies experience a number of schematic patterns that are common to different perceptual modalities, such as vision, touch, and hearing. In one experiment, for instance, Meltzloff and Borton[18] gave blindfolded three-week-olds one of two pacifiers to suck on. One was spherical and the other had nubs protruding from it. After the baby had sucked on one of the nipples, the blindfold was removed and the two nipples were placed side by side. After a brief visual inspection, the infant would look more at the nipple it had just sucked. The baby was somehow able to correlate the structure of what it had *felt* (touched through sucking) with what it *saw*.

Stern surveys a number of experiments that tested different kinds of cross-modal perception, and he concludes that

> Infants thus appear to have an innate general capacity, which can be called *amodal perception*, to take information received in one sensory modality and somehow translate it into another sensory modality. . . . These abstract representations that the infant experiences are not sights and sounds and touches and nameable objects, but rather shapes, intensities, and temporal patterns—the more "global" qualities of experience. And the need and ability to form abstract representations of primary qualities of perception and act upon them starts at the beginning of mental life; it is not the culmination or a developmental landmark reached in the second year of life.[19]

The key point here is that the infant's first experience of making sense of things consists almost entirely in its experience of cross-modal patterns of its perceptual, emotional, and bodily interactions. These structures of activity and experience are the "stuff" of the baby's world, insofar as that world gradually develops into a place that is an arena of action and communication for the baby.

(2) **Physiognomic Perception**: As early as 1948 Heinz Werner[20] suggested that various cross-modal shapes, contours, and other features of people and things are experienced by infants directly in terms of basic categoreal affects or feelings, such as feelings of being happy, sad, angry, and so forth. The crucial idea is that the infant's world is primarily a world of affect attached to various shapes and dimensions of its ongoing experience.

(3) **Vitality Affects**—Stern observes that there exists a vast domain of affective experience beyond what Darwin had described as the discrete categories of affect (such as happiness, sadness, fear, anger, disgust, surprise, interest, shame, or any combination of these). This hitherto uncharted continent of our emotional life consists of the vitality affects that attend the dynamic, kinetic, active aspects of our experience. Stern notes that, lacking adequate terms to describe these affective contours, we use words such as surging, fading away, fleeting, explosive, crescendo, bursting, drawn out, floating, rushing, and so forth. These affective dimensions are not the discrete emotions, like anger or fear, but rather they are the felt quality of the anger or fear—the "rush" of fear, the "crescendo" of anger that leads to an angry "outburst," the "fading away" of one's joyful exuberance.

Such vitality affects are typically contours of activation over time. They are the recurring patterns of changes in the affective quality of an experience over a period of time. As such, they are not restricted to any single sensory modality, but instead characterize what Suzanne Langer called the "vital import" of our experience. Consider the following example: A parent comforting an infant might characteristically say "there, there, there," with a soothing tone, placing more emphasis on the initial "th" than on the rest of the word. But the very same pattern of activation occurs when the parent silently strokes the baby's back or head, applying more pressure at the onset of the stroke, gradually releasing that pressure as the stroke trails off. In both cases, the baby is soothed by the very same activation contour.

Another good example is the THUMB-TO-MOUTH schema. In the infant's early uncoordinated trials at moving its thumb to its mouth, there is increased arousal as the thumb moves jerkily toward the mouth, followed by a rapid falling off of tension once the thumb reaches the mouth and the smooth functioning of the sucking schema takes over. The sensorimotor schema that develops here eventually becomes so habitual and smoothly executed that it may lose its strong affective contour. But this very same arousal schema or activation contour of building intensity occurs across all our sensory modalities, carrying with it the same affective quality of build-up followed by release.

Both William James and John Dewey saw the importance for all our thinking and reasoning of what Stern is here calling vitality affect contours. Each of them gave extensive analyses of the ways in which affective contours are part of the quality that defines any particular experience. And, since thinking and deliberating are themselves experiences, they, too, involve patterns of amodal perception and affective contours. James's nice phrase "the sentiment of rationality" suggests the intimate intertwining of affective, sensorimotor, and inferential structures in all normal thinking.

The point in all of this so far is that the infant makes sense of and reasons about her world via structures that emerge in her embodied experience, and these are neither propositional nor linguistic in their first appearance. These patterns of her corporeal logic are schematic, cross-modal, and blended with affect contours that depend on the nature of our bodies and brains. When the child begins to use language, these embodied modes of understanding do not simply cease to exist; on the contrary, they are what situate, make possible, and give meaning to what we call our higher-level propositional operations and linguistic performances.[21] Without this embodied meaning, there would be no propositional contents or propositional attitudes. Nor would there be any complex sentential structure.[22]

The Image-schematic Basis of Reason

Stern's account of both amodal perception and vitality affects has close parallels with the account of "image schemas" that is being developed in second-generation cognitive science. Primarily on the basis of evidence concerning syntax, semantics, and inference structure, many researchers in cognitive semantics[23] have argued that human conceptualization and reasoning are grounded in recurring patterns of our embodied interactions that can be characterized by cross-modal schemas such as CONTAINMENT, SOURCE-PATH-GOAL, COMPULSIVE FORCE, ATTRACTION, BALANCE, VERTICALITY, SCALARITY, and so forth. The evidence suggests that these image schemas arise from the nature of our sensorimotor activities and that the image schemas are metaphorically extended to structure abstract concepts and acts of reasoning. It is in this sense that human conceptualization, understanding, and reasoning can be said to be embodied.

What Stern's account of vitality affects adds to the concept of an image schema is the crucial affective dimension that orients, motivates, and gives force to our conceptual thinking. Vitality affects give flesh and blood to our more skeletally defined image schemas, thereby giving substance and life to our theory of embodied imaginative structures of human understanding.

This also allows us to understand why image schemas are so important to our sense of our world and ourselves, and it explains why they can have the emotional and motivating force they have.

As an example of a typical kind of image schema, consider the following pattern of our embodied experience. Hundreds of times each day we move our bodies through space to achieve some goal, such as, walking to the refrigerator to get some food, or moving to a door to exit a room. We also track the movements of other people and objects as they move across our perceptual space, from some initial point, over a series of contiguous points, to some destination, in order to achieve some purpose they have. The recurring imaginative structure in these experiences is a SOURCE-PATH-GOAL image schema that is manifest both in our felt sense of our own bodily movement and also in our tracking of objects through our perceptual field. The SOURCE-PATH-GOAL schema, like all image schemas, is cross-modal, existing kinesthetically, visually, tactilely, and auditorily (e.g., when we follow the movement of a melody).[24]

The SOURCE-PATH-GOAL schema is an imaginative structure that we have because of the nature of our bodily capacities. If we did not have bodies that move through space, or if we did not have perceptual organs that can track moving objects, we would not experience and understand our world via a SOURCE-PATH-GOAL schema. In general, our experience of the world, and the ways we are able to reason about it, are based on a massive, mostly unconscious, body of image-schematic structures that bind our modes of thinking together via our embodiment.

V. CONCEPTUAL METAPHOR AND EMBODIMENT

Conceptual metaphor is one of the principal means by which we imaginatively extend the embodied and image-schematic concepts that define most of our concrete experience. A conceptual metaphor is a conceptual mapping of entities and structure from a domain of one kind (the "source" domain)[25] to a domain of a different kind (the "target" domain). We appropriate our knowledge of the source domain to conceptualize and reason about the target domain. In this way the bodily-based meaning of the source domain is carried over into our understanding of more abstract concepts.

As an example of the bodily grounding of conceptual metaphor, let us examine the way in which metaphors such as Moral Strength, Uprightness, Light/Dark, Nurturance, Obedience, Discipline, Growth, and so forth, form the fabric of our moral understanding and experience.[26]

Consider what we call moral strength. This concept is based on a mapping of physical strength onto the domain of moral reasoning and will.

Strength and weakness are things we experience in our bodies. If we lack sufficient physical strength, we cannot lift certain objects or accomplish certain tasks. Our understanding of such experiences maps onto our moral willing. Evil is understood as a strong force (either internal or external) that you must struggle to overcome. If the evil is powerful, it can overwhelm you, knock you down, and make you "fall." When evil is understood metaphorically as an internal force, we then conceptualize ourselves as split, with our higher (moral and rational) selves at war with our lower (immoral and irrational) selves. In our culture, and in many cultures around the world, that "lower," immoral self is tied to the body—to its needs, desires, passions, feelings, etc. Being moral is thus understood as marshalling the requisite strength of will needed to overcome the forces of evil and temptation.

Consider, next, the metaphor in which immoral activity and evil are understood as darkness, while moral activity is light. We say, for example, "Hyde was overcome by his dark side," "The *forces of darkness* must be resisted at all cost," "The Prince of *Darkness* is always waiting to overcome you," "His *shady* financial dealings got him in trouble." Why should we align darkness with evil, sin, and immorality? This is clearly not merely an optional conceptual mapping that we use as a convenience; rather, it is our felt experience of darkness and night that carries over into our understanding of morality. There is a human tendency to fear the darkness, because we tend to associate darkness with bad things that might happen. It is not just that in the darkness things are hard to see, or that it is hard to get around in the dark. Instead, our felt bodily sense of being in darkness plays a crucial role in our correlation of darkness with immorality and evil. This feeling quality of the experience of darkness is present, at least on the horizon, in our conceptualization of evil and immorality.

Another example is the metaphor of Moral Nurturance, in which moral action is understood as the kind of action a nurturant parent gives his child. The metaphor maps the physical nurturance that is essential for all of us onto the idea of moral caring and concern. This is such a powerful metaphor because every human being is utterly dependent, from birth, on the nurturance he or she receives from caregivers. When that nurturance is present, and when it is given in a loving manner, we are happy, fulfilled, and we grow. When nurturance is absent, we are frustrated, sad, incapacitated, and dysfunctional. This experiential cluster of feelings, emotions, expectations, and inferences underlies the Moral Nurturance metaphor and gives it its life and force. Nurturance requires empathy, concern for the growth and well-being of the other, and active care for that person. Feminist "ethics of care" is thus based on defining our moral relations to others by means of the model of nurturance between parent and child, caregiver and care-recipient. Our bodily experience of nurturance, both the giving and receiving of it, is activated via the Moral Nurturance metaphor and is therefore present in the meaning of those moral concepts that are understood through the metaphor.[27]

VI. CONCEPTUAL METAPHOR AND EMBODIED REASONING

Conceptual metaphor is one of the basic imaginative devices by which we employ spatial logics and grounded bodily meaning to understand concepts that are either more abstract or less well conceptually articulated. We reason on the basis of such metaphorical mappings, which let us use the inference patterns of the source domain to reason in the target domain. For example, basic metaphoric structures by which we experience and conceptualize mental phenomena in terms of bodily phenomena lie at the heart of our understanding of human cognition. They form a vast generic metaphoric system that Eve Sweetser has named the Mind As Body metaphor.[28] A number of recent studies have focused on the fact that the vast majority of our conceptions of mind and reasoning are grounded on some bodily-based metaphor system. Our conceptions of mind,[29] memory,[30] knowledge,[31] reason,[32] and logic[33] are all defined by image-schematically grounded metaphors.

To elaborate this key point, consider one of our most important conceptions of mental activity, in which we understand Reasoning As Motion Along A Path. We see ourselves as reasoning *from one point to another. At a certain point in our argument* we can see the conclusion *that we are coming to*. We *move step-by-step* through someone's argument. Here, it is an image schema of goal-directed bodily movement through space (the SOURCE-PATH-GOAL schema) that structures our understanding of reasoning to a conclusion, according to the following mapping:

Spatial Domain	*Mental Domain*
Spatial locations	Ideas
Moving from pt. A to pt. B	Thinking/reasoning
Force that moves you	Reason
Going over the same territory	Remembering the argument
Guiding to a destination	Communication
Discovering a new place	Creativity

Understood in this way, we reason from one idea (initial location) to another idea (second location), moving finally to a conclusion (ultimate destination). As we reason, we *cover ground*, which we may need to *go back over again*, in order to *check the steps* of our reasoning. Argument consists in a projectible *path*, a path we *follow* as we reason, a path we can *lose along the way*, and a path we can *get back on*.

The apriorist—the purist—will object that this is merely a metaphorical way of talking about the essential structure of pure reason. The purist will accuse me of confusing our language ("the words we use") with the nature of reason itself. But I reply that there is no understanding or experience of reasoning independent of some system of metaphors. Classical logic, for example, is a logic of *containment*, one based on the metaphor of Concepts As Containers for the entities that *fall within* them. Spatial containment has its own logic: If object A is in container B, and if container B is in container C, then object A is in container C. Therefore, in syllogistic logic in its classical form, as a logic of containment, the spatial logic of image-schematic containment structures our abstract formal logic: if A is *in* B, and B is *in* C, then A is *in* C. To get a fuller sense of the pervasive, constitutive nature of metaphorical concepts, consider the following chart, which sets out some of the most important Mind as Body metaphors that define mental activity for us. What this chart shows is some of the ways in which various basic types of bodily activity provide source domains for metaphors by which we understand abstract concepts for types of mental activity, such as reasoning, remembering, and creative thinking. (See table 1)

Notice that, for each source domain drawn from the things we do with our bodies, there are patterns of inference in the target domain concerning how the mind works. With the source domain of manipulation, it follows from the structure of our bodily activity in that domain that *grasping* and *working* (forming) objects is the appropriate form of manipulation. Therefore, in the mental domain what we "do" with idea-objects must either be some form of *taking hold of* ("apprehending") the ideas, or else some form of *working* or *shaping* those idea-objects. If moving is our source domain, then all mental operations must be understood as various types of motion.

The apriorist will, no doubt, reply that such metaphors do not *define* inference patterns, but exist only because reason has the essential structure that it does. In other words, the apriorist will claim that the metaphors merely present various aspects of what is a pre-existent, transcendent rationality.

This gambit will not work, because the various metaphors by which we understand and experience mental functioning are themselves often mutually inconsistent. That is, the ontology of one bodily source domain, such as spatial movement, does not map completely onto the entities in another source domain, such as eating. Moving from point A to point B is not the same sort of thing as digesting food. These metaphor systems are not simply different ways of looking at one and the same independent entity that

TABLE 1.

THE MIND IS THE BODY

	PERCEIVING	MANIPULATING	MOVING	EATING	PROCREATING
IDEAS	physical objects	physical objects	locations	food	offspring
THINKING	observing/ perceiving	manipulation of object	moving from pt. A to B	digestion/ preparation	gestation
REASON	light source/ ambient conditions	grasping	force that moves you	capacity to digest	fertility
MEMORY	re-viewing re-perceiving	storage (recalling or retrieving)	going over same territory	regurgitation	
COMMUNICATION	showing	sending	guiding	feeding	intercourse
CREATIVITY	seeing from a new perspective (in a new light)	re-making re-forming	discovery	cooking up new combinations	giving birth

we call "reason." Rather, each metaphor system constitutes its own partial understanding of reasoning. We can only determine the relevant inference structure relative to specific metaphorical mappings for reasoning.

VII. EMBODIED MIND

My chief claims about the bodily basis of conceptualization and reasoning are these: Image schemas and vitality affect contours are the earliest and most primitive bases for the infant's emerging sense of the world. Such structures of bodily experience are nonpropositional and arise prior to language, and yet they are what make it possible for the child to make some sense of its surroundings and to act intelligently to achieve its ends. Because embodied structures of this sort organize our emerging world, they correlatively organize and form our emerging and always developing sense of self. If our bodies were different, and if we therefore had different bodily experiences and different kinds of interactions with our multiple and multidimensional environments, then we would have a different sense of self and different ways of understanding and reasoning.

These embodied patterns are the primitive, nonpropositional structures of our developing selfhood, and so they determine the ways we can make sense of and reason about things. We conceptualize and reason not only with spatial schemas, but also via metaphor and metonymy; we extend image schemas with their spatial logics to structure abstract concepts and inference. Our rationality is embodied in the sense that it is built on and grows out of these affect-rich image schemas. Reason develops as it does primarily because of the nature of our bodies and the range of organism-environment interactions that are possible for the kinds of embodied beings we are. In this way our reason is situated, and it may evolve throughout the history of the human race.

Rationality is thus not a static external structure that we come to grasp or know, as though it pre-existed independently and only awaited discovery by each new infant. Rationality is not a universal structure "wired" into us that we simply activate over time. Rather, our reason is an ongoing, developing activity by which we understand things, and this activity emerges for organisms of the sort we are, organisms with certain constraints on perception, movement, and cognitive processing. We conceptualize and reason the ways we do because of the kinds of bodies we have, the kinds of environments we inhabit, and the symbolic systems we inherit, which are themselves grounded in our embodiment. There are all sorts of constraints on this constructive process—constraints set by our sensorimotor system, our cognitive processing capacities, our interests, and aspects of our environments. These constraints limit the ways we can make sense of things and reason about them. However, in spite of such bodily constraints on meaning and inference, our imaginative capacities (such as metaphor) give rise to variation in the ways we elaborate and reason about our abstract concepts.

Reason, according to this embodied view, is universal only insofar as there are shared perceptual and sensorimotor structures, shared environments, and shared stable contexts that define the ways we conceptualize and draw inferences. In short, human conceptualization and reasoning are bodily activities. We understand and reason starting with, and never leaving behind, the patterns, feelings, and significance of our bodily experience. Our reason is an embodied reason.

NOTES

1. Good examples of work at this level are Patricia Churchland, *Neurophilosophy: Toward a Unified Science of the Mind/Brain* (Cambridge, MA: MIT Press, 1986); Paul Churchland, *A Neurocomputational Perspective: The Nature of the Mind and the Structure of Science* (Cambridge, MA: MIT, 1989); F. Varela, E. Thompson, and E. Rosch, *The Embodied Mind: Cognitive Science and Human Experience* (Cambridge, MA: MIT, 1991); Antonio Damasio, *Descartes' Error: Emotion, Reason, and the Human Brain* (New York: G.P. Putman's Sons, 1994); and Terry Regier, *The Human Semantic Potential* (Cambridge, MA: MIT Press, 1996).

2. Good surveys of this type of cognitive theory are George Lakoff, *Women, Fire, and Dangerous Things: What Categories Reveal About the Mind* (Chicago: University of Chicago Press, 1987); Raymond Gibbs, *The Poetics of Mind* (Cambridge: Cambridge University Press, 1994).

3. The relations of these three levels are discussed extensively in George Lakoff and Mark Johnson, *Philosophy in the Flesh: The Embodied Mind and Its Challenge to Western Thought* (New York: Basic Books, 1998).

4. See, for example, Drew Leder, *The Absent Body* (Chicago: University of Chicago Press, 1990).

5. The dismissal of the body in Fregean semantics is described in Mark Johnson, *The Body in the Mind: The Bodily Basis of Meaning, Imagination, and Reason* (Chicago: University of Chicago Press, 1987), introduction.

6. Here, I think, Merleau-Ponty is the wonderful exception, rather than the rule. His *Phenomenology of Perception* is a model of the blending of phenomenological description, neurophysiology, and even some discussion of conceptual structure and language.

7. But see, Antonio Damasio, *Descartes' Error: Emotion, Reason, and the Human Brain* (New York: G.P. Putman's Sons, 1994) and George Lakoff and Mark Johnson, *Philosophy in the Flesh* (1998).

8. A survey of the types of evidence for this view of the embodied mind can be found in Johnson, *The Body in the Mind,* and also in Raymond Gibbs, Jr., *The*

Poetics of the Mind: Figurative Thought, Language, and Understanding (Cambridge: Cambridge University Press, 1994).

9. Gibbs, *The Poetics of Mind* is especially good at setting out the variety of bodily constraints on the development of meaning that have so far been discovered.

10. Relevant work is summarized in Chapter 8 of F. Varela, E. Thompson, and E. Rosch, *The Embodied Mind.*

11. Thompson, Evan, Palacios, Adrian, and Francisco Varela, "Ways of Coloring: Comparative Color Vision as a Case study for Cognitive Science," *Behavioral and Brain Sciences* 15 (1992): 1–74.

12. Brent Berlin, and Paul Kay, *Basic Color Terms: Their Universality and Evolution* (Berkeley: University of California Press, 1969).

13. See Lakoff, *Women, Fire, and Dangerous Things*, Chapter 2.

14. Eleanor Rosch, "On the International Structure of Perceptual and Semantic Categories." In *Cognitive Development and the Acquisition of Language*, T. Moore, ed. (New York: Academic Press, 1973), and Eleanor Rosch, "Principles of Categorization." In *Cognition and Categorization*, E. Rosch and B.B. Lloyd, eds. (Hillsdale, NJ: Lawrence Erlbaum, 1978).

15. The concept of an image schema is first articulated in Mark Johnson, *The Body in the Mind* and in George Lakoff, *Women, Fire, and Dangerous Things*, but its roots lie in Kant's notion of the schematism of the understanding, as set forth in his *Critique of Pure Reason* (1781/1787, pp. A137/B176–A147/B187).

16. Daniel Stern, *The Interpersonal World of the Infant: A View from Psychoanalysis and Developmental Psychology* (New York: Basic Books, 1985).

17. Daniel Stern, *The Interpersonal World of the Infant*, p. 46.

18. A.N. Meltzoff and W. Borton, "Intermodal Matching by Human Neonates." *Nature* 282 (1979): 403–404.

19. Stern, *The Interpersonal World of the Infant*, pp. 51–52.

20. H. Werner, *The Comparative Psychology of Mental Development* (New York: International Universities Press, 1948).

21. Eugene Gendlin, "Thinking Beyond Patterns: Body, Language, and Situations," in B. den Ouden and M. Moen, eds. *The Presence of Feeling in Thought* (New York: Peter Lang, 1991).

22. For an account of how syntactic and semantic structure might be tied to image schemas, see George Lakoff, *Women, Fire, and Dangerous Things.*

23. Mark Turner, *Reading Minds: The Study of English in the Age of Cognitive Science* (Princeton: Princeton University Press, 1991); Raymond Gibbs, *The Poetics of Mind*; Zoltan Kovecses, *Emotion Concepts* (Springer-Verlag, 1990); Steven Winter, "Transcendental Nonsense, Metaphoric Reasoning, and the Cognitive Stakes for Law," *University of Pennsylvania Law Review* 137, No. 4 (1989): 1105–1237.

24. A more thorough treatment of the SOURCE-PATH-GOAL image schema and its various metaphorical extensions can be found in Mark Johnson, *The Body in the Mind*, chapters 2 and 5. The use of this schema in moral reasoning is examined in Mark Johnson, *Moral Imagination: Implications of Cognitive Science for Ethics* (Chicago: University of Chicago Press, 1993).

25. Conceptual metaphor was first defined in George Lakoff and Mark Johnson, *Metaphors We Live By* (Chicago: University of Chicago Press, 1980), and has subsequently been explored in a large number of studies, several of which are discussed in George Lakoff, "The Contemporary Theory of Metaphor," in A. Ortony, ed., *Metaphor and Thought* (Cambridge: Cambridge University Press, 2nd. ed., 1993).

26. Extensive treatments of the metaphors that define our moral concepts can be found in Mark Johnson, *Moral Imagination* and George Lakoff, *Moral Politics: What Conservatives Know that Liberals Don't* (Chicago: University of Chicago Press, 1996).

27. George Lakoff, in *Moral Politics*, has shown how a nurturant parent model of the family is elaborated via several metaphors for morality (such as Moral Empathy, Moral Growth, and Moral Strength) to define various forms of political liberalism.

28. Eve Sweetser, *From Etymology to Pragmatics* (Cambridge: Cambridge University Press, 1990).

29. Robert Sternberg, *Metaphors of Mind: Conceptions of the Nature of Intelligence* (Cambridge: Cambridge University Press, 1990); D. Gentner and J. Grudin, "The Evolution of Mental Metaphors in Psychology," *American Psycologist* 40 (1985): 181–92; Michael Kearns, *Metaphors of Mind in Fiction and Psychology* (Lexington: University of Kentucky Press, 1987).

30. Henry Roediger, "Memory Metaphors in Cognitive Psychology," *Memory and Cognition* 8 (1980): 231–46.

31. Richard Rorty, *Philosophy and the Mirror of Nature* (Princeton: Princeton University Press, 1979).

32. Steven Fesmire, "Aerating the Mind: The Metaphor of Mental Functioning as Bodily Functioning," *Metaphor and Symbolic Activity* 9, No. 1 (1994): 31–44; Mark Johnson, *The Body in the Mind.*

33. George Lakoff, *Women, Fire, and Dangerous Things.*

SIX

THE CHALLENGE OF MERLEAU-PONTY'S PHENOMENOLOGY OF EMBODIMENT FOR COGNITIVE SCIENCE

HUBERT L. DREYFUS
STUART E. DREYFUS

Cognitive scientists have much to learn from Merleau-Ponty. This paper explicates two central, but rarely discussed, notions in Merleau-Ponty's *Phenomenology of Perception*: the *intentional arc* and the tendency to achieve a *maximum grip*. The intentional arc names the tight connection between body and world, viz. that, as the active body acquires skills, those skills are "stored," not as representations in the mind, but as dispositions to respond to the solicitations of situations in the world. Maximum grip names the body's tendency to refine its discriminations and to respond to solicitations in such a way as to bring the current situation closer to the optimal gestalt that the skilled agent has learned to expect. Neither of these "body-functions" requires that the body have any particular size or shape. However, if one tries to implement Merleau-Ponty's understanding of skill acquisition in a neural network, one finds that, in order to learn to generalize input/output pairs to new situations the way human beings do, a network needs to share crucial aspects of the human body-structure.

To begin with we need to distinguish two different accounts of embodiment in *Phenomenology of Perception*. The first is advanced as a refutation of Sartre's view that human beings have total freedom to interpret the world any way they choose as long as they are willing to take the consequences. Merleau-Ponty answers that the basic structure of the body is not up for interpretation and, since perception depends on the body, neither is the perceptual world. On this account, embodiment refers to the actual shape and innate capacities of the human body—that it has arms and legs, a certain size, and certain abilities. Merleau-Ponty notes:

> In so far as I have hands, feet, a body, I sustain around me intentions which are not dependent upon my decisions and which affect my surroundings in a way which I do not choose. These intentions are general . . . they

originate from other than myself, and I am not surprised to find them in all psycho-physical subjects organized as I am.[1]

Merleau-Ponty points out in his critique of Sartre's extreme view of freedom that, no matter how we choose to interpret them, mountains are tall for us, and that where they are passable and where not is not up to us but is a function of our climbing capacities. That the given shape and physical capacities of the body are reflected willy-nilly in what we see is a powerful argument against Sartre's over-estimation of human freedom, but it plays no further explicit role in *Phenomenology of Perception*.

A related view, however, that as we refine our skills for coping with things, things show up as soliciting our skillful responses, so that as we refine our skills, we encounter more and more differentiated solicitations to act, does play a crucial role in Merleau-Ponty's book. That will concern us in a moment. But we must first make one more distinction. J.J. Gibson, like Merleau-Ponty, sees that characteristics of the human world (e.g., what affords walking on, squeezing through, reaching, etc.) are correlative with both our innate bodily capacities and acquired skills, but he then goes on to add that mail boxes afford mailing letters.[2] This kind of affordance calls attention to a third aspect of embodiment. Affords-mailing-letters is clearly not a cross-cultural phenomenon based solely on body structure, nor on body structure plus a skill all normal human beings acquire. It is an affordance that comes from experience with mail boxes and the acquisition of letter-mailing skills. The cultural world is thus also correlative with our body; this time with our acquired cultural embodiment.

These three ways our bodies determine what shows up in our world—innate structures, general acquired skills, and specific cultural skills—can be contrasted by considering how each contributes to the fact that to Western human beings a chair affords sitting. Because we have the sort of bodies that get tired and that bend backwards at the knees, chairs can show up for us—but not for flamingos, say—as affording sitting. But chairs can only solicit sitting once we have learned to sit. Finally, only because we Western Europeans are brought up in a culture where one sits on chairs, do chairs solicit us to sit on them. Chairs would not solicit sitting in traditional Japan. By embodiment, Merleau-Ponty intends to include all three ways the body opens up a world:

> The body is our general medium for having a world. Sometimes it is restricted to the actions necessary for the conservation of life, and accordingly it posits around us a biological world; at other times, elaborating upon these primary actions and moving from their literal to a figurative meaning, it manifests through them a core of new significance: this is true of motor habits such as dancing. Sometimes, finally, the meaning aimed at

cannot be achieved by the body's natural means; it must then build itself an instrument, and it projects thereby around itself a cultural world.[3]

The notion of intentional arc is meant to cover all three ways our embodied skills determine the way things show up for us. In *Phenomenology of Perception* Merleau-Ponty tells us that

> The life of consciousness—cognitive life, the life of desire or perceptual life—is subtended by an "intentional arc" which projects round about us our past, our future, our human setting, our physical, ideological and moral situation.[4]

In this paper we would like to explain, defend, and draw out the implications of this claim. Since the intentional arc is supposed to embody the interconnection of skillful action and perception, we will first lay out an account of skill acquisition that makes explicit what Merleau-Ponty's claim presupposes. We will then show how this description of skill acquisition supports Merleau-Ponty's account of the relation of perception and action and thereby allows him to criticize cognitivism. Finally, we will suggest that neural-network theory supports Merleau-Ponty's phenomenology, but that it still has a long way to go before it can instantiate an intentional arc.

I. SKILL ACQUISITION: THE ESTABLISHMENT OF THE INTENTIONAL ARC

To see how our embodied skills are acquired by dealing with things and situations and how these skills in turn determine how things and situations show up for us as requiring our responses, we need to lay out more fully than Merleau-Ponty does how our relation to the world is transformed as we acquire a skill. Many of our skills are acquired at an early age by trial and error or by imitation, but to make all possible stages of skill development as explicit as possible we will consider the case of an adult acquiring a skill by instruction.[5]

Stage 1: Novice

Normally, the instruction process begins with the instructor decomposing the task environment into context-free features which the beginner can recognize without previous experience in the task domain. The beginner is then given rules for determining actions on the basis of these features, like a computer following a program.

For purposes of illustration, let us consider two variations: a bodily or motor skill and an intellectual skill. The student automobile driver learns to recognize such interpretation-free features as speed (indicated by the speedometer) and is given rules such as shift to second when the speedometer needle points to ten miles an hour.

The novice chess player learns a numerical value for each type of piece regardless of its position, and the rule: "Always exchange if the total value of pieces captured exceeds the value of pieces lost." She also learns to seek center control when no advantageous exchanges can be found, and the player is given a rule defining center squares and one for calculating extent of control. Most beginners are notoriously slow players, as they attempt to remember all these rules and their priorities.

Stage 2: Advanced Beginner

As the novice gains experience actually coping with real situations, he begins to note perspicuous examples of meaningful additional aspects of the situation. After seeing a sufficient number of examples, the student learns to recognize these new aspects. Instructional maxims now can refer to these new situational *aspects*, recognized on the basis of experience, as well as to the objectively defined nonsituational *features* recognizable by the inexperienced novice.

The advanced beginner driver uses (situational) engine sounds as well as (nonsituational) speed in his gear-shifting rules. He learns the maxim: Shift up when the motor sounds like it is racing and down when it sounds like its straining. Engine sounds cannot be adequately captured by words so words cannot take the place of a few choice examples in learning these distinctions.

With experience, the chess beginner learns to recognize overextended positions and how to avoid them. Similarly, she begins to recognize such situational aspects of positions as a weakened king's side or a strong pawn structure despite the lack of precise and situation-free definition. The player can then follow maxims such as: Attack a weakened king's side.

Stage 3: Competence

With more experience, the number of potentially relevant elements that the learner is able to recognize becomes overwhelming. At this point, since a sense of what is important in any particular situation is missing, performance becomes nerve-wracking and exhausting, and the student might well wonder how anybody ever masters the skill.

To cope with this overload and to achieve competence, people learn, through instruction or experience, to devise a plan, or choose a perspective, that then determines which elements of the situation are to be treated as important and which ones can be ignored. As they restrict themselves to only a few of the vast number of possibly relevant features and aspects, decision making becomes easier.

The competent performer thus seeks new rules and reasoning procedures to decide upon a plan or perspective. But these rules are not as easily come by as the rules given beginners in texts and lectures. Indeed, there are a vast number of situations differing from each other in subtle, nuanced ways. There are, in fact, more situations than can be named or precisely defined, so no one can prepare for the learner a list of what to do in each possible situation. Competent performers, therefore, must decide for themselves what plan to choose without being sure that it will be appropriate in the particular situation.

Now, coping becomes frightening rather than exhausting, and the learner feels great responsibility for his actions. Prior to this stage, if the learned rules didn't work out, the performer could rationalize that he hadn't been given adequate rules rather than feel remorse because of a mistake. Now the learner feels responsible for disasters. Of course, often, at this stage, things work out well, and the competent performer experiences a kind of elation unknown to the beginner. Thus, learners find themselves on an emotional roller coaster.

A competent driver leaving the freeway on an off-ramp curve, after taking into account speed, surface condition, criticality of time, etc., may decide he is going too fast. He then has to decide whether to let up on the accelerator, remove his foot altogether, or step on the brake. He is relieved if he gets through the curve without mishap and shaken if he begins to go into a skid.

The class A chess player, here classed as competent, may decide after studying a position that her opponent has weakened his king's defenses so that an attack against the king is a viable goal. If she chooses to attack, features involving weaknesses in her own position created by the attack are ignored, as are losses of pieces not essential to the attack. Pieces defending the enemy king become salient. Successful plans induce euphoria, while mistakes are felt in the pit of the stomach.

As the competent performer becomes more and more emotionally involved in his tasks, it becomes increasingly difficult to draw back and to adopt the *detached* rule-following stance of the beginner. While it might seem that this involvement would interfere with detached rule-testing and so would inhibit further skill development, in fact just the opposite seems to be the case. As we shall soon see, if the detached rule-following stance of the novice and advanced beginner is replaced by involvement, one is set for further advancement, while resistance to the acceptance of risk and responsibility can lead to stagnation and ultimately to boredom and regression.

Stage 4: Proficient

If, as the learner practices her skill, events are experienced with involvement, the resulting positive and negative experiences will strengthen successful responses and inhibit unsuccessful ones. The performer's theory of the skill, as represented by rules and principles, will thus gradually be replaced by situational discriminations accompanied by associated responses. Proficiency seems to develop if, and only if, experience is assimilated in this atheoretical way and intuitive behavior replaces reasoned responses.

As the brain of the performer acquires the ability to discriminate among a variety of situations, each entered into with concern and involvement, plans are intuitively evoked and certain aspects stand out as important without the learner standing back and choosing those plans or deciding to adopt that perspective. Action becomes easier and less stressful as the learner simply sees what needs to be achieved rather than deciding, by a calculative procedure, which of several possible alternatives should be selected. There is less doubt that what one is trying to accomplish is appropriate when the goal is simply obvious rather than the winner of a complex competition. In fact, at the moment of involved intuitive response there can be no doubt, since doubt comes only with detached evaluation of performance.

Remember that the involved, experienced performer sees goals and salient aspects, but not what to do to achieve these goals. This is inevitable since there are far fewer ways of seeing what is going on than there are ways of responding. The proficient performer simply has not yet had enough experience with the wide variety of possible responses to each of the situations he can now discriminate to respond automatically. Thus, the proficient performer, seeing the goal and the important features of the situation, must still decide what to do. To decide, he falls back on detached rule following.

The proficient driver, approaching a curve on a rainy day, may realize intuitively that he is going dangerously fast. He then decides whether to apply the brakes or merely to reduce pressure by some selected amount on the accelerator. Valuable time may be lost while a decision is consciously chosen, or time pressure may lead to a less than optimal choice. But this driver is certainly more likely to negotiate the curve safely than the competent driver who spends additional time *deciding* (based on speed, angle of bank, and felt gravitational forces), that the car's speed is excessive.

The proficient chess player, who is classed a master, can recognize a large repertoire of types of positions. Recognizing almost immediately and without conscious effort the sense of a position, she then deliberates to determine which move will best achieve her goal. She may, for example, know that she should attack, but she must calculate how best to do so.

Stage 5: Expertise

The proficient performer, immersed in the world of his skillful activity, sees what needs to be done, but *decides* how to do it. The expert not only knows what needs to be achieved, thanks to a vast repertoire of situational discriminations, he knows how to achieve his goal. Thus, the ability for more subtle and refined discrimination is what distinguishes the expert from the proficient performer. Among many situations, all seen as similar with respect to plan or perspective, the expert has learned to distinguish those situations requiring one action from those demanding another. That is, with enough experience in a variety of situations, all seen from the same perspective but requiring different tactical decisions, the brain of the expert performer gradually decomposes this class of situations into subclasses, each of which shares the same decision, action, or tactic. This allows the immediate intuitive situational response that is characteristic of expertise.

The expert chess player, classed as an international master or grandmaster, experiences a compelling sense of the issue and the best move. Excellent chess players can play at the rate of five to ten seconds a move and even faster without any serious degradation in performance. At this speed they must depend almost entirely on intuition and hardly at all on analysis and comparison of alternatives. It has been estimated that a master chess player can distinguish roughly fifty-thousand types of positions. For such expert performance, the number of classes of discriminable situations, built up on the basis of experience, must be comparably large.

A few years ago we performed an experiment in which we required a former world junior chess champion, Julio Kaplan, to add numbers presented to him at the rate of about one number per second as rapidly as he could while at the same time playing chess against a slightly weaker, but master level, player. Even with his analytical mind almost completely occupied by adding numbers, Kaplan more than held his own against the master in a series of games. Deprived of the time necessary to see problems or construct plans, Kaplan still produced fluid and coordinated, long-range strategic play.

Kaplan's performance seems somewhat less amazing when one recognizes that a chess position is as meaningful, interesting, and important to a professional chess player as a face in a receiving line is to a professional politician. Almost anyone can add numbers and simultaneously recognize and respond to faces, even though the face will never exactly match the same face seen previously, and one supposes politicians can recognize thousands of faces. Likewise, Kaplan can recognize thousands of chess positions similar to ones previously encountered.

Automobile driving probably involves the ability to discriminate a similar number of typical situations. The expert driver, generally without any awareness, not only knows by feel and familiarity when slowing down on an off-ramp is required; he or she knows how to perform the appropriate action without calculating and comparing alternatives. What must be done, simply is done.

It seems that a beginner calculates using rules and facts just like a heuristically programmed computer, but that with talent and a great deal of involved experience, the beginner develops into an expert who intuitively sees what to do without applying rules. The tradition has given an accurate description of the beginner and of the expert facing an unfamiliar situation, but normally experts do not *calculate*. They do not solve *problems*. They simply do what normally works and, of course, it normally works.

Given this account we must now make a qualification that may seem to run counter to Merleau-Ponty's body-rhetoric, but which is in accord with his most fundamental and original insights. A disembodied being could acquire chess mastery by playing mental chess on an imagined board. Its ability to discriminate and respond to the solicitations of more and more subtle patterns, and so its ability to play better and better chess, would thus not require that it have a body structured like ours. But to acquire a skill at all it must have some kind of perception or imagination and some way to act in response to what is presented to it so as to change the presented situation. Thus, the intentional arc must at least be embodied in the sense that the know-how we acquire is reflected back to us in the solicitations of situations correlative with our dispositions to respond to them. It is this attenuated, but still important, sense of embodiment that interests Merleau-Ponty. That is why he speaks of the body as an "I can," not a structure, and why reading *Phenomenology of Perception* one gets so little sense of the body's actual shape.[6]

II. MAXIMUM GRIP: INTENTIONALITY WITHOUT REPRESENTATION

Trying to find out what Merleau-Ponty means by the "I can" leads us to a second crucial feature of embodiment: *motivation*. Merleau-Ponty has an original account of what leads one to act on the basis of the skills one has, and to acquire new ones. The philosophical tradition since Plato has held that what motivates animals and people to acquire skills and act on them is the desire to achieve certain goals.[7] These goals are worth achieving because they are associated with certain satisfactions. But, as we have seen, once one has a skill one is solicited to act without needing to have in mind any goal at all. Thus, Merleau-Ponty is interested in exploring a more basic kind of motivation.

According to Merleau-Ponty, in everyday, absorbed, skillful coping, acting is experienced as a steady flow of skillful activity in response to one's sense of the situation. Part of that experience is a sense that when one's situation deviates from some optimal body-environment relationship, one's activity takes one closer to that optimum and thereby relieves the "tension" of the deviation. One does not need a goal or intention to act. One's body is simply solicited by the situation to get into equilibrium with it.

> Whether a system of motor or perceptual powers, our body is not an object for an "I think," it is a grouping of lived-through meanings which moves towards its equilibrium.[8]

When everyday coping is going well, one experiences something like what athletes call flow, or playing out of their heads. One's activity is completely geared into the demands of the situation. Aron Gurwitsch offers an excellent description of this absorbed activity:

> [W]hat is imposed on us to do is not determined by us as someone standing outside the situation simply looking on at it; what occurs and is imposed are rather prescribed by the situation and its own structure; and we do more and greater justice to it the more we let ourselves be guided by it, i.e., the less reserved we are in immersing ourselves in it and subordinating ourselves to it.[9]

To get the phenomenon in focus, consider a tennis swing. If one is a beginner or is off one's form one might find oneself making an effort to keep one's eye on the ball, keep the racket perpendicular to the court, hit the ball squarely, etc. But if one is expert at the game, things are going well, and one is absorbed in the game, what is experienced is more like one's arm going up and its being drawn to the appropriate position, the racket forming the optimal angle with the court—an angle we need not even be aware of—all this so as to complete the gestalt made up of the court, one's running opponent, and the oncoming ball. One feels that one's comportment was caused by the perceived conditions in such a way as to reduce a sense of deviation from some satisfactory gestalt.

Such skillful coping does not require a mental representation of its goal. It can be *purposive* without the agent entertaining a *purpose*. As Merleau-Ponty puts it:

A movement is learned when the body has understood it, that is, when it has incorporated it into its "world," and to move one's body is to aim at things through it; it is to allow oneself to respond to their call, which is made upon it independently of any representation.[10]

Merleau-Ponty would like basketball player Larry Bird's description of the experience of passing the ball in the midst of a game:

[A lot of the] things I do on the court are just reactions to situations. . . . A lot of times, I've passed the basketball and not realized I've passed it until a moment or so later.[11]

To help convince his reader that no representation of the final gestalt is needed in order for the skilled performer to aim at it, Merleau-Ponty uses the analogy of a soap bubble. The bubble starts as a deformed film. The bits of soap just respond to local forces according to laws which happen to work so as to dispose the entire system to end up as a sphere, but the spherical result does not play a causal role in producing the bubble. The same holds for the final gestalt of body and racket in our example. Indeed, I cannot aim at turning my racket the appropriate amount since I do not know what I do when I return the ball. I may once have been told to hold my racket perpendicular to the court, and I may have succeeded in doing so, but now experience has sculpted my swing to the situation in a far more subtle and appropriate way than I could have achieved as a beginner following this rule.

An even more striking case, where the goal the skilled perceiver is being led to achieve is not available to the actor as something to aim at, will make the point clear. Instructor pilots teach beginning pilots a rule determining the order in which they are to scan their instruments. The instructor pilots teach the rule for instrument scanning that they themselves were taught and, as far as they know, still use. At one point, however, Air Force psychologists studied the eye movements of the instructors during simulated flight and found, to everyone's surprise, that the instructor pilots were not following the rule they were teaching, in fact their eye movements varied from situation to situation and did not seem to follow any rule at all. They were presumably responding to changing situational solicitations that showed up for them in the instrument panel thanks to their past experience. The instructor pilots had no idea of the order in which they were scanning their instruments and so could not have entertained the goal of scanning the instruments in that order.

The phenomenon of purposive action without a purpose is not limited to bodily activity. It occurs in all areas of skillful coping, including intellectual coping. Many instances of apparently complex problem solving that seem to implement a long-range strategy, as, for example, a masterful move in chess as we have seen, may be best understood as direct responses to familiar perceptual gestalts. Here the question arises: How can the expert initiate and carry through long-range strategies without having assessed the situation, chosen a perspective, made a plan, and formed expectations about how the situation will work out? To answer this question the tradition has assumed that goal-directed action must be based on conscious or unconscious *planning* involving beliefs, desires, and goals. However, after years of seeing chess games unfold, a chess grandmaster can play master level chess simply by responding to the patterns on the chess board while his deliberate, analytic mind is absorbed in something else. Such play, based as it is on previous attention to thousands of actual and book games, incorporates a tradition which determines the appropriate response to a situation, and then to the next etc., and therefore makes possible long-range, strategic, purposive play, without the player needing to have in mind any plan or purpose at all. In general, if the expert responds to each situation as it comes along in a way which has proven appropriate in the past, his behavior will achieve the past objectives without his having to have these objectives as goals in his conscious or unconscious mind. Thus, although comportments must have logical conditions of satisfaction[12], i.e., they can succeed or fail, there need be no mentalistic intentional content, i.e., no representations of a goal.

If one can act without representing one's goal, what motivates skillful action? According to Merleau-Ponty, higher animals and human beings are always trying to get a *maximum grip* on their situation. Merleau-Ponty's inspiration for his notion of maximum grip comes from perception and manipulation. When we are looking at something, we tend, without thinking about it, to find the best distance for taking in both the thing as a whole and its different parts. When grasping something, we tend to grab it in such a way as to get the best grip on it.

> For each object, as for each picture in an art gallery, there is an optimum distance from which it requires to be seen, a direction viewed from which it vouchsafes most of itself: at a shorter or greater distance we have merely a perception blurred through excess or deficiency. We therefore tend towards the maximum of visibility, and seek a better focus as with a microscope.[13]
>
> My body is geared into the world when my perception presents me with a spectacle as varied and as clearly articulated as possible, and when my motor intentions, as they unfold, receive the responses they expect from the world.[14]

As an account of skillful action, maximum grip means that we always tend to reduce a sense of disequilibrium. What is experienced as disequilibrium and equilibrium depends, of course, on what skills have been acquired. In the tennis example, the situation on the court requires my arm to go up and move in a certain way. Thus, the "I can" that is central to Merleau-Ponty's account of embodiment is simply the body's ability to reduce tension or, to put it another way, to complete gestalts. This is why Merleau-Ponty holds that perception and skill acquisition require an active body.

In addition, the body not only moves to complete a good gestalt in any skill domain, it also tends to improve what counts as a good gestalt in that domain. As we have seen, the involved performer tends to discriminate more and more refined situations and pair them with more and more appropriate actions. Thus, the intentional arc is steadily enriched and refined. But this is not a goal-directed activity. One is no doubt consciously motivated to acquire a skill like tennis, but one does not try consciously to discriminate more and more subtle tennis situations and pair them with more and more subtle responses.[15] All one can say is that in order to improve one's skill one must be involved, and get a lot of practice. The body takes over and does the rest outside the range of consciousness. This capacity is for Merleau-Ponty a further manifestation of the body's tendency to acquire a maximum grip on the world. Only because there is a tendency towards maximum grip in this fundamental sense is there an intentional arc.

III. THE NEURAL BASIS OF THE INTENTIONAL ARC

A cognitivist—Merleau-Ponty's intellectualist—would say that in spite of appearances the mind/brain of the expert *must* be acquiring more and more sophisticated rules and then making millions of rapid and accurate inferences like a computer. After all, the brain is not "wonder tissue" and how else could it work?

Husserl has a similar view. He needs mental machinery to explain the way past experience modifies the perceptual world. For example, he explains the fact that when I see an object from one side I see it as having a similar other side, as follows:

> The similar reminds me of the similar, and by analogy with what was given with the similar on the one side, I expect something similar on the other side. It is associated with it and "reminds" me of it, . . . All thingly apperception and all apperception of unities of the nexus of several things and thingly processes would have their source in associative motivations.[16]

Here Husserl is making the typical empiricist assumption that events that once played a role in my experience, are somehow "remembered" and play an unconscious role in my current perceptions and responses. But this is an unwarranted construction. Indeed, it may well be incoherent since, as Merleau-Ponty points out, there are many dimensions in which experiences can be similar, so the empiricist cannot explain why one experience calls up a specific memory as similar to the current one.

> An impression can never by itself be associated with another impression. Nor has it the power to arouse others. It does so only provided that it is already *understood* in the light of the past experience in which it co-existed with those which we are concerned to arouse.[17]

No mentalistic model, whether idealist or empiricist, can answer this objection, but fortunately, there are other models of what might be going on in the hardware that make no use of empiricist association nor of the sort of symbols and rules presupposed in rationalist philosophy and artificial intelligence (AI) research. Such models are called simulated neural networks. According to these models, memories of specific situations are not stored. Rather, the connections between "neurons" are modified by successful behavior in such a way that the same or similar input will produce the same or similar output.

Neural networks provide a model of how the past can affect present perception and action without the brain needing to store specific memories at all. It is precisely the advantage of simulated neural networks that past experience, rather than being stored as a memory, modifies the connection strengths between the simulated neurons. New input can then produce output based on past experience without the net having to, or even being able to, retrieve any specific memories. The point is not that neural networks provide an explanation of association. Rather they allow us to give up seeking an associationist explanation of the way past experience affects present perception and action.

Some psychologists claim that neural-network modeling is no more promising than rule-based AI, since it is just a new version of associationism, which has already failed as a model of how the mind/brain produces intelligence. But they overlook the capacities of the most sophisticated neural networks. The hidden nodes of these networks are always already in a particular state of activation when input stimuli are received, and the output that the network produces depends on this initial activation. Thus, input *plus initial activation* determines output. If the input corresponds to the experience of the current situation, the prior activation of the hidden nodes which is determined by inputs leading up to the current situation might be said to correspond to the expectations and perspective that the expert brings to the situation, in terms of which the situation solicits a specific response. This would distance the neural-network model from passive associationism and make it a perfect candidate for the neural basis of the phenomenon Merleau-Ponty calls the intentional arc.

Networks also enable us to explain skill acquisition without appeal to AI's symbols and rules. While it is easy to see how traditional philosophy and conventional AI explain the feature detecting and inference making of the novice, and hard to see how a network could implement the required step-wise processing, when we turn to the expert, things are reversed. Once a network has encountered a particular situation from a particular perspective and has performed an appropriate action, the same or similar situation, seen in the same way, will tend to produce the same or similar appropriate behavior. So a connectionist account of learning by examples seems much more natural than any conventional AI account.

Consider the case where a network is used to map inputs representing chess positions into outputs that represent associated moves. Any new chess position which is not identical with any previous learned input will produce some new output. If that output is similar to the action output associated with some other given input position, one can say that the system has recognized the new input position as similar to that earlier position. Moreover, such a net can be said to respond to similarity without using a predefined similarity measure—without asking and answering the question: "Similar with respect to what?" "A similar situation" simply means whatever situation the net responds to in a similar way due to its past training. Sometimes the net's outputs will not be interpretable as representations of any move. Then the system can be said to recognize that the current input is not similar to any input to which it has been exposed. In the above way, a large enough net should be able to discriminate the approximately fifty-thousand different board positions that a grandmaster needs to distinguish, and to respond to a new position as similar to one of these, or else, as outside its intuitive expertise.

Still, there are many important ways in which neural nets differ from embodied brains. Some of them seem to be limitations that can be overcome by further research. Thus, nets now depend for their learning on people giving them examples by pairing input with output, but work is underway on reinforcement learning techniques in which the nets can learn by feedback from the target domain.

A more fundamental difficulty, however, is endemic to net-learning, whether the net learns by being given appropriate situation-action pairs or by finding for itself which pairings work. To learn to recognize the sorts of situations and things we recognize and to respond appropriately, a network must respond to the same similarities human beings do. But everything is similar to everything else and different from everything else in an indefinitely large number of ways. We just do not notice it. This leads to the problem of generalization. Neural-network modelers agree that an intelligent network must be able to generalize. For example, for a given classification task, given sufficient examples of inputs associated with one particular output, it should associate further inputs of the same type with that same output. But what counts as the same type? The network's designer usually has in mind a specific definition of type required for a reasonable generalization and counts it a success if the net generalizes to other instances of this type. But when the net produces an unexpected association, can one say it has failed to generalize? One could equally well say that the net has all along been acting on a different definition of type, based on different perceived similarities, and that that difference has just been revealed.

But a neural net must respond to the same types of situations as similar that human beings respond to, otherwise it will not be able to learn our skills and so will fail to find its way about in our world. There seems to be a puzzle here. How do human beings—let alone networks—ever learn to generalize like other human beings so they can acquire the skills required to get around in our shared human world? If everything is similar to everything else in an indefinitely large number of ways, what constrains the space of possible generalizations so that trial and error learning has a chance of succeeding? Here is where the body comes in.

We pointed out that in *Phenomenology of Perception* Merleau-Ponty put aside any talk of body-structure except as an argument against Sartrean freedom. To understand how we generalize, however, body-structure becomes crucial. There are three ways the body constrains the space of possible generalizations. The first is due to the brain; the other two are due to actual body-structure.

First, the possible responses to a given input must be constrained by brain architecture. This innate structure accounts for phenomena such as the perceptual constants that are given from the start by the perceptual system as if they had always already been learned. Merleau-Ponty calls these "déjà monté."

But this alone would not be enough to constrain the generalization-space so that all human beings learned to respond to the same inputs as similar. It turns out, however, that the order and frequency of the inputs further constrains how a net will generalize. This order is determined by the trainer in what is called supervised learning, but if the net is to learn by itself, that is, if its connection strengths are to be allowed to adjust themselves on the basis of the input-output pairs it encounters, then the order and frequency of inputs will depend on the interaction of the structure of the embodied network and the structure of the world. For example, things nearby that afford reaching will be experienced early and often. Their various ways of being reachable and the kind of grip and satisfaction they provide will be an obvious source of shared similarities. Thus, body-dependent order of presentation provides the second constraint on generalization.

The third constraint depends on what counts as success. In reinforcement learning, what counts as success in each specific domain is defined by the researcher. For an organism in the world, however, success would depend on some measurement of satisfaction. Merleau-Ponty claims that this satisfaction is not defined most generally by the pain/pleasure feedback of the behaviorists, but by the sense of equilibrium experienced when an organism is able to cope successfully with its environment. Thus, those input/output pairs will count as similar that move the organism towards maximum grip, which is itself a function of body-structure.

These three body functions may be all that is needed to explain why all human beings generalize in roughly the same way and so acquire the skills necessary for getting around in the shared human world whose affordances their self-moving bodies both constitute and reproduce.[18]

All this puts disembodied neural networks at a serious disadvantage when it comes to learning to cope in the human world. Nothing is more alien to our life-form than a network with no up/down, front/back orientation; no interior/exterior distinction; no preferred way of moving, such as moving forward more easily than backwards and grasping what is in front of it;[19] no tendency towards acquiring a maximum grip on its world; and no emotional response to failure and success. The odds are overwhelming against such a net being able to classify situations and affordances as we do, to distinguish what for us is relevant and irrelevant, to pick up on what is obvious to us. In our world the cards are stacked to enable entities that share our embodied form of life to learn to cope in a way we find intelligent, while leaving all disembodied creatures looking to us hopelessly stupid.

The moral is that the way brains acquire skills from input-output pairings can be simulated by neural networks, but such nets will not be able to acquire our skills until they have been put into robots with a body-structure like ours. So it seems that we must supplement Merleau-Ponty's account of the "I can" and the tendency towards maximum grip by an account of those aspects of our body-structure that lead us to respond to certain inputs as similar if we are finally to understand how human beings are able to project a shared world around themselves in what Merleau-Ponty calls an intentional arc. Until cognitive scientists recognize this essential role of the body, their work will remain a mixed bag of ad hoc successes and, to them, incomprehensible failures.

NOTES

1. Maurice Merleau-Ponty, *Phenomenology of Perception*, trans. C. Smith, Routledge & Kegan Paul, 1962, p. 440.
2. J.J. Gibson, *The Ecological Approach to Visual Perception*, Houghton Mifflin, 1979, pp 160–161.
3. Merleau-Ponty, op. cit., p. 146.
4. Merleau-Ponty, op. cit., p. 136.
5. For a detailed treatment of the phenomenology of skill acquisition, see H. Dreyfus and S. Dreyfus, *Mind Over Machine*, Free Press, 1982.
6. There is a temptation to say at this point that know-how is embodied because it is made possible by a modification of the brain. But this is to trivialize the notion of embodiment completely. Even computers used as physical symbol systems are embodied in this sense. They require computer chips to function, but they do not respond to situational solicitations.
7. For Heidegger what sets human beings apart from all animals is that they are ultimately motivated by a need to take a stand on their being. In Heidegger's famous example one exercises the skill of hammering in order to fasten pieces of wood together towards building a house, but ultimately for the sake of being a carpenter. That is, what ultimately motivates all learning and all action according to Heidegger is that only through action does one get an identity, and having an identity, a way to be, is what being human is all about. For Merleau-Ponty, on the contrary, as we shall see, human action, like animal action, is, at its most basic level, motivated by a need to get a grip on the world.
8. Merleau-Ponty, op. cit., p. 153.
9. Aron Gurwitsch, *Human Encounters in the Social World*, Duquesne University Press, 1979, p. 67. Since Merleau-Ponty attended Gurwitsch's lectures in Paris explaining Heidegger's account of comportment in terms of gestalt perception, there may well be a direct line of influence here.
10. Merleau-Ponty, op. cit., p. 139.
11. Quoted in L.D. Levine, *Bird: The Making of an American Sports Legend*, New York: McGraw Hill, 1988.
12. John Searle formulates both a logical and phenomenological requirement for something to be an intentional state. The logical requirement is that each intentional state represents its *conditions of satisfaction* [See J. Searle, *Intentionality* (1983) London, England: Cambridge University Press.]. My intentional state is satisfied if what I believe is true, or what I remember happened, or what I perceive is in front of me causing my visual experience, or what I expect occurs, etc. The *phenomenological* requirement is that these conditions of satisfaction be *represented in the mind*, i.e., that they are structures of a conscious subject separate from, and standing over-against, an object.

Merleau-Ponty would not dispute the logical requirement, but he would reject the phenomenological requirement. The question is whether *all* intentional content is *mental* content. If it were, one could describe the conditions of satisfaction of all mental intentional states apart from the question whether those conditions were satisfied, i.e., one could study the intentional correlates of all types of acts of consciousness in isolation from the world. Such intentional content would be the condition of the possibility of objective experience in general, so Husserl would be justified in his "imperturbable conviction" that, by a detailed description of the intentional structure of consciousness, he could develop a transcendental phenomenology. Merleau-Ponty's rejection of mental intentional content thus underlies his rejection of Husserl's transcendental reduction.

13. Merleau-Ponty, op. cit., p. 302.
14. Ibid., p. 250.
15. We would not know how to try to do such a thing. Indeed, in some cases, like that of the instructor pilots, there can be no awareness of one's eyes responding to more and more subtly discriminated situations.
16. Edmund Husserl, *Ideas II*, Kluwer, 1989, p. 237.
17. Merleau-Ponty, op. cit., p. 14.
18. For a phenomenological version of this argument, see Chapter 7 of H. Dreyfus, *What Computers Still Can't Do*, MIT Press, 1991.
19. For a worked out account of our human body-structure and how it is correlative with the structure of the human world, see Samuel Todes, *The Human Body as Material Subject of the World*, Garland Publishing, 1990.

SEVEN

AFFORDANCES:
AN ECOLOGICAL APPROACH TO FIRST PHILOSOPHY[1]

JOHN T. SANDERS

The idea of "embodiment," as stressed in the philosophical work of Maurice Merleau-Ponty[2] and as elaborated by more recent authors, is a complex one. As the title of this volume indicates, it involves, at the very least, consideration of the influence of both nature and culture.[3]

This fact about the idea of "embodiment," in turn, has two immediate consequences: In the first place, it indicates—especially on the side of supposed cultural influences—how embodiment is to be distinguished from mechanistic materialism. But in the second place, much is left rather vague. What *are* the influences of nature and culture? Indeed, how is each of these to be defined? "Nature" has to include both physiology and physical environment. "Culture" is construed, by most of those who write about embodiment, as considerably more than just an array of influences that come from the human part of the physical environment. Both history and ideology—perhaps combined to produce something like what Pierre Bourdieu has called "habitus"—are important in understanding the cultural aspect of (or contribution to) embodiment.[4] Finally, it is important to understand that, for those who have turned to "embodiment" as key to understanding the human condition, embodiment is entirely misunderstood if it is cast as no more than a passive resultant of several more or less causal forces. Central to the idea of "embodiment" is the notion of *agency*.

The importance of these several complications has led some to prefer expressions like "embodied agency" or even "engaged agency" to "embodiment" by itself.[5] Even Merleau-Ponty, in turning to expressions like "the flesh" and "chiasm," showed some discomfort with "embodiment" as the preferred term.[6] Without a great deal of explanation and qualification, embodiment comes perilously close to sounding materialistic, or at least behavioristic. For virtually all authors in the growing embodiment tradition, it is vital to avoid this implication. Materialism and behaviorism are held by these authors to make people out to be too mechanical, too passive.[7]

This concern over embodiment, and over how best to express the implications of embodiment, is no parochial question, of interest only to a few philosophers. It confronts perceptual psychologists, developmental psychologists, and psychotherapists. It may not be surprising that it has also become an important issue to some students of history and sociology, and to linguists, literary theorists, and aestheticians. But that is not all. As physicists—working within the very bastion of "objective" analysis—have tried to espress what seems to be going on in the domain of subatomic nature, they have begun to suggest that physical description itself is inevitably *situated*. And within the study of artificial intelligence, support is growing for the contention that intelligence cannot be understood entirely formalistically. Intelligence must at least be embodied—it must somehow display "engaged agency"—if it is to be recognizable as intelligence.[8]

It is within this context that the contribution offered by this essay must be understood. I shall contend that a particular conception—that of "affordances"—can, when suitably qualified, offer a conceptual tool of exceptional value in the construction of a positive theory of embodied agency, and of its philosophical consequences.

I am aware that positive theories are not much in fashion in late twentieth century philosophy, but it seems to me high time that this part of the philosopher's responsibility be more consistently met. Socratic challenge, analytic criticism, Wittgensteinian philotherapy, continental deconstruction, all are quite vital to the enterprise of making things as clear as possible, which I take to be the central aim of philosophy.[9] But that enterprise is only half the story. Even those who criticize must try to elucidate the nature of the platform from which they mount their critique.

The positive theory of embodied agency advanced in the present essay is designed to offer a language that can be used to talk about how things are without commitment to a rigid subject/object dichotomy. In the construction of this theory, as with all constructions, it will be necessary to do some work to prepare the ground. In the case of a theory that hopes to bridge the subject/object gap, it will be necessary to clear away rubble from both sides of the gap before the new theory can be deployed. It is partly in aid of this preliminary demolition that I have chosen for this essay a title that I hope will be provocative.

FIRST PHILOSOPHY

The idea of "first philosophy"[10] is closely associated with that of "foundationalism." And foundationalism, one might think, is surely dead. Perhaps this is as much a hope as anything else.[11]

Foundationalism is the view that there is some (relatively) small set of basic truths which has some special role to play in explaining things. What that role is supposed to be, however, may be the subject of lively debate. Perhaps the truths represent some basic facts about the universe as it really is, and these features of the universe are then jointly sufficient to determine many or all of the less basic features of the world. This kind of alleged primacy may be called metaphysical primacy, and such foundations are metaphysical foundations. Alternatively, the small set of basic truths may be truths about human knowing, and these may be held to be jointly sufficient for determining certain necessary features of all human knowledge, certain impossible features, and may even yield considerable insight into what sorts of things are (generally speaking) probable features of human knowledge. This kind of primacy may be called epistemological primacy, and such foundations are epistemological ones.

If foundationalism is dead, then that would mean that it is unnecessary—foolish, even—not only to seek foundations of either of these two kinds, but to seek any foundations at all for our understanding of our lives and our world.

There are some reasons to think that foundationalism *is* dead, or close enough as to make no difference. The quest for fundamental *metaphysical* truths about the universe as it really is, apart from how it appears to some observer, real or hypothetical, seems hopeless. Indeed, it has become less and less clear what such a "perspectiveless" perspective could possibly even mean. To this extent, those who say that human standards of meaningfulness are partly a product of (historical or developmental) cultural factors seem to be right. We are no longer sure what one is after if one searches for "metaphysical foundations."

The situation is not really so much better, though, for the notion of epistemological foundationalism. Immanuel Kant tried out a handful of basic "categories of the understanding" as allegedly necessary for human knowing, but among these were some that seemed pretty early on to be dispensable, at least at *some* level of understanding. Not only could mathematicians work comfortably with non-Euclidean geometries, for example (which straightforwardly failed to conform to Kantian categories), but physicists like Albert Einstein could propose (and find good reason to believe) the thoroughly anti-Kantian view that our universe is basically non-Euclidean. Such things are not easy to visualize, it is true, but it certainly does not seem impossible to articulate and accept such views at some level of understanding. Thus, whatever may be said about human powers of picturing or visualizing the world, there seem to be pretty decisive reasons for rejecting the idea that Kant's categories are fundamental to human *knowing*, and the process by which his particular proposal got overturned serves to discourage any renewed attempts at offering modern, up-to-date lists of fundamental human categories.

Perhaps, then, foundationalism should be abandoned—and with it, the ideal of "first philosophy." Perhaps we should not even hope to figure out any basic or fundamental truths about the world. Perhaps we should rest content with whatever more or less particular truths (or hypotheses) we can glean about the world, however it is we come by these (and if there are any to be gleaned). In some ways, this might be nice. The quest for truth is a bit less demanding if we no longer need to worry about which truths are *fundamental* in some sense. Truths in the plural would then be all we would care about, and our hope would be to bring these into some coherent arrangement. Perhaps this would be a manageable task.

It is possible, then, at least to *wish* that foundationalism were dead—or to wish that its demands would go away—so that a particular kind of vexing question might disappear. It seems especially appropriate to wish this given the apparent bankruptcy of attempts to figure out the fundamental truths.

The urge for foundations does not go away that easily, though, and I contend that it cannot. That, indeed, is one of the fundamental truths about knowing. It is not just coherence we need to seek among our beliefs . . . we need some weighting as to relative certainty. We need this in our private efforts at understanding our world, so that we may have some beliefs to rely on while we examine others;[12] and we need this as we interact with others in order to make successful interaction even possible: we need some common basis in belief for our interaction.[13] As will become clearer in what follows, such weighting not only serves to distinguish between beliefs that are (at least for the moment) to be relied upon and other beliefs that are to be treated with some circumspection, it also serves to indicate how questions of coherence among beliefs are to be resolved. Where conflict arises among beliefs, the ones that are less certain are the ones to be investigated, reassessed, modified, etc. For this reason we *must* arrange our beliefs as to relative certainty—even if only tacitly—and the more certain ones operate very much like foundational truths. While it is possible, therefore, to consign "foundationalism" to history if one defines that term in such a way as to make it a term of art referring to particular adventures in the history of philosophy, this is hardly illuminating. In a broader sense—the sense in which what is sought is some relatively small set of truths that shed special light on how things are—foundationalism will not, cannot, go away.[14]

A second point that must be made immediately is that, as possible as it is that the choice of which truths to treat as fundamental could be arbitrary and idiosyncratic (or "only" culturally determined, or otherwise conventional), this is not, at least, the whole story. There are good reasons for thinking that some truths really are more fundamental than others. These truths will be rather abstract, to be sure, and they may be about belief formation itself. But they will be no less fundamental for all that. Indeed, there is a curious possibility here that needs to be examined (if only to be rejected, in the end): it may be that the fundamental truth . . . the truth that will allow us to evaluate all further claims to human knowledge of the world . . . is that human belief is formulated in a completely arbitrary (or completely culture-bound) way. This is not an alternative to foundationalism. It is a candidate foundation.

In some sense, then, foundationalism cannot be dead. What may be dead are certain brands of foundationalism. If the argument of the last few paragraphs is correct, we must seek to secure all our beliefs as best we can, we must rank them at least implicitly in terms of their relative (and perhaps changing) certainty, and we must do this especially to serve our efforts at bringing coherence among our beliefs. We must all do this at some level or another. Those who have or wish to arrive at beliefs about knowing itself (and about the metaphysical conditions for knowing itself) must do it at *that* level.[15]

THE FUNDAMENTAL TRUTHS

Where shall we start, then? Shall we talk about the world that we find ourselves in? Shall we talk about big bangs and evolution and the like? Surely there is some justification for this, since human beings . . . perceivers . . . arrive on the scene pretty late, and (contemporary theories would further have us believe) what humans (and their powers of observation) *are* is a function of the demands placed upon them as growing and functioning organisms (and members of evolving species) in particular environmental niches. Shall we start, then, with physics, biology, or perhaps metaphysics?

The reference to contemporary theory should generate some discomfort. We know that there has been disagreement about these theories. Are they right? Can we rely on them at the outset in our search for fundamental truths? How can this be acceptable? Perhaps we should explore epistemology first . . . perhaps we should figure out what the criteria of acceptability are supposed to be before we blithely accept some theory about the world as our starting point. Our efforts to begin with metaphysics lead us to take up epistemology, and our efforts to dig into epistemology suggest that we need to have already taken care of the metaphysics. Where can we begin?

The question is not about *temporal* priority, of course, it is about *logical* priority. Which questions are most fundamental? The epistemological ones or the metaphysical ones? This is the most important issue of first philosophy. What is the most fundamental kind of question, in order to get our whole inquiry up and running?

Neither a purely metaphysical approach nor a purely epistemological one will suffice. At least that is the answer that will be suggested here. First philosophy must be "ecological" in at least two senses. The first sense would be question-begging, if it were not for the second sense.

In the first sense of the term, first philosophy must be ecological in that it must consider human beings, and the way they perceive and understand their world, as functioning in an environment. Understanding the world is a species of interacting with it . . . it is not something that can be adequately understood as a passive undertaking that goes on inside a person's head. Organisms are the products of an evolutionary process, and their lives are spent in an interaction with the world that both instantiates and models that process. The ways people have of coming to terms cognitively with their world (along with the very fact that they *must* come to terms with it cognitively) are themselves the products of selection processes of this kind. Some of the ways they deal with the world are characteristic of the species, some may be contributed by cultural or social factors, and some are idiosyncratic. But all are the products of interactions of organisms in environments. None arises out of a vacuum, or a quasi-divine whim. There are qualifications to be offered to this picture, but as it stands it will do for now. First philosophy must be ecological because its subject is dually dependent on factors inside and outside of the organism.

Surely, though, if this is all that could be said on the subject, we would be relying upon a biological theory that is itself part of what we are supposed to be providing foundations for.

Thus, more must be said. There is a slightly different sense in which first philosophy ought to be ecological. It is a metatheoretic sense, and does not presume the truth of any biological (or other putatively empirical) theory. Instead, it is only *inspired* by the particular way of looking at things that is characteristic of modern approaches to evolutionary biology. Ecological biology serves thus as a *model* for ecological first philosophy.

THE ECOLOGICAL APPROACH AS "METATHEORY"

To suggest that an ecological approach is the best way to proceed in a particular domain of inquiry is a strategic proposal, first and foremost. If a particular strategic proposal in first philosophy (for example) is followed, then it may very well have numerous consequences for metaphysics and epistemology, but the proposal itself must find its justification in its fruitfulness, measured along some fairly clear dimension. In what way might an ecological approach bear fruit?

An ecological approach acknowledges that some domains of inquiry are best tackled by understanding them not solely as collections of discrete and autonomous objects interacting in clean, singular exchanges of causes and effects, but as full-fledged systems, within which influences are continuous and reciprocal, and within which the lines that distinguish objects from one another—and even objects from the observer—are not solely a matter of objective fact, but are rather—at least partially—a function of the purposes of whoever describes the situation. Furthermore, it explicitly acknowledges that human learning (or even "knowing") is something that goes on in particular settings, with particular constraints, and with particular purposes.

The approach outlined above might very well be called a "holistic" approach (indeed, holistic approaches to this and that usually offer the same sort of critique of alternatives that is common among partisans of the ecological approach), but this expression does not sufficiently emphasize the dynamic interaction that characterizes the world and the encounters we humans make with that world. The word "ecological" is much better in this respect.

There are a number of strikingly similar critiques of the traditional subject/object dichotomy arising from various perspectives. Elizabeth Fee, for example, offers a critique of "dominant/dominated power relations articulated and reproduced within scientific knowledge."[16] Fee points to the similarity between "feminist" critiques of science and epistemology and other critiques offered from African, Native American, Chinese, and working-class perspectives.

While Fee herself generally follows the usage that refers to this critique as "feminist," she not only points out the similarity among this divergent array of criticisms of the "dominant" epistemological approach, she notes also that the sharp distinction between subject and object, at least as canonized in the traditional ideal of scientific "objectivity," has really been dominant for only the last few hundred years, and that it is to be identified, not with science as such, but with particular traditions in science. The question concerning what to *call* the approach that tries to avoid rigid subject/object distinctions is not too pressing, really, and Fee's opting for the label "feminist" is perfectly apt for the purposes she has in mind (especially since she herself calls attention to the problem of nomenclature).

Whatever conclusions one arrives at about the proper way to characterize the approach that I am calling "ecological," the large critical literature that exists on this subject (whether holistic, Marxist, feminist, phenomenological, anticolonialist, postmodern, pragmatist, or something else) will be of

127

great value, in the discussion that follows, insofar as the critique of the subject/object distinction is their common cause.[17]

The upshot of this section, then, is that the "ecological" approach to first philosophy is not one that relies upon findings in evolutionary biology. At a metatheoretic level, we may certainly learn valuable methodological lessons from that discipline, but we are not begging the questions most basic to first philosophy by adopting an ecological approach. An ecological approach to first philosophy no more presupposes the truth of contemporary evolutionary biology than a more transparently foundational approach presupposes the empirical adequacy of, say, Euclidean geometry.

As suggested by the title of this essay, though, the ecological approach to be taken here does rely upon "affordances." I take it that it is reasonably clear by now what I mean by an "ecological approach to first philosophy." It will be the objective of the next two sections to explain what is meant by an "affordance."

ONTOLOGY DEOBJECTIFIED

Ontologies—maps of the metaphysical terrain—are usually formulated in terms of arrays of independent objects of some kind, fully separate—at least in *some* dimensions—from one another and from those who create or use the maps. Thus, a fairly rigid subject/object distinction has been included in the traditional conception of ontology itself. It is no wonder, then, that rigid subject/object distinctions seem nearly impossible to avoid in substantive ontologies: the very project of mapping the metaphysical world has seemed to presuppose them.

Rigid subject/object distinctions are troublesome, however. In physics, they have become questionable both in attempts to characterize what occurs in the quantum domain—and as a result of quantum phenomena in the macroscopic domain—as well as in attempts to characterize the laws of physics in as general a way as possible. In psychology, they have caused problems in attempts to understand both perception and conception. In cognitive science, they seem to be responsible for apparently intractable dilemmas concerning the seemingly disparate realms of the mental and the physical. In more generally philosophical areas, rigid subject/object distinctions have spawned radical idealism, radical behaviorism, doctrines of immortal souls, mechanical animals, magical pineal glands, and a great deal more that has, to put the matter modestly, been difficult to swallow. As many have noted from a variety of philosophical and more practical traditions, it would be nice to be able to avoid rigid subject/object distinctions.[18]

A reasonable place to look for remedies to this situation may be in the area of basic ontology. For however widespread the tendency has been to understand ontology in terms of arrays of independent objects at arms length from (when not in principle completely inaccessible to) observing subjects—and these latter as somehow nonmaterial yet physically efficacious—there is nothing necessary about such an equation. Ontology, as I shall show in the next section, need not be conceived in this way.

AFFORDANCES AND ONTOLOGY

The term "affordance" evolved in the course of J. J. Gibson's attempt over thirty years and more to reconceive perceptual psychology. Affordances may be defined, for present purposes, as opportunities for action in the environment of an organism.[19]

Gibson traced the ancestry of the concept of affordances back to a term coined by Kurt Lewin in 1926, "Aufforderungscharakter."[20] This term was translated a few years later into English variously as "invitation-character" and as "valence," the latter gaining the widest acceptance. Kurt Koffka, who was a colleague of Gibson's at Smith College from 1928 to 1941, and whose influence on Gibson was profound, used the term "demand-character" in 1935 to encompass the same basic idea.[21]

Koffka used the notion of demand-character to capture his suggestion that mailboxes "invite" the mailing of letters, handles "want" to be grasped, chocolate "wants" to be eaten, etc. The idea is that things in our experience are not just neutral lumps to which we cognitively attach meaning. The things we experience "tell us what to do with them."[22]

All this would be fine, according to Gibson, if it were not for the fact that Aufforderungscharaktere were held by Lewin to be elements of a "phenomenal field," rather than in the physical world, and Koffka understood his demand-characters to be part of what he called the "behavioral" environment rather than the "geographical" environment.

Gibson insisted that affordances, as contrasted with these other notions, are in the world. They are opportunities for action in the environment of the organism. These opportunities are "picked up" by organisms as they negotiate the world. Affordances, he argued, do not change as the moment-to-moment needs or moods of the observer change. Affordances in the environment are offered by things like surfaces that can be stood upon, places that present opportunities for hiding, things that are reachable, and things that are climbable. While which things are reachable depends in large measure on characteristics of the organism (what is reachable for me is not necessarily reachable for my thirteen-year-old son

Dylan, although the differences between us in this regard are presently changing rapidly), and while these may change from time to time in the organism's life, they do not vary just as a function of psychological state.

> The positive affordance of an object can be perceived whether or not the observer needs to take advantage of it. It offers what it does because it is what it is. The uses of things are directly perceived, as Lewin and Koffka sometimes realized, but this is not because of a force between the object and the ego in the phenomenal field, as they believed; it is only because the substance and the layout of the object are visible and these determine its use.[23]

While the *concept* of affordances has not caused people much trouble, the way Gibson and his followers have deployed the concept has been quite controversial. Most of Gibson's critics would probably grant that the notion of affordances is an interesting and useful one. What has not gone over so well is the idea that it is *these*, rather than rocks and tables and chairs and the like—and rather than sense data—that are the primitive objects of perception.

Furthermore, Gibson claims that affordances are perceived *directly*. While his critics have been able to accept much of the rest of this "ecological" approach to the study of visual perception, they reject the claim that the perception of affordances is not mediated by a more primitive perception (or sensation) of objects (or sense data).

The upshot is this: the typical critic argues that Gibson is right that organisms perceive affordances in the environment, and that this is an important feature of perception. He is held to be wrong in his characterization of how this works. Organisms do not perceive affordances directly (i.e., unmediated by either neutral sense data or neutral object recognition). Instead, an organism first is barraged with data, some of which it can pick up with its perceptual organs. Some of this data is converted to images and patterns of various kinds: more or less coherent patches of color, noises, etc. These sensations, then, are themselves processed and sorted into objects, thus providing the organism with a minimal perceptual perspective on its world. Finally, the organism focuses attention on portions of that world as it recognizes the opportunities and dangers presented by the several objects it perceives. Far from being direct, the critic would argue, the recognition of an affordance is the result of a fairly high-level perceptual process, requiring recognition and evaluation mechanisms that work with data provided by sensory mechanisms.

While Gibson and his followers have written volumes in response to this kind of criticism, that response finally comes down to a few rather simple theses.

First, they argue that this "internal processing" model is circular. It requires that the internal processors be able to do the very things that are supposedly being explained. For example, the internal processing model suggests that an organism is able to recognize that certain things in its environment are important to it because it has an internal processor that recognizes this.[24]

Second, Gibsonians argue that there is no neurophysiological evidence (i.e., no non-question-begging evidence) that supports the notion that the human brain is functionally arranged into "processors" of the relevant kind.[25] Thus, the internal processing model can be evaluated only in the same *systematic* way as the direct perception model, and the internal processors must be regarded as nothing more than theoretical constructs like egos, ids, and superegos.[26]

Third, those who favor the idea of direct perception argue that such an approach highlights the active involvement of the organism with its environment even in perception, has much in common with lines of research that have proven illuminating in other areas of research (e.g., evolutionary biology, philosophy of science, quantum mechanics, more general work in perceptual psychology), and does not require the postulation of internal processors for which there is little or no neurophysiological evidence.

Whatever the merits of Gibson's approach to perceptual psychology, however, the style of his argument makes it extraordinarily interesting in connection with first philosophy. Thus, I now turn to an examination of the bearing that affordances have in this area.[27]

AFFORDANCES AS ONTOLOGICAL PRIMITIVES

I propose that affordances can be taken as fundamental ontological entities; that they may be taken, indeed, as being *ontologically* prior to objects and events. Attention to affordances as fundamental ontological "objects" seems to me to direct attention away (in a useful manner) from consideration of such things as quarks and electrons and fields of force as being ontologically fundamental. Thus, it is not just rocks and chairs and tables—and sense-data—that are at risk of being deposed, if this approach to ontology is correct.

Here is what I have in mind. There are, of course, rocks and trees. But like hiding places, they are picked up and individuated against their backgrounds because of their use value. Indeed, the same is true of quarks and electrons, black holes and super-novae. They are identified as individuals, and they become prime foci of attention within the environments they inhabit, because of their affordances in a particular domain of possible action.

Merleau-Ponty distinguished among different modes or styles of animal behaviors on the basis of the sophistication with which this was done:

> [I]t should be possible—and it is necessary—to classify behavior, no longer into elementary and complex behavior as has often been done, but according to whether the structure in behavior is submerged in the content or, on the contrary, emerges from it to become, at the limit, the proper theme of activity. From this point of view, one could distinguish "syncretic forms," "amovable forms" and "symbolic forms." These three categories do not correspond to three groups of animals: there is no species of animal whose behavior *never* goes beyond the syncretic level nor any whose behavior *never* descends below the symbolic forms. Nevertheless, animals can be distributed along this scale according to the type of behavior which is most typical of them.[28]

The idea in Merleau-Ponty, as it was for Gibson, is that animal behavior is best understood in terms of alertness to opportunities for action. While all animals move through their worlds in a kind of attunement with affordances, different animals show different degrees of complexity in their appreciation of multiplicities of affordances available in particular parts of the surrounding environment. He suggests that some animals are better able than others, in a given circumstance, to see that an item that has just been used for the achievement of one goal could also immediately be used for the achievement of another.

Merleau-Ponty uses the behavior of chimpanzees as an example.[29] They seem to be able to use a box either for leaning on (on some occasions) or for climbing on (on others). But just having leaned on it, it is not perceived as climbable-on, and vice versa. It is as if what is seen is thing-to-lean-on or thing-to-climb-on (but not both at the same time), rather than the "box" that *we* see, which is capable of both usages.

Now, to see that something is a box—indeed, simply to see a box—is, on the approach I am recommending, simply to see a particular constellation of affordances. Similarly with rocks and trees. One *could* work within an analytical framework that portrays rocks and trees as being primitive objects, and affordances as being derivative. That, of course, is the traditional—even commonsensical—approach: that we see rocks and trees and (derivatively) see *that* they afford certain actions. But this approach misunderstands not only the way perception works, I maintain, but the entire way we and other animals approach our worlds—and thus it misunderstands the way worlds (in the plural) of objects, events, and the like are carved out of the world (in the singular). All animals perceive affordances. Some animals are better able than others to see subtle multiplicities of affordances in specific parts of their environments.[30] This is not *causally* related to the different behavioral capacities of different organisms; rather, it is a logical consequence of, or another way of expressing, these different capacities.

Rocks and trees would not *be* objects for organisms so constructed as to be offered no opportunities for action by them. *That* they are objects—i.e., that they are picked out as significant individuals and kinds from the background—reflects their affordance character. This relationship between what there is and the behavioral capacities of organisms shows basic ontology to be in one sense relativized, yet in another sense objective. As it was for Einstein and Bohr in physics, so it is for us in metaphysics/epistemology: while ontology must be relativized to what different observers can do in terms of affordances, this is no mere matter of what the observer *thinks* or *believes*. It is a function of what the observer *can do*, and this may be as objective a matter as anyone could hope.

Understanding ontology in terms of affordances thus bridges gaps that would otherwise leave room for questions of relative priority between epistemology and metaphysics. One cannot talk about affordances without talking about *both* metaphysics and epistemology at the same time (or alternately, at least). Indeed, where affordances are the things being discussed, metaphysics and epistemology turn out to be disciplines that address the same basic array of issues from two different partially abstracted points of view: to use the contrast often discussed in connection with certain results of contemporary quantum mechanics, the points of view are those of the observer and of the observed.[31] Within ecological psychology, the contrast would be between the organism and its environment. For *any* way of characterizing the contrast, the important feature to be noted is that neither contrasted pole (or "point of view") can be characterized independently of the other. "Environments" just *are* organism-indexed parts of the world. "Organisms" are just parts of the world distinguished, for present purposes (whatever they may be), from what they are embedded in. "Observers" and the "things" or "processes" or "systems" that they observe are just portions of the world that are set apart or distinguished from one another for particular investigative or narrative (or other) purposes. Different purposes may very well require different parsings of the world.[32] What is real is an infinitely complex array of use-potential—or affordances—which can be spoken about in terms of "relationships" only once someone has crystallized *some* of the potential into objects (or other entities) that can stand in relations to other similarly constituted "things."

The deployment of affordances as metaphysical/epistemological primitives helps also in the expression of some well-known themes in epistemology and philosophy of science. It has been argued by some that "all observation is theory-laden." This theme has had an important role to play in efforts to understand the ways theory and observation interact in science, but it has considerably broader application than just this. While the theme has occasionally been taken to implausible extremes, most commenters have agreed that there is considerable truth to the claim that observation is often, anyway, affected by antecedent belief.[33] What a scientist sees in an experimental setting will be affected, to some extent, by what is expected (i.e., in particular, by what the scientist is *led* to expect by theory).

The broader application extends to all of us in our perception of our environments. The argument goes that we see what we expect to see. The unexpected is often suppressed, in perception.

Clearly, this is only part of the story. We cannot arrange to see what we want, simply by arranging our expectations appropriately. Our expectations are often disappointed, and our observations often yield, much to our chagrin, puzzles that we do not understand. As Abner Shimony has pointed out, while it is true that one *can* document the effects of perceptual readiness in experimental tests of human observation of controlled scenes, it is equally plain in such perceptual research that perception *resists* the influence of beliefs, on occasion.[34]

Nevertheless, there can be no doubt that there is an interesting relation between *conception* (especially the beliefs we have about how the world works, about what sorts of things are to be found in the world, etc.) and *perception*. The literature concerning the theory-ladenness of observation has led fairly conclusively to the abandonment of the once-popular view that observation can provide a neutral, objective test of theory (or, more broadly again, of antecedent belief in general). While there has been considerable argument about the extent of the theory-ladenness of observation, few who have involved themselves in this discussion would deny, by now, that observation is fallible as a test. What we perceive—or observe— is, to some extent at least, infected by our beliefs, by the category schemes that we are accustomed to deploying, by our expectations. While such factors may not be *decisive* in observation, they cannot be ignored.

The idea that observation or perception is at least *influenced* by beliefs and "category schemes" seems uncontroversial, once we see what is meant in this suggestion. The problem has been to understand the extent to which there is anything *un*influenced in this way. Kant's well-known solution already noted that there was little to nothing that could be *said* about the noumenon (whatever there was in the world that was independent of the experiencer) that was not infected by the categories that were brought to experience by the observer. But Kant thought that the pure forms of intuition and the categories of judgment were fixed in advance, by the necessary nature of knowledge and experience as such, for all potential observers. Thus, there was something "given" about certain *forms*, such that they could be counted on to inform all possible experience.

All this is familiar. But it is in connection with this set of issues that it is easiest to understand the felicitous role that affordances play in first philosophy. Contrary to Kant's vision, the perceptual readiness or theoretical set with which we frame particular experiences varies not only from time to time and from culture to culture, it varies from moment to moment in any individual's life as a function of interest, purpose, desire, and the like. It is relative to this changing background that the world gets cast in terms of opportunities and risks—in terms, that is, of affordances. In short, it is the logic of affordances that provides detail in the account of how theory is packed into observation, how conception affects perception, how behavioral orientation, intention, or purpose exerts its powerful influence over the way environments are parsed among things and events, the way figure emerges against ground, and the way attention is directed.

Affordances serve, finally, as analytical units of embodiment. It is not an embodiment that is merely physical—the language of affordances relativizes ontology not simply to the physical body, but to what an agent *can do*. The "environment" within which affordances may be deployed is not only the perceptual environment, but the entire universe of potential action.[35] What it is comprised of and how it is parsed will be a function of affordances. The embodied agent is "embodied" precisely insofar as the agent's capacities and functions are understood as deriving in vital part from activity, rather than from a priori gift or passive assimilation of external messages.

As analytical units of embodiment, affordances emphasize the fundamental character not only of subjective reality, but of any way that worlds could be at all. The sense in which worlds are made rather than found is the sense in which worlds are (and must be) *parsings* of the potential that is available to embodied agents as they engage and are engaged by the world. This is emphatically *not* just a matter of clarifying the necessary conditions for *characterizing* the world, since to *be* a world just is to be a parsing of that potential. And, of course, the last few sentences (these ways of understanding the world, which parse the world into bare potential and parsers) do not escape these constraints. They explicitly cast the world in terms of opportunities for action in the environment of engaged agents—in terms, once again, of affordances.

Affordances thus help to elucidate both the theoretical insight and the dynamic implications of the idea of embodiment and engaged agency. They further the project of pursuing philosophical understanding of ourselves in our world without invoking a rigid subject/object distinction, and they do it in a way that is on the one hand considerably less mystifying than "the flesh" and "chiasm," while on the other hand at least is consistent with fruitful recent work in both natural and social sciences.

Affordances, in short, deserve to be given a leading role in the fully ecological first philosophy that one hopes will finally emerge from the ashes of traditional dualism.

NOTES

1. This paper was read and discussed at the University of Helsinki in November 1995. A longer and substantially different version was presented at the University of Waterloo, Ontario, in February 1994. Earlier versions of parts of the essay were read and discussed at the Niels Bohr Centennial Symposium, Rochester Institute of Technology, May 1985, and at SUNY College at Buffalo, April 1988, and parts of the essay were discussed at the Fifth International Conference on Event Perception and Action, Miami University, Ohio, July 1989, and at the International Workshop on Formal Ontology in Conceptual Analysis and Knowledge Representation, Padova, Italy, March 1993. I am grateful to the participants at these several meetings for their comments and suggestions, to David B. Suits for an especially thoughtful reading of an early version, to Gail Weiss for more recent suggestions, and to Marx Wartofsky and Marjorie Grene for calling my attention, two decades ago and more, to J.J. Gibson in the first place. Finally, I owe thanks to Hubert Dreyfus and David Hoy, the organizers of the 1994 NEH Summer Institute on "Embodiment," which not only was the catalyst for this volume, but which also helped me to see how my thoughts on affordances might be brought to bear on problems I hadn't yet dreamt of. I would like to honor, in this paper, the memory of Honi Haber, Ed Reed, Sam Todes and Marx Wartofsky.

2. See especially Merleau-Ponty, *Phenomenology of Perception* (London: Routledge, 1992), pp. 67–199.

3. The "at least" serves as a cautionary marker for my discomfort with a general neglect of *particularity* in most recent discussions of embodiment, in favor of a perhaps too Platonist leaning toward the influence of the general. There will be some occasion in what follows to hint at my own conviction that "nature" and "culture"—taken, as they usually are, as general, even rule-governed influences—cannot entirely account for what any one of us is, thinks, says, or does. I do not have magic in mind as an alternative, of course. I mean to emphasize the idiosyncratic—the *particular*. In a suitably broad sense, I would acknowledge that *everything* is natural. But this broad sense is not the one typically indicated in the arguments of those who regard individuals as entirely shaped by nature and culture. Such arguments usually have general natural and cultural shaping forces in mind, sometimes quite specific ones. I am convinced that there is also a (natural) something there that is shaped, that offers *resistance* to such forces, as well. This topic is plainly too big to confront in this essay, which is (after all) devoted to another issue. For thought-provoking discussion of embodiment that takes seriously the particularity of the embodied agent, see Samuel Todes, *The Human Body*

as Material Subject of the World (New York: Garland Publishing, 1990).

4. See Bourdieu, *The Logic of Practice* (Stanford: Stanford University Press, 1990), especially pp. 52–65.

5. See, for example, Charles Taylor, "Lichtung or Lebensform: Parallels between Heidegger and Wittgenstein," in his *Philosophical Arguments* (Cambridge, MA: Harvard University Press, 1995), pp. 61–78, especially pp. 22–25 and 62–63. Taylor suggests that embodiment proper may best be considered a particular *aspect* of engaged agency, and compares this latter to what Heidegger called the "finitude" of the knowing agent.

6. Merleau-Ponty, *The Visible and the Invisible* (Evanston, IL: Northwestern University Press, 1968), especially pages 130–55.

7. Whether *Skinnerian* behaviorism, with its focus on *operant* conditioning, is really guilty of this charge is an extremely interesting question that really ought to be addressed carefully by someone who knows Skinner's work well. See B.F. Skinner, *Science and Human Behavior* (New York: The Free Press, 1953).

8. The prime mover in this area has been Hubert Dreyfus. See his *What Computers Still Can't Do* (Cambridge, MA: MIT Press, 1993). See also John Hauge-land, "The Plausibility of Cognitive Psychology," *The Behavioral and Brain Sciences*, Vol. 1, No. 2.; Charles Taylor, "Cognitive Psychology," in his *Human Agency and Language: Philosophical Papers I* (Cambridge: Cambridge University Press, 1985), pp. 187–212; John T. Sanders, "Experience, Memory and Intelligence," *The Monist*, October 1985; and Sanders, "An Ecological Approach to Cognitive Science," *The Electronic Journal of Analytic Philosophy*, Issue 4 (Spring, 1996). URL http://www.phil.indiana.edu/ejap.

9. And philosophy, as it seems to me *should* go without saying, is hardly the private property of those with advanced degrees in the academic discipline that has been given the *name* "Philosophy." Twentieth-century academic philosophy is marred by far too much attention to the questions: Which particular array of questions are really philosophical? What is the proper activity of the philosopher, which distinguishes philosophy from all other disciplines? As far as I can see, philosophy has always been just the activity of trying to gain clarity on questions that have (at some place and time) thus far eluded clear resolution (or, in many cases, even expression). The philosophical questions in any area of inquiry—or of life— are the ones that even the "experts" debate. When philosophical discussion of some issue yields a resolution that is widely agreed upon, whether in the form of a relatively clear answer or in the form of a way of looking at things that avoids the original puzzle, then the issue largely ceases to be a philosophical problem. This has at least two interesting consequences. First, problems that have not yet been resolved in any satisfactory way after centuries of discussion may look like they will *never* be resolved, and people who are interested in those problems might appear to be a bit dotty. This may not be the case, of course; but, then again, it may. Second, though, now that academic inquiry has been disciplinized, the *new* philosophical problems that arise may very well appear in disciplines other than academic philosophy. That is perfectly normal—it's the way things always have been. This doesn't make "philosophy" archaic, it just makes it senseless to try to contain philosophy within some arbitrary academic boundaries.

10. Or "prima philosophia," as in Jürgen Habermas, "Themes in Postmetaphysical Thinking," in his *Postmetaphysical Thinking: Philosophical Essays* (Cambridge, MA: MIT Press, 1992), pp. 28–51; or "philosophy of origins" ("Ursprungsphilosophie"), as in Theodor Adorno, *Against Epistemology: A Metacritique* (Oxford: Blackwell, 1982).

11. For the most unequivocal renunciation of foundationalism, see the works of Richard Rorty. Especially interesting in this connection are his *Philosophy and the Mirror of Nature* (Princeton: Princeton University Press, 1979) and the essays collected in his *Objectivity, Relativism, and Truth: Philosophical Papers Volume 1* (Cambridge: Cambridge University Press, 1991). See also the essays by Rorty in Józef Niznik and John T. Sanders (eds.), *Debating the State of Philosophy: Habermas, Rorty, and Kotakowski* (Westport, CT: Greenwood, 1996).

12. Beliefs, that is, that are relatively far from what W.V.O. Quine referred to as the "sensory periphery" ["Two Dogmas of Empiricism," in his *From a Logical Point of View* (New York: Harper Torchbooks, 1961), pp. 20–46], or (in science, anyway) relatively close to what Imre Lakatos called the "hard core" of a research program ["Falsification and the Methodology of Scientific Research Programmes," in Imre Lakatos and Alan Musgrave (eds.), *Criticism and the Growth of Knowledge* (Cambridge: Cambridge University Press, 1970), pp. 91–196].

13. For exhaustive discussion of the dynamics of communication, common understanding, and common action, see the works of Jürgen Habermas. Especially useful is his *The Theory of Communicative Action* (Boston: Beacon Press, 1984 & 1987), published in two volumes. A good place to begin might be the section in Volume One entitled "Intermediate Reflections: Social Action, Purposive Activity, and Communication," pp. 273–344. See also Habermas, "An Alternative Way out of the Philosophy of the Subject: Communicative versus Subject-Centered Reason," in his *The Philosophical Discourse of Modernity* (Cambridge, MA: MIT Press, 1987), pp. 294–326.

14. While clearly trying to distance himself from "foundationalism" construed in the narrow sense, Charles Taylor urges a kind of extension of traditional philosophy which is quite in congruence with the kind of foundationalism I espouse. See his "Overcoming Epistemology," in *Philosophical Arguments*, pp. 1–19, especially p. 14.

15. Jürgen Habermas argues (correctly, in my view) that a renunciation of transcendent philosophical ambitions need not lead to Rortyan "ethnocentrism." Habermas urges that Rorty's attempt at avoiding any appeal to something other than what he and his peers agree to (where these peers are actually defined in terms of Rorty's beliefs, rather than in terms of Rorty's *ethnos*) must fail, and is indeed a symptom of unselfconscious philosophizing. His contention that in all serious discourse there *must* be some allusion to standards at least alleged to be independent of that discourse is akin to my argument, here in the text, that foundations by any other name are still foundations. See Habermas, "Coping with Contingencies: The Return of Historicism," in Niznik and Sanders, *Debating the State of Philosophy*.

16. Elizabeth Fee, "Critiques of Modern Science: The Relationship of Feminism to Other Radical Epistemologies," in Ruth Bleier, ed., *Feminist Approaches to*

Science (Elmsford, NY: Pergamon, 1986), pp. 42–56, p. 53.

17. I am grateful to Deborah Johnson for calling my attention to Fee's extremely interesting essay.

18. This does not imply, of course, that there is anything that is everywhere and always *wrong* about a subject/object distinction made in a fairly rigid, a priori way. As is the case for any other theoretical distinction, whether a rigid subject/object distinction is apt will depend upon the theoretical circumstances. My argument, then, is that such a distinction is emphatically *in*apt given the circumstances faced at present in first philosophy, and that these circumstances are themselves in many respects the results of developments in science, in culture, and even in other areas of what continues to be called "philosophy" (presumably for want of a widely agreed-upon method of resolution).

19. These "opportunities" are not always beneficial to the organism, of course. Some of them, in fact, are likely to be quite threatening. Thus, "opportunity" is probably not the best word to use. I welcome suggestions of terms that are more apt. The best single source, though, for Gibson's own discussion of affordances is *The Ecological Approach to Visual Perception* (Boston: Houghton Mifflin, 1979). For discussion of the interestingly close parallel between the development of Gibson's ideas, on the one hand, and the development of the thought of Merleau-Ponty, on the other, see John T. Sanders, "Merleau-Ponty, Gibson, and the Materiality of Meaning," *Man and World*, July 1993.

20. Kurt Lewin, "Untersuchungen zur Handlungs- und Affektpsychologie II. Vorsatz, Wille und Bedürfnis," *Psychologische Forschung* 7, 330–85. For Gibson's discussion of this history, see his "Notes on Affordances," in Edward Reed and Rebecca Jones (eds.), *Reasons for Realism: Selected Essays of J.J. Gibson* (Hillsdale, NJ: Lawrence Erlbaum, 1982), 401–18, especially pp. 409–10.

21. Koffka, *Principles of Gestalt Psychology* (1935).

22. See Koffka, *Principles of Gestalt Psychology*, p. 353, and Gibson, "Notes on Affordances," p. 409.

23. Gibson, "Notes on Affordances," p. 409.

24. For a criticism of such an argument as used in explanations of memory, see John T. Sanders, "Experience, Memory and Intelligence." For what is surely the most heroic effort to make this kind of argument work, see Daniel Dennett, *Consciousness Explained* (Boston: Back Bay Books, 1991).

25. A good example involves the "storage model" of human memory. The storage model has been uncritically adopted by *most* researchers, to the point where the locution "memory storage" seems to be taken by many people to be simply *synonymous* with "memory." Thus, for example, when discussing research that seems very promising in terms of explaining neurophysiological mechanisms that underlie memory in humans, Daniel L. Alkon consistently speaks of these mechanisms as comprising "*storage*" facilities (see Alkon, "Memory Storage and Neural Systems," *Scientific American*, July 1989). This does not follow at all. When I flick the wall switch for my overhead light with a movement of my hand, I change the state of the electrical system in a clear-cut way; there is a perfectly plain mechanical explanation for what has happened and why the system (in particular, the lightbulb) now behaves differently. But it is an extremely

stretched metaphor that would have it that the movement of my hand is now "stored" in the electrical system. For all its prettiness as a metaphor, it is quite inapt for purposes of clear explanation of what is going on. It is the state of the system that has changed. This is most evident, in the case of the electrical system, in the fact that no mechanism need be postulated for the purpose of "retrieving" or "recovering" the information that is supposedly stored. That "information" is now implicit in the state of the system. The same story, I would argue, can be told of the "internal processor" or "indirect" model of memory and, more generally, of the corresponding model of perception. It seems to me that a large part of the problem involves the dogged commitment of many or most people in cognitive science to the idea that the things that happen to us must somehow be internally *represented* if they are going to do us any good as experiences. Andy Clark tries to handle some of these issues by distinguishing between "encoding" conceptions of representation, on the one hand, and "control" conceptions. See Clark, "Moving Minds: Situating Content in the Service of Real-Time Success," in J. Tomberlin (ed.), *Philosophical Perspectives 9: Connectionism, AI and Philosophical Psychology* (1995), pp. 89–104. While I agree that one *can* talk in this way, I think such insistence on "representation" talk is part of what keeps cognitive science in the Cartesian Theater. See Sanders, "An Ecological Approach to Cognitive Science." For an interesting alternative general theory of perceptually guided action and practical intelligence, see David John Hilditch, "At the Heart of the World: Merleau-Ponty and the Existential Phenomenology of Embodied and Embedded Coping," unpublished Ph.D. dissertation, Washington University of St. Louis, 1995.

26. This is not to say, of course, that there is anything wrong with theoretical constructs of this kind. Rather, the point is that competing sets of theoretical constructs must be evaluated as such, using criteria that attempt to clarify both systematic advantages and disadvantages of each.

27. The extension of the idea of affordances into areas beyond the ones discussed by Gibson himself is quite natural. For a very elegant explanation of the extension of affordances into the area of social perception, one which is as natural as it is powerful, see Harry Heft, "Affordances and the Body: An Intentional Analysis of Gibson's Ecological Approach to Visual Perception," *Journal for the Theory of Social Behavior*, vol. 19, no. 1 (March 1989), pp. 1–30. The move beyond Heft's proposal to the application of affordances as ontological primitives seems to me to be similarly natural and similarly powerful. It is certainly similarly motivated.

28. Merleau-Ponty, *The Structure of Behavior*, trans. Alden L. Fisher (Boston: Beacon Press, 1963), p. 168. For discussion, see John T. Sanders, "Merleau-Ponty on Meaning, Materiality, and Structure," *The Journal of the British Society for Phenomenology*, vol. 25, no. 1 (January 1994): 96–100.

29. While there is good reason to think that Merleau-Ponty and his contemporaries were somewhat mistaken about the capabilities of chimpanzees, the chimp example does a fine job of showing what Merleau-Ponty meant. And while he may have been wrong about the details concerning which things chimpanzees could and couldn't do, he was certainly right in thinking that the scale of comparison he

was working with—which in Gibson's terms is clearly a scale involving the degree to which affordance-complexity can be appreciated—was of vital importance.

30. As Merleau-Ponty was aware, it is probably wrong to think that there is a simple continuum of increasing sophistication among different animal species. The ability of one species to appreciate subtlety of use-potential in a particular part of their environments may be balanced by inabilities in other areas, compared to other species.

31. Although the terms "observer" and "observed" are the ones that have been standard in discussing some of the curiosities of quantum mechanics, these terms do not really capture the real sense of what is at issue. What's really at stake are boundaries that distinguish between what's inside and what's outside a system. In the now infamous "Schrödinger's Cat" saga, the suggestion is made that, on the Copenhagen interpretation of quantum mechanics, there is no fact of the matter about whether physical events have occurred or not (insofar as they are determined by events at the quantum level) until some observation is made of the system. This is inexact. Take your favorite system of cat-in-box-cum-death-ray (or whatever). Call this system "S." Whenever the events within S lead to effects outside of S, a new, larger "system" is invoked: the larger system includes S, but it also includes these effects that are external to S. Call this new, larger system "S'." The issue of whether the cat is alive or dead is *closed with respect to S'* whenever the events within S have effects within S'. When this latter system includes an experimental physicist (or Humane Society investigator), we may rightly speak of "observation."

32. For a "nominalist" perspective on the matter of parsing the world in terms of "projectible predicates," and for a discussion of the relation of all this to "inductive inference," one simply *must* see Nelson Goodman, *Fact, Fiction, and Forecast* (Indianapolis: Bobbs-Merrill, 1965), pp. 59–83. For some moderating considerations regarding Goodman's claims, see Patrick Grim's unpublished essay "Tangled Up in Grue." Since Patrick hasn't worked very hard at getting this essay published, it would be entirely appropriate for people to harass him for copies by mail. He can be contacted at the Department of Philosophy, SUNY at Stony Brook.

33. One very influential source for this view within mid-twentieth century philosophy of science has been N.R. Hanson, *Patterns of Discovery* (Cambridge: Cambridge University Press, 1958). Hanson's view has powerful traditional antecedents, going back at least to Kant.

34. For a very nice corrective to some Hansonian excesses, see Abner Shimony, "Is Observation Theory-Laden? A Problem in Naturalistic Epistemology," in Robert G. Colodny (ed.), *Logic, Laws, and Life; Some Philosophical Complications* (Pittsburgh: University of Pittsburgh Press, 1977); reprinted in David L. Boyer, Patrick Grim and John T. Sanders (eds.), *The Philosopher's Annual: Vol. I - 1978* (Totowa, NJ: Rowman & Littlefield, 1978), pp. 116–45.

35. See John T. Sanders, "An Ontology of Affordances," *Ecological Psychology*, vol. 9, no. 1 (1997): pp. 97–112.

EIGHT

Embodiment and Cultural Phenomenology

Thomas J. Csordas

BODY AND EMBODIMENT

If embodiment is an existential condition in which the body is the subjective source or intersubjective ground of experience, then studies under the rubric of embodiment are not "about" the body per se. Instead, they are about culture and experience insofar as these can be understood from the standpoint of bodily being-in-the-world. They require what I would call a *cultural phenomenology* concerned with synthesizing the immediacy of embodied experience with the multiplicity of cultural meaning in which we are always and inevitably immersed.

We can begin to elaborate this position with an anecdote from Maurice Leenhardt's classic 1947 ethnography of New Caledonia, *Do Kamo: Person and Myth in a Melanesian World*. Leenhardt was both anthropologist and Christian missionary, with an exceptional sensibility to the existential realities of New Caledonian life. He reports a conversation between himself and an elderly indigenous philosopher about the impact of European civilization on the cosmocentric world of the Canaques in which Leenhardt suggested that the Europeans had introduced the notion of "spirit" to indigenous thought. His interlocutor said on the contrary, we have "always acted in accord with the spirit. What you've brought us is the body." For Leenhardt this is a startling pronouncement—startling because it upends a stereotype that presumes the body lies on the side of nature and spirit on the side of culture, that the body lies on the side of the primitive and spirit on the side of the civilized. Leenhardt interprets the elderly philosopher's remark as follows:

> [The body] had no existence of its own, nor specific name to distinguish it. It was only a support. But henceforth the circumscription of the physical being is completed, making possible its objectification. The idea of a human body becomes explicit. This discovery leads forthwith to a discrimination between the body and the mythic world.

This passage vividly suggests that the very possibility of individuation, the creation of the individual that we understand (following Louis Dumont and others) as the core of the ideological structure of Western culture, has as its condition of possibility a particular mode of inhabiting the world as a bodily being. It suggests that prior to European dominance the body was for the Canaques neither a subject of experience nor an object of discourse. In Leenhardt's view this had profound implications for the nature of the person in Canaque culture, and by extension it challenges the generalizability of conventional Euro-American understandings of a person articulated in phrases like having a body, being a body, made up of body and mind, or being a mind in a body.

This unstable and culturally variable relation between person and body raises two general and quite consequential possibilities. First is that the body is a cultural and historical phenomenon as well as a biological and material one. This is an assertion that may already be familiar to many: from Foucault on the history of discursive formations and Carolyn Walker Bynum on the history of religion, to Emily Martin and Donna Haraway on the development of immunology, the body as we understand it in the human sciences has become increasingly unstable as an object of knowledge. On this level, the anecdote from Leenhardt simply helps us again to pose some increasingly important basic questions: Is the body a determinate object, or must it somehow be considered as subject as well? Is biology itself determinate, or does it somehow change along with our knowledge of it? If we object to the idea that the body is a tabula rasa upon which culture inscribes its meaning, should we base that objection on the argument that biology gives us disposition and temperament prior to culture, or on the argument that the body is never a tabula rasa because it is always already cultural as well as biological in the first place?

The second possibility inverts the terms of the first with the suggestion that culture and history are bodily phenomena as well as the product of ideas, symbols, and material conditions. If, as is suggested in Leenhardt's example, the person as a cultural category depends on the way people inhabit their bodies, perhaps other domains of culture are also grounded in bodiliness. To examine this possibility productively, I think, requires a methodological distinction that will allow us to capitalize on the body's instability as an object of knowledge. Let's reflect a moment on Leenhardt's interpretation of the elderly Canaque's remark, because the move we are going to make depends on distinguishing between the sense in which the New Caledonians "had no bodies" prior to European intrusion, and the sense in which "of course they had bodies"—don't we all? For the New Caledonians, the body was "just a support" and the European influence "made possible its objectification." The issue is the manner in which the body is an existential condition of life. Of course we have bodies, but there are multiple modes of embodiment and styles of bodily objectification that are critical for the understanding of culture.

It is this methodological distinction between body and embodiment that I think is important. What is salient in this distinction is precisely analogous to what for some might be a more familiar distinction between text and textuality. Recall Barthes's distinction between the work as a material object that occupies space in a bookstore or on a library shelf, and the text as an indeterminate methodological field that exists caught up within a discourse and that is experienced as activity and production (1986: 57–68). For Barthes's work and text I am substituting text and textuality, and to them I would like to juxtapose the parallel figures of the body and embodiment—the body, then, as a biological, material entity and embodiment as an indeterminate methodological field defined by perceptual experience and by mode of presence and engagement in the world.

EMBODIMENT AND TEXTUALITY

The parallel I have drawn between textuality and embodiment is by no means fortuitous or coincidental. In the 1970s the interpretive turn, the linguistic turn, the move to cultures defined as systems of symbols, were in full swing. One of the most powerful elements of this movement was understanding the nature of culture via the metaphor of the text as borrowed from Paul Ricoeur and disseminated into anthropology by the persuasive and eloquent voice of Clifford Geertz. This notion of culture as a system of symbols that could be read as a text gave way to a stronger view that what we recognize as culture is in fact an artifact of ethnographic practice, that is, the product of the genre conventions that define texts called ethnographies. Along with the broad appeal of structuralism and then poststructuralism these developments had the profound consequence of making the methods of literary criticism available and relevant to anthropology, and of stimulating a wave of interdisciplinary thinking in at least two ways. It became possible to conceive ethnology, the comparative study of cultures, and comparative literature as cognate disciplines; and it offered a channel of communication between historians, who worked through texts, and anthropologists, who worked through the metaphor of the text.

Over the past decade or so it has perhaps become less common to use terms like signs and symbols than terms like discourse and representation, but if anything the general trend toward semiotics broadly conceived has become even more prominent and productive in the human sciences. In fact, textuality has become, if you will, a hungry metaphor, swallowing all of culture to the point where it became possible and even convincing to hear the deconstructionist motto that there is nothing outside the text. It has come to the point where the text metaphor has virtually (indeed, in the sense of virtual reality) gobbled up the body itself—certainly we have all heard phrases like "the body as text," "the inscription of culture on the body," "reading the body." I would go so far as to assert that for many contemporary scholars the text metaphor has ceased to be a metaphor at all, and is taken quite literally.

Having made this assertion about the hungry metaphor, let me hasten to acknowledge that notions like textuality, discourse, and representation have made it possible to launch the reflexive critique of ethnography that has been so productive and influential in the past decade. However, at the height of this move to text and structure—at least in my home discipline of anthropology through the 1970s and 1980s—the notion of "experience" virtually dropped out of theorizing about culture, and indeed might be said to have been purged from theoretical discourse. The radical epistemological move was that representation does not denote experience, but constitutes it. This move closes the gap between language and experience, and thereby eliminates a dualism, but does so not by transcending the dualism but by *reducing* experience to language, or discourse, or representation. It allows for a very powerful critique of specific representations, but does so by insulating representation as a mode of knowledge from epistemological critique. That is, it makes difficult the posing of questions about the limits of representation, or whether there is anything beyond or outside representation, implying that to ask "representation of what" is fallaciously essentialist. The consequences are large. For example, in comparative religion, a field with which I have been concerned, it makes quite a difference whether one is dealing with religious symbols or religious experience, with mythic texts or mythic worlds.

There is an alternative that does not reduce experience to language—it comes from the phenomenological tradition, and is captured by Heidegger's dictum that language can *disclose* experience. When this tack is chosen, the key theoretical term that comes to take its place alongside representation is *being-in-the-world*. I emphasize the word "alongside" because my argument is not that representation should be replaced or overturned as a methodological figure, but that it will in the long run benefit from a dialogical partner that keeps it intellectually in check—that allows us to pose the alternatives that representation constitutes experience and reality as a text *or* that it discloses their embodied immediacy.

Within the phenomenological tradition there are quite a few variants, and among those variants there are a number of thinkers who have in some respect highlighted embodiment, including Maurice Merleau-Ponty, Martin Heidegger, Helmut Plessner, Gabriel Marcel, Herbert Pflugge, and Max Scheler. Among these, Merleau-Ponty (1962, 1964) has had the most influence on recent work. He defined phenomenology as a science of beginnings, and so insisted that the starting point for philosophical, historical, and cultural analysis of how we are in the world be perception. For Merleau-Ponty perception is basic bodily experience, where the body is not an object but a subject, and where embodiment is the condition for us to have any objects—that is, to objectify reality—in the first place. His work suggests that culture does not reside only in objects and representations, but also in the bodily processes of perception by which those representations come into being. These creative processes are closely bound up with intentionality, which throughout his work Merleau-Ponty describes with phrases like a tending toward the world, a taking up of the world, a sense of intentional threads that trace the connections between ourselves and our worlds, an image of perception as tracing an intentional arc through the world—all meant to convey a sense of existential meaning beyond representational meaning. My suggestion is that this tradition offers us being-in-the-world as a dialogical partner for representation. In brief, the equation is that semiotics gives us textuality in order to understand representation, phenomenology gives us embodiment in order to understand being-in-the-world.

If language can be understood either in terms of representation or of being-in-the-world—that is, as something that constitutes experience or that discloses experience—so our understanding of the body differs when it is construed as representation or as being-in-the-world. We are much more familiar with the former: the body as source of representations à la Mary Douglas, or as the product of representation à la Foucault. It is when we begin to think of the body as being-in-the-world that we find ourselves no longer interested in "the body" per se, but in embodiment as an existential condition. In other words, if we are not studying the body per se, neither are we studying embodiment, but studying culture and self in terms of embodiment, just as we can study culture and self in terms of textuality. Thus, to work in a "paradigm of embodiment" (Csordas 1990) is not to study anything new or different, but to address familiar topics—healing, emotion, gender, or power—from a different standpoint.

How embodiment appeals to being-in-the-world in distinction to representation is perhaps best illustrated anecdotally and experientially (see Csordas 1994c for a more theoretical account). Consider a discussion that took place during the defense of a Ph.D. prospectus in which a student was proposing a study of modern dance from the standpoint of embodiment. In an effort to grasp what the student was really getting at one examiner unfamiliar with the approach asked how embodiment might deal with a series of paintings by Joshua Reynolds he had recently seen. These paintings portray portly and highly successful eighteenth century gentlemen and their families. My colleague noted that a marked portliness and prominent paunch were characteristic of the people in these portraits, and also that he had a difficult time personally relating to the social personae they projected. For my part of the discussion, I called attention to how, as he was speaking, he had made a gesture and repositioned his body in a way that both imitated/incorporated his sense of the identity of these gentlemen and expressed a certain distaste for their overbearing arrogance. This bodily action had in fact more precisely captured their mode of being-in-the-world than his verbal description of the mode of their representation on canvas. Through that action he had gone beyond understanding the paunch as a semiotic convention to identify a manner of inhabiting space as a phenomenological essence—not a universal essence, but an essence of the particular, of cultural and historical specificity. The point is that although the painting can and should be read as a text about social status, it also allows us more immediately to grasp or recognize a set of socially salient bodily dispositions of posture, bearing, and physique.

This anecdote raises an important methodological question. How important was it for my colleague himself to experience a bodily concrete distaste in order to grasp the bodily groundedness of culture in those paintings by Reynolds? There are really two issues embedded in this question. The first is whether doing cultural phenomenology grounded in embodiment requires a special, different, or particularly bodily kind of data. If this means attending to "nonverbal" rather than "verbal" behavior the answer is no. Neither can it be said that there is an absolute methodological gulf between representation and being-in-the-world, such that nothing of being-in-the-world can be understood from representations like the paintings of Reynolds, or that we must devise a technique to measure mysterious essential existential emanations of being from the body. This is because embodiment is about neither behavior nor essence per se, but about experience and subjectivity, and understanding these is a function of interpreting action in different modes and expression in different idioms. This is a point I find it necessary to make repeatedly when students come to ask how to study embodiment. There is no special kind of data or a special method for eliciting such data, but a methodological attitude that demands attention to bodiliness even in purely verbal data such as written text or oral interview.

Nevertheless, there are certain domains in which the experiential immediacy required by a cultural phenomenology grounded in embodiment is, as it were, closer to the surface and more apparently accessible to study. Hence it is no surprise that a paradigm of embodiment is advancing unevenly along the front of cultural analysis. Indeed, it is perhaps best elaborated in the cultural study of health and illness, where bodiliness is most overtly problematized, moreover in a way that has broad and pervasive cultural relevance. The explicit influence of phenomenological writers is evident across a variety of writings in this field: Arthur Kleinman's (1995) efforts to develop a general theory of human suffering; Byron Good's (1994) narrative approach to the phenomenology of illness experience; studies in the United States by Gelya Frank describing the bodily synthesis and experience of wholeness of a congenital amputee with undeveloped limbs and by Jean Jackson (1994) analyzing the subject-object problem in the experience of chronic pain sufferers whose bodies are otherwise intact; studies in Italy by Deborah Gordon (1990) of urban cancer patients and by Mariella Pandolfi (1990, 1991) of psychotherapy patients in a mountain village; and studies in China by Thomas Ots (1990, 1991, 1994) of contemporary Chinese medicine and healing cults in practice and by Scott Davis (1996) in his attempt to reconcile structure and experience in the constitution of the classical medical system. What these works have most in common is a sensibility for the body as existential ground of culture, such that their arguments are rarely limited to disease per se but also teach us about broader issues of self, emotion, religion, meaning, transformation, social interaction, institutional control of experience, and the human interface with technology.

The second issue has to do with the mode in which the scholar engages the data—whether it is sufficient to attend to the body or whether one must in addition attend with the body, now understood as a tool for research. In the above anecdote, my colleague's gestures constituted a pre-reflective version of the latter: first puffing himself up in incorporative imitation of paunch and stuffiness, then shaking it off as if shedding an uncomfortable mode of being-in-the-world or of inhabiting the world. Is there a sense in which this kind of experience can or should be raised to the consciously reflective level of method? The historian Morris Berman poses the issue like this: "History gets written with the mind holding the pen. What would it look like, what would it read like, if it got written with the body holding the pen?" (1989: 110) Berman advocates a "visceral history" that not only takes into account that history is made and experienced with the body, but requires the experiential engagement of the historian in the matter of history. A twinge in the gut as an indicator of inner accuracy of interpretation, or the experience of anger as a grounding for writing a history of anger, are examples he cites of bringing bodiliness into method. In ethnography, this agenda has been approached in remarkably similar ways by Paul Stoller (1989) and Michael Jackson (1989), who quite independently of one another have proposed a marriage between Merleau-Ponty's existential analysis and Dewey's radical empiricism. Jackson's analyses of initiation ritual and bodily metaphors illustrates the theme "that ideas have to be tested against the *whole* of our experience— sense perceptions as well as moral values, scientific aims as well as communal goals" (1989: 14). Stoller's discussions of the social dialogue carried on through the taste of sauces prepared with food and of the constitution of lived space among Songhay merchants offer examples of how ethnography can "enter the sensual world of evocation" (1989: 153).

Explicit recognition of this methodological issue can contribute directly to the contemporary struggle to clarify ethnographic practice. The critique of ethnography associated with postmodernism in anthropology is an effort to locate cultural sensibility not in the representation of reality but in an evocation of reality, not in the representational relation between signifier and signified but in the dialogical relation between ethnographer and indigenes as interlocutors (Clifford and Marcus 1986, Marcus and Fischer 1986, Tyler 1987). This effort is made under the sign of the *reflexive*, both in the sense that the author figures into the text in a self-conscious way and in the sense that the text includes a dialogue with the voice of the indigene. This change of ethnographic practice remains thoroughly textual in orientation, and thus constitutes a restructuring of representation rather than offering an alternative to the primacy of representation. In contrast, we could say that the work invoking being-in-the-world that I cited in the preceding paragraph moves forward under the sign of the *reflective*. Here prereflective gut feeling and sensory engagement are raised to the level of methodological self-consciousness by insertion of a phenomenological sense of embodiment into the ethnographic enterprise. In this precise sense, the reflexive and reflective can be understood as complementary contributions from textuality and embodiment to the reformulation of ethnographic practice.

Another context in which these issues are relevant is vis-à-vis the cognitive approach to ethnography in which culture is described as a form of knowledge, specifically what one needs to know to live within a society (Goodenough 1957). This approach has grown increasingly sophisticated, describing knowledge in the more elaborate representational terms of schemas, cultural models, or parallel processing networks (Holland and Quinn 1987, D'Andrade and Strauss 1992). Despite its sophistication, this is inherently an understanding limited to what we might call culture from the neck up. Recent work has introduced the notion that the cognitive categories on which cultural knowledge is based are themselves grounded in the body (Johnson 1987, Lakoff 1987), and this has led to an understanding of culture as the body in the mind. This is surely an advance, but it allows the body to remain merely a source, the objective raw material of representations rather than the seat of subjectivity and ground for intersubjectivity. A case in point is the treatment of metaphors, which in the recent cognitive work are abstracted from their bodily origins and transported to the representational structures of mind. From the standpoint of embodiment, such metaphors in contrast, are phenomena of intelligent and intelligible bodies that animate lived experience (Jackson 1989, Kirmayer 1989, 1992, Fernandez 1990, Low 1994, Jenkins and Valiente 1994). In this respect, to embrace the paradigm of embodiment as a move from representation toward being-in-the-world would be to endorse a further step in the progression from "culture from the neck up" to "the body in the mind," moving finally to recognition of "the mind in the body."

TOWARD A CULTURAL PHENOMENOLOGY

In the foregoing discussion I have indicated the complementarity between textuality and embodiment, and between representation and being-in-the-world. I have suggested the value of elaborating a cultural phenomenology that can contribute to realizing the potential of these complementarities in the face of an already more fully developed problematic on the side of textuality and representation (see Hanks 1989). With this in mind, in this final section I will present a synopsis of several constructs that I think constitute a step toward fleshing out a methodological standpoint for the analysis of culture and self from the standpoint of embodiment.

First is the notion of somatic modes of attention (Csordas 1993, 1994a), defined as culturally elaborated ways of attending to and with one's body in surroundings that include the embodied presence of others. The most vivid examples of somatic modes of attention come from ritual healing. In the healing system of the religious movement known as the Catholic Charismatic Renewal, there is a phenomenon called the "word of knowledge," understood as a spiritual gift from God by means of which healers come to know facts about their patients through direct inspiration and without being told. These inspirations often occur in specific sensory modalities. The healer may see the afflicted organ or the name of the organ, may hear the name of the organ or a sound like a snapping sound that indicates healing taking place in an afflicted ear, may experience pain (either physical or emotional, as in the dual senses of "heart" pain) in the same area of the body that is afflicting the patient. The healer may also experience heat in a body part that indicates healing is occurring, queasiness or agitation that indicates the presence of an evil spirit, or an unexpected sneeze or a yawn that indicates that a spirit is passing out of a patient through the healer. These are not mere signs or representations generated in the minds of healers, though from a semiotic point of view many have the form of what could be called, following Charles Sanders Peirce, indexical icons. From the standpoint of embodiment, cultural phenomenology would highlight the engagement of sensory modalities in these phenomena, an engagement that defines a mode of intersubjective perception and attention to the distress of another.

A similar somatic mode of attention is elaborated among healers in the tradition of Puerto Rican Espiritismo, although the phenomena is symbolically elaborated in different terms (Harwood 1977, Koss 1992). Espiritistas do not regard the inspirations as direct experiences of divine power but as the work of spirits that enter or possess the healer, and they experience the manifestations according to their own cultural mode of embodiment associated with such notions as *ojo oculto*, *ojo malo*, *boca del estomago*, and *fluidos* that course through a humorally defined system. Despite these differences, the experiences are notably similar, and occur in categories distinguishing engagement of multiple senses: seeing the spirits (*videncias*), hearing the spirits (*audiciones*), sensing immediately what is on the client's mind (*inspiraciones*), and feeling the pain and distress of the client (*plasmaciones*).

Somatic modes of attention can also be identified in forms of healing that are not explicitly religious. For example, E. Valentine Daniel (1984) reports that practitioners of Siddha medicine in South Asia do not reach a final diagnosis until experiencing a state called *cama nilai* in which their own pulse becomes confluent and concordant with that of their patient. Some forms of countertransference in contemporary psychotherapy also count as somatic modes of attention, in which, as Andrew Samuels has reported, there is a "physical, actual, material, sensual expression in the analyst of something in the patient's psyche" (1985: 52). Beyond the domain of healing entirely, Anne Becker (1994) has recently described the situation in Fiji where, as in Leenhardt's New Caledonia, the body is not a function of the individual self but of the community. She describes an ongoing surveillance, monitoring, and commentary on body shape that includes changes due to hunger vs. being well fed, and changes that begin at the onset of pregnancy. For Fijians, not revealing a pregnancy is spiritually dangerous, and can both cause destructive events and be manifest in the bodily experience of others. Becker reports that this phenomenon was fully cultivated as a somatic mode of attention by one woman who typically experienced an itch in her breast whenever a member of her family became pregnant. In a less explicitly elaborated form in the United States, Cathy Winkler (1994) describes her identification of a rapist by a visceral sense of terror and recognition of his bodily form in the absence of an ability to identify his face.

A related construct I have been working with as a step toward developing embodiment as a methodological stance is that of embodied imagery (Csordas 1994), a term which appears quite redundant as soon as its meaning is grasped. When we invoke the term imagery in the psychological sense, I think it is typical to assume that it refers to "mental imagery," and then further to assume that we are talking about visual imagery in the form of pictures or representations. But thinking in terms of the mental-visual-representational biases the discussion from the outset toward something quite abstract. When we pause a moment to realize that imagery can occur in all the other sensory modalities and not just the visual, and we realize that imagery processes are concrete and sometimes profound and vivid engagements of the sensory modalities, we understand that all imagery can be interpreted as embodied imagery—hence the redundancy of the term.

From this standpoint, the Charismatic words of knowledge I discussed above can be understood as revelatory embodied imagery. It has been widely observed that Euro-American cultures are largely visual in orientation, with other dimensions of the sensorium less elaborated (Howes 1991). It is then not surprising that visual imagery predominates among North American Catholic Charismatic healers. What I found, however, was that healers also experience a substantial amount of imagery in other sensory modalities. Specifically, of eighty-seven healers I interviewed, 54% had experienced visual revelatory imagery, 35% some type of haptic, kinesthetic, or proprioceptive imagery; 28% auditory imagery; and 22% olfactory imagery, though none reported gustatory imagery (Csordas 1994a: 88). Healers also occasionally reported multisensory imagery, that is, complex images in more than one modality at a time. Consider the following interview excerpt:

> HL: One time I was praying over a man [for healing]. He had a brain tumor and the doctor had sent him home and said, "Forget it. It's all over." And I had a very strong picture of the tumor actually shrinking. And when he left the tumor hadn't, the tumor was still, see, but I felt, when I had my hand on his head, I felt as if it was like a ball on my hand and it got smaller and smaller. And I just, not only through sensory, but through a picture in my mind, I felt it was shrinking. Well, I think it was a week or two later, and [he came back and] said the doctors just don't know what happened. It went away. It was gone.
>
> TC: Wait a minute, you felt it with your hand, shrinking as well.
>
> HL: It wasn't shrinking in reality, the growth was still there [inside of his head]. But I sensed it in my hand. I felt it in my hand shrinking. But it wasn't in reality. And I had, and then I had a picture of it shrinking, as well, in my mind.
>
> TC: It was all the way in his head, or could you feel it from the outside?
>
> HL: Yeah, he had a lump on his head. I actually felt the lump. And I did

sense strongly that he was going to be healed, and I remember sharing with that [i.e., telling him about it]. And he came back and it was gone, totally gone. The doctors were baffled.

Here is a healer struggling to sort out the strands of sensory perception (feeling a lump) from imagery in the tactile and visual modalities (a complex image of the tumor shrinking).

This example highlights the intimate connection between touch and sight in a way that appeals directly to the notion of embodiment as the existential ground of culture and self. Certainly "the tactile senses combine with sight to register depth and distance when these are presented in the visual field" (Ong 1991: 25), but what are they registering when presented in the imaginal field? Michael Taussig, in elaborating Walter Benjamin's ideas on Dadaism, film, and architecture, also suggests that "tactility, constituting habit, exerts a decisive impact on optical reception" (1992: 144). For him, however, this "tactile optics" is closely bound up with mimesis, which "implies *both* copy and substantial connection, both visual replication and material transfer" (1992: 145). In the case of the Charismatic healer the mimetic image is not mere representation, but has a materiality grounded in bodily experience that is at once constitutive of divine power and evidence of efficacy. That materiality is all the more compelling in that it marshals for performance the existential intertwining of the tactile and the visual, described by Merleau-Ponty:

> There is a circle of the touched and the touching, the touched takes hold of the touching; there is a circle of the visible and the seeing, the seeing is not without visible existence; there is even an inscription of the touching in the visible, of the seeing in the tangible—and the converse; there is finally a propagation of these changes to all the bodies of the same type and of the same style which I see and touch—and this by virtue of the fundamental fission or segregation of the sentient and the sensible which, laterally, makes the organs of my body communicate and founds transitivity from one body to another (1968: 143).

Further analysis of embodied imagery can lead toward clarification not only of intersensory constitution (in this case with respect to revelatory experience) of the bodily synthesis through imagination, but also of the imaginal constitution of intersubjectivity and transitivity (in this case between healer and patient) through mimesis.

Despite the importance of such examples, however, embodiment is not exhausted by sensory experience conceived strictly in terms of the five major sensory modalities. Some of the imagery experienced by Charismatic healers I interviewed, for example, could not be classed under specific sensory modalities, though they appeared no less embodied. Again, of the eighty-seven healers, 32% reported images of a type I labelled "intuitive" that were constituted by experiencing a "sense" about a person or situation. Another 14% reported what I called "affective" images constituted by experiencing a specific emotion that mirrored or participated in the state of the patient. Finally, 7% reported "motor" images constituted by an impulse to speak or act, and 6% (a relatively small proportion compared to healers in some societies studied by anthropologists) reported dream images relevant to a patient's problem.

The nature of these images suggests that the deployment of senses and sensibility, and not only their content, is emphatically cultural. This point is well made by Robert Desjarlais (1992) in his study of trance and healing performed by Yolmo shamans in Nepal. Learning how to use his body in an everyday way was a prerequisite to experiencing culturally meaningful embodied imagery in ritual settings. Insofar as these images had revelatory content that allowed him to "tap into tacit realms of knowledge" concerning others (1992: 24), they also offer evidence of a somatic mode of attention. Similarly, Carol Laderman (1994) describes her own incorporation of Malay bodily postures and practices as a prerequisite for her own experience of *semangat* (Spirit of Life) and *angin* (Inner Winds) as components of her self.

These types of images are also related in nature to the category of cultural phenomena described by some authors as embodied metaphors. Setha Low, for example, discusses the "senses of body" associated with the condition of "nerves" (Spanish *nervios*) across cultures, suggesting that "the bodily experiences are metaphors of self/society relations, with the body acting as the mediating symbolic device" (1994: 157). Janis Jenkins and Martha Valiente have described the experience of intense heat (*el calor*) among Salvadoran women refugees as an embodied metaphor characterized by an indeterminate status midway between being a burning physical sensation and an emotional metaphor for anger and fear. They argue that "the indeterminacy of these tropes reveals them not so much as cultural meanings imposed on experience as fleeting, evanescent disclosures of inexhaustible bodily plenitude" (1994: 170). In his discussion of a gynecological healing ritual among the Yaka people of the Congo, Rene Devisch (1985) shows how the metaphor of the body as a weaving loom is grounded in bodily process, with the body as enactive source and agent, rather than as an inchoate medium upon which symbolic meaning is imposed or inscribed. Such examples recall the important point made by Laurence Kirmayer that bodily metaphors are often enactive rather than representational, and that embodied meaning is to be found primarily in "modes of action or ways of life" (1992: 380).

EMBODIMENT, BIOLOGY, HISTORY

Where can this program of inquiry lead, and what is the next step? In this essay I have concentrated on sketching out a methodological trajectory toward a cultural phenomenology, moving dialogically between textuality and embodiment and between representation and being-in-the-world. The examples I have given are intended to locate embodiment in relation to some of the interests of interdisciplinary studies in the grounds of culture and self. I am convinced that constructs like somatic modes of attention and embodied imagery are essential for developing a cultural phenomenology, and will go a long way toward addressing the often-expressed concern that phenomenology is often too dense and abstract to grasp comfortably. For the present there remain two questions that I want to address, or at least pose, in this concluding remark. The first has to do with the relation between embodiment and biology, the second with the relation between embodiment and more global processes of culture and history.

First, if the body is a thoroughly cultural phenomenon, and embodiment is of importance as the existential ground of culture, does this not throw the biology out with the bathwater? Is this not the result when Emily Martin describes the immune system as an "emerging entity" (1994: 47), or when Atwood Gaines argues that cross-cultural differences in biomedicine or scientific medical systems represent divergent "local biologies"? (1992: 190) If we for the sake of argument allow these phrases intentionally to be taken out of context, Martin's could certainly be read as referring *either* to an entity emerging into existence through the process of social construction, *or* to a preexisting empirical entity emerging from obscurity into the light of scientific knowledge. Gaines could be taken to mean either that there is no general translocal biology, or that biological science requires principles of ecology that seriously attend to local conditions. These observations suggest that a mature understanding of the relativizing tendency in much contemporary scholarship on the body and embodiment must precisely pose the question of which of the alternative interpretations is most accurate. This does not mean that scholarship must deny biology, but that it must bring biology into the problematic of cultural and historical change.

Consider the following case study from work I did on the experience of Navajo cancer patients (see Csordas 1994d for a full account). The case is that of a young Navajo man afflicted with a cancer of the brain. His story cannot be understood solely in terms of the organic lesion and its consequences, but must include how he brought to bear the symbolic resources of his culture and of biomedicine to create meaning for a life plunged into profound existential crisis. He constructed this meaning around the loss and gradual recovery of his ability to speak and understand. An experience of hearing words he attributed to the Navajo deities or Holy People, followed by a new and almost compulsive ability and need to utter long prayers, led him to conclude that his survival was a sign that he was to become a medicine man and help others through his words.

A cultural phenomenology of this case must draw together several intertwined dimensions of understanding. First is that there are real experiential consequences of the kind of biological lesion suffered by the patient. Specifically, neurology suggests that hyperreligiosity expressed linguistically is a common symptom of an "interictal behavior syndrome" characteristic of people with temporal lobe lesions such as this (Waxman and Geschwind 1975). Second are findings about the effects of peyote (Denber 1955), which this patient ingested as part of his healing process, along with cultural understanding of the long and impassioned prayers that characterize American Indian peyote ritual. Third is the performative nexus among knowledge, thought, and speech characteristic of Navajo culture and ritual, where speech bears both the substance and identity of the speaker and a concrete efficacy for creation or destruction (Witherspoon 1977). Fourth is the analysis of the embodied, speaking person taking up an existential position in the world elaborated in phenomenological writing, insofar as meaningful utterance is not only semiotic text but verbal gesture (Merleau-Ponty 1962). In such an exercise, biology does not disappear, but a cultural phenomenology of embodied experience helps us to question the difference between biology and culture, thereby transforming our understanding of both. In other words, both biology and culture (or more specifically in this case, neuropathology and religion) are forms of objectification or representation, and discussion of embodied being-in-the-world must be threaded between these two poles of objectification.

Here is the second general question: If phenomenology offers an understanding of embodiment at the microanalytic level of individual experience, can it also address global issues of cultural politics and historical process? The issue is really one of whether phenomenology can be cultural in this broad sense, and reciprocally whether cultural analysis can in fact be authentically phenomenological in method, consisting of something more than a subject grafted onto a Foucauldian analysis of power in discursive formations. Merleau-Ponty himself was convinced that embodiment could be the starting point for the existential analysis of culture and history, and explicitly described his masterwork, the *Phenomenology of Perception*, as a preliminary study in this direction. However, he did not get far enough in his own work to demonstrate this conviction, and his political writings remain somewhat distinct from his philosophical ones in this respect.

I think it is worth picking up his project and seeing where it leads (Csordas 1997; see also the various contributions to Csordas 1994b). Certain contemporary cultural developments may also be especially fruitful sites for a cultural phenomenology grounded in embodiment. In particular, I have in mind changes instigated by information and biomedical technologies that allow conceptualization of topics such as the self in cyberspace, virtual reality and the senses, or cyborg anthropology (Benedikt 1991; Haraway 1991; Brook and Boal 1995; Gray 1995; Stone 1995; Turkle 1995; Aronowitz, Martinsons, and Menser 1996). These issues are of a nature such that working through them can help in at least two ways to bridge the gap between an apparently ego-focused, psychological-minded, individual-centered phenomenology and a phenomenology of cultural and historical process. First, they challenge the very notion of bodily boundaries and discrete elements of identity, problematizing them rather than presuming them as essential to the constitution of subjectivity and intentionality. These boundaries dissolve at the interfaces between humans as biological organisms and machines that is the image of the cyborg, between perception and the technological simulation of perception that is virtual reality, and between the social person and the persona interacting in a community defined by shared computer linkups. Second, these processes appear indeed to be generalized cultural and historical ones. They are thus, at least in potential, transformative not of isolated individual subjectivities and intersubjectivities but of modes of subjectivity and intersubjectivity characteristic of broad segments of the global population. Finally, they are necessarily both driven by and responsive to the broader forces of political economy that increasingly bind local interests and global concerns.

I think that both of these themes—the relation between biology and culture and the study of broader cultural and historical processes—can be enriched by a cultural phenomenology grounded in embodiment. By the same token, such a cultural phenomenology can only be worked out fully by grappling with these issues. What matters is the methodological starting point and the way questions are framed. To reiterate, in closing, one of the central points of the present essay, although much contemporary cultural analysis of such issues takes place in the mode of representation, with the methods of semiotics broadly conceived, and in the paradigm of textuality, our understanding can be complemented and enriched by analysis in the mode of being-in-the-world, drawing on the methods of phenomenology, and guided by the paradigm of embodiment. Highlighting the interplay between these interpretive poles is not the only problematic available, but it is certainly worth seeing where it can take us.

REFERENCES

Aronowitz, Stanley, Barbara Martinsons, and Michael Menser, eds. 1996. *Technoscience and Cyberculture*. New York: Routledge.

Barthes, Roland. 1986. *The Rustle of Language*. Trans. R. Howard. New York: Hill and Wang.

Baudrillard, Jean. 1983. *Simulations*. Trans. Paul Foss, Paul Patton, and Philip Beitchman. New York: Semiotext.

Becker, Anne. 1994. "Nurturing and Negligence: Working on Others' Bodies in Fiji." In Thomas J. Csordas, ed. *Embodiment and Experience*. Cambridge: Cambridge University Press, 100–15.

Benedikt, Michael, ed. 1991. *Cyberspace: First Steps*. Cambridge, MA: MIT Press.

Berman, Morris. 1990. *Coming to Our Senses: Body and Spirit in the Hidden History of the West*. New York: Simon and Schuster.

Brook, James and Iain Boal, eds. 1995. *Resisting the Virtual Life: The Culture and Politics of Information*. San Francisco: City Lights Books.

Clifford, James and George E. Marcus, eds. 1986. *Writing Culture: The Poetics and Politics of Ethnography*. Berkeley: University of California Press.

Csordas, Thomas J. 1990. "Embodiment as a Paradigm for Anthropology". *Ethos* 18: 5–47.

———. 1993. "Somatic Modes of Attention." *Cultural Anthropology* 8: 135–56.

———. 1994a. *The Sacred Self: A Cultural Phenomenology of Charismatic Healing*. Berkeley: University of California Press.

———. 1994b. ed. *Embodiment and Experience: The Existential Ground of Culture and Self*. Cambridge and New York: Cambridge University Press.

———. 1994c. "Introduction: The Body as Representation and Being-in-the-World." In Thomas J. Csordas, ed. *Embodiment and Experience: The Existential Ground of Culture and Self*. Cambridge: Cambridge University Press, 1–24.

———. 1994d. "Words from the Holy People: A Case Study in Cultural Phenomenology." In Thomas J. Csordas, ed. *Embodiment and Experience: The Existential Ground of Culture and Self*. Cambridge: Cambridge University Press, 269–90.

———. 1997. *Language, Charisma, and Creativity: The Ritual Life of a Religious Movement*. Berkeley: University of California Press.

D'Andrade, Roy and Claudia Strauss, eds. 1992. *Human Motives and Cultural Models*. Cambridge: Cambridge University Press.

Daniel, E. Valentine. 1984. "The Pulse as an Icon in Siddha Medicine." *Contributions to Asian Studies* 18: 115–26.

Davis, Scott. 1996. "The Cosmobiological Balance of the Emotional and Spiritual Worlds: Phenomenological Structuralism in Traditional Chinese Medical Thought." *Culture, Medicine, and Psychiatry* 20: 83–123.

Denber, Herman C.B. 1955. "Studies on Mescaline III. Action in Epileptics: Clinical Observations and Effects on Brain Wave Patterns." *Psychiatric Quarterly* 29: 433–38.

Desjarlais, Robert. 1992. *Body and Emotion: The Aesthetics of Illness and Healing in the Nepal Himalayas*. Philadelphia: University of Pennsylvania Press.

Devisch, Rene. 1993. *Weaving the Threads of Life: The Khita Gyn-Eco-Logical Healing Cult Among the Yaka.* Chicago, IL: University of Chicago Press.

Fernandez, James. 1990. "The Body in Bwiti: Variations on a Theme by Richard Werbner." *Journal of Religion in Africa* 20: 92–111.

Frank, Gelya. 1986. "On Embodiment: A Case Study of Congenital Limb Deficiency in American Culture." *Culture, Medicine, and Psychiatry* 10: 189–219.

Gaines, Atwood. 1992. "Medical/Psychiatric Knowledge in France and the United States: Culture and Sickness in History and Biology." In A. Gaines, ed. *Ethnopsychiatry: The Cultural Construction of Professional and Folk Psychiatries.* Albany: SUNY Press, 171–201.

Good, Byron. 1994. *Medicine, Rationality, and Experience: An Anthropological Perspective.* Cambridge: Cambridge University Press.

Goodenough, Ward. 1957. "Cultural Anthropology and Linguistics." In P. Garvin, ed., *Report of the Seventh Annual Round Table Meeting in Linguistics and Language Study.* Monograph Series on Language and Linguistics, No. 9. Washington, D.C.: Georgetown University, pp. 141–66.

Gordon, Deborah. 1990. "Embodying Illness, Embodying Cancer." *Culture, Medicine, and Psychiatry* 14: 275–97.

Gray, Chris Hables, ed. 1995. *The Cyborg Handbook.* New York: Routledge.

Hanks, William. 1989. "Text and Textuality." *Annual Review of Anthropology* 18: 95–127.

Haraway, Donna. 1991. *Simians, Cyborgs, and Women: The Reinvention of Nature.* New York: Routledge.

Harwood, Alan. 1977. *Rx: Spiritist as Needed: A Study of a Puerto Rican Mental Health Resource.* New York: John Wiley.

Holland, Dorothy and Naomi Quinn, eds. 1987. *Cultural Models in Language and Thought.* Cambridge: Cambridge University Press.

Jackson, Jean. 1994. "Chronic Pain and the Tension between Body as Subject and Object." In Thomas J. Csordas, ed. *Embodiment and Experience: The Existential Ground of Culture and Self.* Cambridge: Cambridge University Press, 201–228.

Jackson, Michael. 1989. *Paths Toward a Clearing: Radical Empiricism and Ethnographic Inquiry.* Bloomington: Indiana University Press.

Jenkins, Janis H. and Martha Valiente. 1994. "Bodily Transactions of the Passions: *El Calor* among Salvadoran Women Refugees." In Thomas J. Csordas, ed. *Embodiment and Experience: The Existential Ground of Culture and Self.* Cambridge: Cambridge University Press, 163–82.

Johnson, Mark. 1987. *The Body in the Mind: The Bodily Basis of Meaning, Imagination, and Reason.* Chicago: University of Chicago Press.

Kirmayer, Laurence J. 1989. "Mind and Body as Metaphors." In M. Lock and D. Gordon, eds. *Biomedicine Examined.* Dordrecht: Kluwer Academic Publishers, 57–94.

———. 1992. "The Body's Insistence on Meaning: Metaphor as Presentation and Representation in Illness Experience." *Medical Anthropology Quarterly* 6: 323–46.

Kleinman, Arthur. 1995. *Writing at the Margin: Discourse between Anthropology and Medicine.* Berkeley: University of California Press.

Koss, Joan. 1992. *Women as Healers, Women as Patients: Mental Health Care and Traditional Healing in Puerto Rico*. Boulder, CO: Westview Press.

Laderman, Carol. 1994. "The Embodiment of Symbols and the Acculturation of the Anthropologist." In Thomas J. Csordas, ed. *Embodiment and Experience: The Existential Ground of Culture and Self*. Cambridge: Cambridge University Press, 183–97.

Lakoff, George. 1987. *Women, Fire, and Dangerous Things: What Categories Reveal about the Mind*. Chicago: University of Chicago Press.

Leenhardt, Maurice. 1947/1979. *Do Kamo: Person and Myth in a Melanesian World*. Trans. Basia Miller Gulati. Chicago: University of Chicago Press.

Lhamon, W.T., Jr. 1976. "Pentecost, Promiscuity, and Pynchon's V.: From the Scaffold to the Impulsive." In George Levine and David Leverenz, eds. *Mindful Pleasures: Essays on Thomas Pynchon*. Boston: Little, Brown, and Co., 69–86.

Low, Setha. 1994. "Embodied Metaphors: Nerves as Lived Experience." In Thomas J. Csordas, ed. *Embodiment and Experience: The Existential Ground of Culture and Self*. Cambridge: Cambridge University Press, 139–162.

Marcus, George and Michael M. J. Fischer. 1986. *Anthropology as Cultural Critique: An Experimental Moment in the Human Sciences*. Chicago: University of Chicago Press.

Martin, Emily. 1994. *Flexible Bodies: The Role of Immunity in American Culture from the Days of Polio to the Age of AIDS*. Boston: Beacon Press.

Merleau-Ponty, Maurice. 1962. *Phenomenology of Perception*. Trans. James Edie. Evanston, IL: Northwestern University Press.

———. 1964. *The Primacy of Perception*. James Edie, ed. Evanston, IL: Northwestern University Press.

———. 1968. "The Intertwining—The Chiasm." In Maurice Merleau-Ponty, *The Visible and the Invisible*. Ed. Claude Lefort, and trans. Alphonso Lingis. Evanston, IL: Northwestern University Press, 130–55.

Ong, Walter. 1991. "The Shifting Sensorium." In David Howes, ed., *The Varieties of Sensory Experience: A Sourcebook in the Anthropology of the Senses*. Toronto: University of Toronto Press, 25–30.

Ots, Thomas. 1990. "The Angry Liver, The Anxious Heart and the Melancholy Spleen: The Phenomenology of Perceptions in Chinese Culture." *Culture, Medicine, and Psychiatry* 14: 21–58.

———. 1991. "Phenomenology of the Body: The Subject-Object Problem in Psychosomatic Medicine and Role of Traditional Medical Systems." In Beatrix Pflederer and Gilles Bibeau, eds. *Anthropologies of Medicine: A Colloquium of West European and North American Perspectives. Special Issue of Curare*. Wiesbade: Wieweg, 43–58.

———. 1994. "The Silenced Body—The expressive *Leib*: On the Dialectic of Mind and Life in Chinese Cathartic Healing." In Thomas J. Csordas, ed. *Embodiment and Experience: The Existential Ground of Culture and Self*. Cambridge and New York: Cambridge University Press, 116–136.

Pandolfi, Mariela. 1990. "Boundaries Inside the Body: Women's Suffering in Southern Peasant Italy." *Culture, Medicine, and Psychiatry* 14: 255–74.

———. 1991. "Memory Within the Body: Women's Narrative and Identity in a

Southern Italian Village." In Beatrix Pflederer and Gilles Bibeau, eds. *Anthropologies of Medicine: A Colloquium of West European and North American Perspectives. Special Issue of Curare.* Wiesbade: Wieweg.

Samuels, Andrew. 1985. "Countertransference, the 'Mundus Imaginalis,' and a Research Project." *Journal of Analytical Psychology* 30: 47–71.

Stone, Allucquere Roseanne. 1995. *The War of Desire and Technology at the Close of the Mechanical Age.* Cambridge, MA: MIT Press.

Taussig, Michael. 1992. "Tactility and Distraction." In Michael Taussig, *The Nervous System.* New York: Routledge, 144–148.

Turkle, Sherry. 1995. *Life on the Screen: Identity in the Age of the Internet.* New York: Simon and Schuster.

Tyler, Stephen A. 1987. *The Unspeakable: Discourse, Dialogue, and Rhetoric in the Postmodern World.* Madison: University of Wisconsin Press.

Waxman, Stephen G. and Norman Geschwind. 1975. "The Interictal Behavior Syndrome of Temporal Lobe Epilepsy." *Archives of General Psychiatry* 32: 1580–86.

Winkler, Cathy (with Kate Wininger). 1994. "Rape Trauma: Contexts of Meaning." In Thomas J. Csordas, ed. *Embodiment and Experience: The Existential Ground of Culture and Self.* Cambridge and New York: Cambridge University Press, 248–68.

Witherspoon, Gary. 1977. *Language and Art in the Navajo Universe.* Ann Arbor: University of Michigan Press.

PART THREE

Rewriting the History of the Body

NINE

Returning the Gaze: The American Response to the French Critique of Ocularcentrism

Martin Jay

Let me ask you to accept on faith what I lack time to demonstrate now, but have tried to spell out in a recent book entitled *Downcast Eyes*[1]: that a wide variety of French thinkers and artists in this century have been conducting, often with little or no explicit acknowledgment of each other's work, a ruthless critique of the domination of vision in Western culture. Their challenge to what can be called the ocularcentrism of that tradition has taken many different forms, ranging from Bergson's analysis of the spatialization of time to Bataille's celebration of the blinding sun and the acephalic body, from Sartre's depiction of the sadomasochism of "the look" to Lacan's disparagement of the ego produced by the "mirror stage," from Foucault's strictures against panoptic surveillance to Debord's critique of the society of the spectacle, from Barthes's linkage of photography and death to Metz's excoriation of the scopic regime of the cinema, and from Irigaray's outrage at the privileging of the visual in patriarchy to Levinas's claim that ethics is thwarted by a visually grounded ontology. Even an early defender of the figural as opposed to the discursive like Lyotard could finally identify the postmodernism that he came to champion with the sublime foreclosure of the visual.

Although there are many nuances in the work of these and other figures of comparable importance who might be added to the list, the cumulative effect of their interrogation of the eye has been a radical challenge to the conventional wisdom that sight is the noblest of the senses. Instead, its hegemonic status in Western culture has been blamed for everything from an inadequate philosophy and idolatrous religion to a pernicious politics and impoverished aesthetics. Often some other sense, usually touch or hearing, or the essentially nonvisual realm of language, has been offered as an antidote to sight's domination. Although at times, attempts have been made to rescue a less problematic version of visual experience, most of the thinkers whose ideas I traced in *Downcast Eyes* would agree with Lacan when he wrote: "The eye may be prophylactic, but it cannot be beneficent—it is maleficent. In the Bible and even in the New Testament, there is no good eye, but there are evil eyes all over the place."[2]

In the recent American appropriation of French thought, the critique of ocularcentrism has, I want to argue, struck a particularly respondent chord. Paradoxically, what has been called the new "pictorial turn"[3] or "visual turn" in cultural studies has been fueled in large measure by the reception of ideas from the antiocularcentric discourse developed most notably in France. As a result, it has often been accompanied by a hostility or at least wariness towards its subject matter, which seems very different from that generally celebratory mood accompanying the previous "linguistic turn."

There have, to be sure, been influences from elsewhere, for example Heidegger's trenchant analysis of the "age of the world picture" and Gadamer's defense of the hermeneutic ear over the scientific eye. Domestic traditions have played their part as well, as shown by the importance of John Dewey's pragmatist critique of the "spectator theory of knowledge," recently revived by Richard Rorty in his widely read *Philosophy and the Mirror of Nature*.[4] American psychologists of visual experience like J.J. Gibson also produced important work that had a potential impact beyond their narrow discipline.[5] And the media theories of Marshall McLuhan and Walter J. Ong, which caused an intense, if short-lived, flurry of excitement in the late 1950s and early 1960s, must also be acknowledged as preparing the ground.[6]

But it was not really until the wave of translations and interpretations of post-1968 French theory washed over the American intellectual scene that a sustained, nuanced, and still by no means exhausted discussion of the dangers of privileging the eye—or at least certain dominant regimes of visuality—gained center stage. Even when the original political momentum of the reception was largely spent, many of its elements remained potent in the debates over postmodernism—and its counterenlightenment dangers—that began in earnest in the early 1980s. Journals like *October*, *Camera Obscura*, *Visual Anthropology Review* and *Screen*—the last although British, having a wide following in America—helped plant the French-inspired suspicion of the visual at the very center of contemporary cultural debate. As a result, to borrow the title of a recent collection, modernity and the hegemony of vision have come to seem inextricably, and for some, ominously, intertwined.[7]

In fact, the variety and range of the American reception of the French critique of that hegemony has been so great that easy generalizations about its contours and tensions are hard to provide. Rather than attempt, therefore, what might be called an Icarian or synoptic overview of the entire field, let me focus on a few salient landmarks within the discourse surrounding the visual arts in the hope of illuminating some of the effects of the recontextualization of the anti-ocularcentric polemic on our side of the Atlantic. In particular, I want to examine developments in recent art history and criticism, which are themselves now in danger of being absorbed into a larger and more amorphous realm of inquiry called visual studies in part because of the importation of ideas about ocularcentrism from France.

As has been widely remarked, the center of gravity of modernism in the visual arts shifted from Paris to New York in the years after 1945, when abstract expressionism emerged as the dominant school at the cutting-edge of artistic innovation. Whether or not, as Serge Guilbaut has provocatively contended, this shift was tantamout to a theft based on the calculated Cold War strategy of purging art of any political implications, it certainly meant purifying the visual of any apparently extraneous interference, such as a narrative, didactic, or anecdotal function, and imbuing it instead with a claim to universal value in itself.[8] Although anxieties about the commodification or functionalization of the visual object can be detected as early as the nineteenth century, when the invention of replicable photographs seemed to threaten aesthetic autonomy,[9] it was only in postwar modernism that the strategy of resisting such incursions by essentializing the opticality of the medium came into its own.

Here the influential criticism of Clement Greenberg, himself a recently disillusioned Trotskyist rapidly shedding his political past, was pivotal in elevating what he called the "purity" of the optical to the defining characteristic of modern art.[10] For Greenberg, genuine avant-garde art should have no truck with the commodified kitsch of mass art, nor should it register the resistant materiality of its supporting media. Pure visuality meant the presence of atemporal, essential form, the old Platonic dream now paradoxically realized—or at least ever more closely manifested—in the world of visual appearance on the flat surface of a canvas. Greenberg's was thus a modernism reminiscent of the strictly self-referential formalism of earlier critics like Roger Fry and Clive Bell, but now for the first time successfully elevated to a position of cultural hegemony.[11] His standards could be applied not only to define genuine art, but also to decide qualitatively between its good and bad exemplars.[12]

Along with this argument for visual purity went a banishment of movements like Surrealism, which Greenberg called a "reactionary tendency" because it attempted to "restore 'outside' subject matter,"[13] such as the unconscious. Others like Dada were also not worth taking seriously because of their radical antiformalism and hostility to the differentiated institution of art in general and painting in particular. Only pure opticality detached from any external inference—whether political, economic, psychological, or even the materiality of media and the artist's own body—

met the highest standard of aesthetic achievement for Greenberg and those he influenced. The defense of photography as high art made by important critics like the Museum of Modern Art's John Szarkowski in the 1960s, to take one prominent example, followed virtually the same line of argument.[14] So too did the critique of debased theatricality in art, its degeneration into spectacles for an audience instead of absolute self-contained presentness, vigorously made by Michael Fried in his celebrated essay "Art and Objecthood" of 1967.[15] Although later Fried vigorously tried to put some distance between his argument and that of Greenberg, which he claimed had been too ahistorically essentialist and based on a privileging of pure opticality he had not himself embraced,[16] he was widely considered his ally at the time.

The Greenbergian consensus began, however, to unravel in the late 1960s and early 1970s with the introduction of new art movements difficult to accommodate in his terms, notably Pop Art, Minimalism, and Conceptualism; a growing politicization of the art world, which found his Cold War liberal universalism jejune; and most important for our purposes, a new openness to theory from abroad, especially from France.[17] Although it would be an exaggeration to attribute developments in American art primarily to the influence of that theory, it would also be wrong to see the theory as nothing but a post facto justification for changes that were happening on the purely practical level. For, as Daniel Herwitz has recently emphasized, virtually from the beginning avant-garde art was developed in intense dialogue with the theories that explained and legitimated it.[18] The result was often, to borrow the title of Joseph Kosuth's 1969 conceptualist manifesto, the production of "art after philosophy."[19]

Put schematically, the new movements of the late 1960s and early 1970s shifted the ground away from the postwar consensus in the following ways. Mocking his belief in standards of artistic quality, Pop Art undermined Greenberg's rigid distinction between high and low, provocatively blurring the difference between commodity and disinterested aesthetic experience. Minimalism—like the performance art and happenings that also came into their own during this period—restored the temporal and corporeal dimensions of aesthetic experience, in defiance of Greenberg's stress on atemporal visual presence and Fried's excoriation of theatricality.[20] Conceptualism increasingly substituted dematerialized ideas or at least language about art for visual presence, impure discursivity for pure opticality. All of these movements, moreover, in one way or another reflected the art world's growing politicization, which encouraged a skeptical reflexivity about the institutions of art—museums, galleries, the art market, etc.—and their relation to larger social forces in place of an internal reflexivity about aesthetic form or the characteristics of the medium itself.

The theories—in most cases French—that were marshalled to explicate and legitimate all of these changes can be usefully divided into three categories, which helps us see the overdetermined nature of the onslaught against the idea of high modernist pure opticality: (1) those that stress the importance of language as opposed to perception, (2) those that emphasize the forgotten role of the (often sexualized) body, and (3) those that stress the political implications of certain visual practices. In reality, of course, many of the arguments in each of these categories were combined by different thinkers in a variety of ways, whose intricacies cannot be adequately reproduced in a survey as brief as this one.

With the American reception of what became known as Structuralism in the late 1960s, identified primarily with Saussure, Lévi-Strauss, and the early Barthes, came a powerful imperative to conceptualize all cultural production in terms of language and textuality. That is, everything could be treated as a sign system based on arbitrary, diacritical signifiers, whose ability to convey significance could be uncoupled from their referential, mimetic function. In visual terms, it thus now seemed possible to "read" rather than simply look at pictures, movies, architecture, photographs, and sculpture. As the British artist and critic Victor Burgin put it in 1976, "the ideological resistance, in the name of the 'purity' of the Image, to the consideration of linguistic matter within and across the photograph is no more or less well founded than that which met the coming of sound in the cinema."[21]

A salient example of the new openness to language from a critic whose other work we will encounter again shortly can be found in Rosalind Krauss's 1978 essay "Sculpture in the Expanded Field."[22] Krauss provocatively identified certain modern, and even more, postmodernist works as negativities rather than positivities, defined by their relationship to what they were not, that is, landscape or architecture. By then reversing these negative terms and relating them in a quaternary field of multiple contradictions, Krauss was able to situate contemporary sculpture in a discursive rather than purely visual context. "The logic of the space of postmodernist practice," she concluded, "is no longer organized around the definition of a given medium on the grounds of its material, or, for that matter, the perception of the material. It is organized instead through the universe of terms that are felt to be in opposition within a cultural situation."[23]

When more so-called poststructuralist versions of language, especially those identified with deconstruction, became available to American critics, the neatness of such diagrams became less compelling,[24] but the textual interference with pure opticality was, if anything, strengthened. Thus, for example, W.J.T. Mitchell in his widely admired *Iconology: Image, Text, Ideology* of 1986 would write that

Derrida's answer to the question, "What is an image?" would undoubtedly be "Nothing but another kind of writing, a kind of graphic sign that dissembles itself as a direct transcript of that which it represents, or of the way things look, or of what they essentially are." This sort of suspicion of the image seems only appropriate in a time when the very view from one's window, much less the scenes played out in everyday life and in the various media of representation, seem to require constant interpretative vigilance.[25]

Although at times, the textual threatened to replace the optical entirely in the reception of structuralist and even post-structuralist modes of thought, more often the result was their mutual problematization. Here a new appreciation for the experiments in verbal and visual punning conducted by the Surrealists emerged, as evidenced by the enthusiastic reception of Foucault's essay on Magritte, *This Is Not a Pipe*, when it was translated in 1983.[26] Combined with the powerful impact of his strictures against panopticism and the medical gaze, Foucault's homage to Magritte's "non-affirmative painting" provided new ammunition in the campaign to disrupt pure opticality through the introduction of discursivity. Comparable lessons were drawn from Lyotard's *Discours, Figure*, still not fully translated, but an evident influence on such widely read works as *Vision and Painting: The Logic of the Gaze* of 1983 by the art historian Norman Bryson, which drew on Derrida, Barthes and Lacan as well.[27]

Bryson's influential book, which was one of several by him in the 1980s showing an evident debt to French thinkers like Lyotard and Lacan,[28] also lamented the suppression of corporeality in the dominant tradition of viewing in the West from the Renaissance through modernism. In what Bryson called the "Founding Perception" of that tradition, "the gaze of the painter arrests the flux of phenomena, contemplates the visual field from a vantage-point outside the mobility of duration, in an eternal moment of disclosed presence; while in the moment of viewing, the viewing subject unites his gaze with the Founding Perception, in a perfect recreation of that first epiphany."[29] In both cases, what is lost is the deictic location of the glancing eye—or more correctly, both eyes—in the body, a body moving temporally through a concrete spatial location rather than somehow suspended above it in an eternal present. Merleau-Ponty's celebrated critique of disincarnated God's-eye views and defense of preobjective experience also could be adduced to support a temporalized rather than static notion of formal abstraction, as Krauss was to argue when she introduced Richard Serra's work to a Parisian audience in 1983.[30]

What is also suppressed in the elevation of opticality to an ideal realm above the temporal body, Bryson, following Lyotard rather than Merleau-Ponty, added, is the power of the desire coursing through the experience of sight.[31] Ocular desire, ever since at least the time of Augustine, has troubled those who want to privilege sight as the noblest of the senses, for it seems to undermine the disinterestedness of pure contemplation. In the French antiocularcentric discourse, it is precisely the inevitability of such impure desiring that undermines the claims of the eye to be dispassionate, cold, and above the fray.

Often this has meant exploring the complicated links between the fetishism of the image and specifically male desire, an exploration carried out in the French feminist critique of visuality most explicit in the work of Irigaray. Not only has this critique had its echoes in Anglo-American film criticism, beginning with Laura Mulvey's now classic essay of 1975 on the male gaze,[32] but it has also played a role in the turn against Greenberg's reading of modernism. Witness again Victor Burgin, who argued in 1984 that "structurally, fetishism is a matter of separation, segregation, isolation; it's a matter of petrification, ossification, glaciation; it's a matter of idealization, mystification, adoration. Greenbergian modernism was an apotheosis of fetishism in the visual arts in the modern period."[33]

So too an awareness of the body as a site of suffering as well as pleasure, of abjection in Julia Kristeva's sense as well as beautiful form, helped call into question the hegemony of the dispassionate eye. As the artist Mary Kelly noted in 1981, "The art of the 'real body' does not pertain to the truth of a visible form, but refers back to its essential content: the irreducible, irrefutable experience of *pain*."[34] Kelly's sensitivity to bodily pain clearly reflected her feminist concerns, especially her resistance to the objectification of women's bodies. A more general theoretical recovery of the desiring body and the suffering body, both of the artist and the beholder, in the post-Greenbergian climate can, however, be most clearly traced to a new appreciation of two French figures from the traditions of Dada and Surrealism who had been scorned by the exponents of abstract expressionism, Marcel Duchamp and Georges Bataille.[35]

The extraordinary American reception of Duchamp, himself a long-time resident in the United States, has been the object of considerable scholarly interest, culminating—at least for the moment—in Amelia Jones's ambitious feminist study, *Postmodernism and the En-gendering of Marcel Duchamp*, Jerrold Seigel's bold attempt to unite life and work in *The Private Worlds of Marcel Duchamp*, Dalia Judavitz's imaginative *Unpacking Duchamp*, and the recent issue of *October* devoted to "The Duchamp Effect."[36] Although the explosive impact of his *Nude Descending a Staircase* at the legendary New York Armory show of 1913 was not entirely forgotten, it was Duchamp's later, very different work that gained center stage in the 1960s. No history of the origins of many movements of the period, including the neo-Dada of Jasper Johns and Robert Rauschenberg, the

Conceptualism of Joseph Kosuth, the Minimalism of Robert Morris, and the Pop Art of Andy Warhol, can ignore his importance. In more general terms, Duchamp's readymades, aggressively "indifferent" to their instrinsic aesthetic value, have been recognized as a powerful challenge to the differentiated institution of art, the traditional privileging of cultivated aesthetic taste, the modernist distinction between high and low, and even the fetish of originality in Western art as a whole. His self-parodic foregrounding of the artist's constructed persona has been praised for effacing the boundary between artwork and performance art, and sometimes blamed for allowing their complete transformation into marketable commodities (e.g. the Warhol phenomenon). And his campy disruption of his own gender identity—Duchamp photographed in drag or signing his works as Rrose Sélavy, among other pseudonyms—has been credited with inspiring the postmodernist assault on modernist assumptions about male creativity, exemplified by the macho posturing of many of the abstract expressionists and their supporters, as well as the modernist figuring of mass culture in misogynist terms as an inferior realm of "feminine" entertainment.[37]

But it is perhaps Duchamp's celebrated disdain for what he called "retinal art," the art of pure opticality and visual appearance, that has most earned him a place in the pantheon of current American critics of ocularcentrism. Here both his apparent withdrawal from the art scene to play chess in the 1920s (his last oil painting was *Tu m'* done in 1918) and the surprising discovery after his death in 1968 that he was all the while preparing the shocking installation or "sculpture-construction" known as *Étant donnés* (*Being Given*) now at the Philadelphia Museum of Art, have combined to make him the leading critic of the voyeuristic assumptions of conventional painting, perspectival realist as well as abstract and two-dimensional. Indeed, he has been enlisted as a weapon in the battle against the society of the spectacle as a whole, even if Debord and Situationists themselves had thought his attempt merely to abolish art, rather than both abolish and realize it, was flawed.[38]

Duchamp also presented a challenge to the Greenbergian defense of pure opticality by directing attention away from the essence of specific arts, visual or otherwise, to the general, sensually abstracted category of "art" as such. As Thierry de Duve recently pointed out, Duchamp foregrounded what Foucault was to call the "enuciative" capacity of language, its ability to make performative statements rather than merely describe what already exists.[39] Although he performatively designated visually accessible objects as art—some of the readymades can, in fact, be looked at and appreciated in formal terms—it was the act of designating that was crucial, as evidenced by his indifference to the found or fabricated quality of the objects themselves. This generalization of the act of aesthetic fiat with no attention to the differences among the arts was a key instance of what Michael Fried had damned as "theatricality" in "Art and Objecthood."[40]

What made Duchamp so powerful a resource for those who wanted to challenge the Greenbergian paradigm was not only his subversion of received notions of aesthetic value, not only, that is, his intellectual stimulus to conceptualism, but also his restoration of the desiring body in much of his work. Duchamp's erotic preoccupations, evident for example, in the undulating optical discs he dubbed "rotoreliefs" or the "Large Glass" (also called *The Bride Stripped Bare by Her Bachelors, Even*), initially invited reductive psychological explanations. But more recently, they have been the stimulus to a very different set of questions, which deal with the interference produced by the intervention of repetitive and unfulfilled desire into the space of the seemingly plenitudinous visual object. Lyotard's 1977 *Les Transformateurs Duchamp* had already addressed some of the same issues, but in America, it was Rosalind Krauss and her collaborators at the journal *October* who most insistently explored their implications.[41]

Krauss's role in the dissemination and elaboration of post-Greenbergian ideas has been central, so much so that Amelia Jones could turn her into "a sort of institutional author-function whose influence on this level has been vast."[42] Although a considerably more personal reading of Krauss's animus towards Greenberg, who had been her teacher in the 1960s, is invited by the bitter evocation of his baleful presence in her recent book *The Optical Unconscious*, it is clear that one of the reasons for their falling out concerns a radical difference in their appreciation of Duchamp.[43] As Krauss recalled, "what Clem detests in Duchamp's art is its pressure towards desublimation. 'Leveling' he calls it. The attempt to erase distinctions between art and non-art, between the absolute gratuitousness of form and the commodity. The strategy, in short, of the readymade."[44]

As early as 1977 and her *Passages in Modern Sculpture*, Krauss was already finding much to admire in Duchamp's challenge to a welter of traditional assumptions about art as sublimation, including those that informed the Greenbergian defense of high modernism. She approvingly acknowledged his debt to the writer Raymond Roussel's demolition of the idea that works of art expressed a creator's interiority by acting as "a transparent pane—a window through which the psychological spaces of viewer and creator are open onto each other."[45] Duchamp's radical antipsychologism, his denial that works reveal the artist's soul or even his intentions, Krauss compared to the antisubjectivism of both the Minimalist artists of the 1970s and the "new novelists" of the same era: "it is no accident that the work of [Robert] Morris and [Richard] Serra was being made at the time when novelists in France were declaring: 'I do not write. I am written.'"[46] In all these cases, the art object was situated in a discursive field rather than understood as a self-sufficient visual presence. For Krauss, the trajectory of contemporary sculpture from Rodin to Robert Smithson increasingly brought to the fore precisely the theatricality and temporality—the "passages" mentioned in her title—that Greenbergian purists like Fried had tried so hard to banish.

The temporality introduced by Duchamp, Krauss later claimed,[47] was that of a blinking eye rather than the fixating stare of the modernist artist/beholder. Anticipating Derrida's famous deconstruction of Husserl's reliance on the instantaneity of the *Augenblick*, Duchamp's work showed that even a blink has duration. And when the blink is repeated, it reveals what Krauss called, in still another essay on this theme, the "im/pulse to see," which expressed the rhythms of erotic desire and its frustration. Now her reading of Duchamp admitted a psychological dimension, but one that revealed a divided, partly formless rather than unified and expressive subject. It was the unstoppable beat repetitively coursing through that disunified subject, she charged, that "modernism had solemnly legislated out of the visual domain, asserting a separation of the senses that will always mean that the temporal can never disrupt the visual from within, but only assault it from a position that is necessarily outside, external, eccentric."[48]

Moreover, the moment when the eye was closed could be understood as providing a screen on which the nonplenitudinous, heterogeneous signs of what Derrida called *écriture* could be projected. Here the figurality of which Lyotard had written in *Discours, Figure* was crossed by discursivity, but both were internal to vision rather than one within and the other without. In still another way, Krauss contended, the purity of visual experience was undermined by the blink of the eye. Like the interruption experienced by the voyeur suddenly caught looking through a keyhole, so trenchantly described in Sartre's *Being and Nothingness*, the body intervened to subvert the illusion of pure, disincarnated sight. Instead, a chiasmic intertwining of viewer and viewed, of the subject and object of the gaze, ensued, which mobilized specular processes of projection and identification.

A similar sensitivity to the ways in which temporality and the body disrupted the ideology of visual presence was evident in Krauss's celebration of Surrealist photography, so long maligned as impure gimmickry by advocates of modernist formalism.[49] Here she employed Derrida's notion of spacing to explain the ways in which internal deferral and doubling subvert seemingly unified individual prints.[50] The result, she argued, was a visual heterogeneity that presents what is seen as always already discursively coded, as in fact, a kind of disseminating *écriture* in the complicated sense of that word introduced by deconstruction.

Even non-Surrealist photography could be understood to deny the visual plenitude, the formal self-sufficiency, assumed by the high modernist defense of the medium. Here the comparison Duchamp once made between his readymades and snaphots was telling, Krauss argued, because it suggested that the photographs also needed some textual supplementation to become fully meaningful. That is, snapshots were empty signifiers, wrested from any narrative coherence and produced by the indexical trace, the brute physical residue, of the objects they reproduced. As a consequence, they needed captions to make them meaningful.

Whether like *écriture* and thus internally coded in heterogeneous ways or like uncoded indices and thus in need of a supplementary text to give them meaning, photographs could be understood to challenge the ideology of pure visual presence promulgated by Greenberg and his followers. In much of the art of the 1970s, including that which seemed an extension of abstract expressionism, Krauss detected the impact of the photograph in precisely this fashion: "Its visual and formal effect," she wrote of one example, "was that of captioning: of bowing to the implied necessity to add a surfeit of written information to the depleted power of the painted sign."[51]

It was not, however, until the introduction of even more explicitly anti-ocularcentric, antisublimating arguments from Bataille in her work of the 1980s that Krauss was able to demonstrate how depleted that power actually was.[52] Krauss first evoked the author of the scandalous pornographic novel *Histoire de l'oeil* in her 1983 essay "No More Play," published in a Museum of Modern Art collection on *Primitivism in 20th Century Art* and reprinted in her enormously influential collection *The Originality of the Avant-Garde and Other Modernist Myths*.[53] Bataille's violent fantasies of enucleation and the metaphoric displacement of the eye by other objects like the sun, eggs, and testicles work, Krauss recognized, to deprivilege vision in general and formal clarity in particular. His introduction of the word *informe* in the Surrealist journal *Documents* in the 1930s indicated a challenge to the formalist bias of high modernism, indeed to any notion of vertical hierarchy as opposed to horizontal leveling. The word denoted, according to Krauss, "what alteration produces, the reduction of meaning or value, not by contradiction—which would be dialectical—but by putrefaction: the puncturing of the limits around the term, the reduction to the sameness of the cadaver—which is transgressive."[54] Here the body as base, unformed materiality, a materiality always susceptible to corruption, mutilation, and decay, was pitted against the elevated, sublimated, timeless body of formal perfection in traditional Western art. Here a "hard" primitivism of transgression and expenditure replaced the "soft" primitivism of aestheticized visual form. Here was undone the alleged superiority of the spiritualizing, formalizing head over the materializing, grotesque body, an acephalic body whose tangled innards mimic the obscurity of the labyrinth.

Perhaps the high-water mark of Krauss's adoption of the antiocular-centric rhetoric emanating from France came in the 1986 issue of *October* dedicated to Bataille, to which she contributed an essay with the straight-forward title "Antivision."[55] Bemoaning what she called the "modernist fetishization of sight,"[56] whose effects she disappointedly detected in Bataille's late book on Manet, Krauss celebrated his earlier embrace of the values of darkness, blindness, and dazzlement in the obscurity of the caves at Lascaux or the labyrinth of the Minotaur. Her essay ended by eagerly anticipating the effects of rereading modernism in antivisual terms, such as "*informe, acéphale, basess*, automutilation and blindness":

> It is not clear what an alternative view of the history of recent art—one operated through Bataille's disruption of the prerogatives of a visual sys-tem—would yield. It is my assumption that in gesturing toward anoth-er set of data, in suggesting another group of reasons, another descrip-tion of the goals of representation, another ground for the very activity of art, its yield will be tremendous.[57]

Ultimately, the simple binary implications of pro- and antivision seem to have proven too restrictive for Krauss, whose most recent book bor-rowed Walter Benjamin's notion of the "optical unconscious" and gave it a Lacanian spin to suggest a split *within* vision itself.[58] Although in some of her earlier work she had adopted ideas about the fractured nature of the visual field developed by Lacan in his *Four Fundamental Concepts of Psychoanalysis*, Krauss now was also able to draw on the research of Jonathan Crary, whose *Techniques of the Observer*, published in 1990, demonstrated the importance of the nineteenth-century recovery of phys-iological optics, the workings of the actual two eyes in the human body, in overturning the dominant model of vision based on the disembodied workings of a camera obscura.[59]

Crary's own debts to Krauss in return and the French critique of ocu-larcentrism are evident in this remarkable study, but he went beyond her in teasing out the explicitly political implications of his material.[60] Situating the modernist rejection of perspectivalist realism in an earlier and more widespread shift in the status of observation, which he dates as early as the 1820s, Crary argued that it was less of a liberation than has been supposed. The new protocols of the observer seemed to allow the body to come back, but actually only permitted the two eyes to return, while still keeping the other senses, especially touch, at bay. "This auton-omization of sight, occurring in many different domains," Crary conclud-ed, "was a historical condition for the rebuilding of an observer fitted for the tasks of 'spectacular' consumption."[61]

Unlike earlier Greenbergian celebrants of modernist visuality, who saw in its emancipation from previous perspectival regimes a genuine liberation, Crary had absorbed enough of the French distrust of all scopic regimes to recognize the insidious implications of high modernist optical purity. Among the many French theoreticians he cites, including Deleuze, Lyotard, Lacan, Bataille and Baudrillard, two in particular stand out for their impact on the political significance Crary wrests from his story: Foucault and Debord. As mentioned above, the allegedly sinister political implications of ocularcentrism were often an important source of the American interest in its subversion, complementing the fascination with language and the body. *Techniques of the Observer* deliberately combines Foucault's celebrated critique of surveillance in the carceral society of panopticism with Debord's attack on the Spectacle, a combination that neither French theorist would have been likely to find felicitous.

For Crary, however, both regimes of visual power have worked in tandem to rationalize vision in the service of the status quo:

> almost simultaneous with this final dissolution of a transcendent foundation for vision emerges a plurality of means to recode the activity of the eye, to regiment it, to heighten its productivity and to prevent its distraction. Thus the imperatives of capitalist modernization, while demolishing the field of classical vision, generated techniques for imposing visual attentiveness, rationalizing sensation, and managing perception. They were disciplinary techniques that required a notion of visual experience as instrumental, modifiable, and essentially abstract, and that never allowed a real world to acquire solidity or permanence.[62]

Once again, the modernist visual regime, which a generation ago during the postwar era, seemed emblematic of emancipation from extraneous constraints, is damned as itself a subtle form of discipline and regimentation, somehow complicitous with the imperatives of capitalist rationalization. Although the alternative strategy of evoking the desublimating effects of Lyotard's sublime or Bataille's *informe* has itself recently been questioned by another member of the *October* circle, Hal Foster, in his new book on Surrealism and the uncanny, *Compulsive Beauty*, it is clear that for anyone who has absorbed the last twenty or so years of French theory in America, there can be no turning back.[63]

Not surprisingly, the most vociferous champions of high modernism in 1990s America, at least in the visual arts, often turn out to be outspokenly conservative figures like Hilton Kramer and Roger Kimball, whose distaste for French theory goes along with their hatred of anything that questions literary canons or subverts the distinction between high and low culture, thus threatening the traditional value hierarchies they so doggedly defend.

Although Paris has not yet stolen back the idea of modern art from New York, or rather recovered its place as the dominant locus of contemporary artistic creation, the infiltration of French theory, in particular its critique of ocularcentrism, has been a powerful weapon in the dismantling of the critical consensus that made the theft seem worth the effort in the first place. What French artists may not have been able to bring about, French theory seems to have ultimately accomplished: the dissolution of the triumphalist reading of modern art as the realization of aesthetic truth in the context of political freedom. We now see things differently on our side of the Atlantic, if indeed we feel able to see anything very clearly at all.

NOTES

Martin Jay's essay, "Returning the Gaze: The American Response to the French Critique of Ocularcentrism" first appeared in *Definitions of Visual Culture II: Modernist Utopias, Post-formalism, and Pure Visuality*, edited and published by Musée d'art contemporain de Montréal (1996) who kindly granted permission for this reprint.

1. Martin Jay, *Downcast Eyes: The Denigration of Vision in Twentieth-Century French Thought* (Berkeley: University of California Press, 1993).
2. Jacques Lacan, *The Four Fundamental Concepts of Psychoanalysis*, ed., Jacques-Alain Miller, trans. Alan Sheridan (New York, Norton, 1981), pp. 118–119.
3. W.J.T. Mitchell, "The Pictorial Turn," *Artforum* (March 1992).
4. Richard Rorty, *Philosophy and the Mirror of Nature* (Princeton: Princeton University Press, 1979). See also his *Consequences of Pragmatism: Essays, 1972–1980* (Minneapolis: University of Minnesota Press, 1982), especially chapter 3, "Overcoming the Tradition: Heidegger and Dewey."
5. J.J. Gibson, *The Perception of the Visual World* (Boston: Houghton Mifflin, 1950).
6. Their importance for the French debate is addressed by Andreas Huyssen, "In the Shadow of McLuhan: Jean Baudrillard's Theory of Simulation," *Assemblage*, 10 (1990). In general, however, McLuhan and Ong rarely find their way into the French theorizing I have examined.
7. David Michael Levin, ed., *Modernity and the Hegemony of Vision* (Berkeley: University of California Press, 1993).
8. Serge Guilbaut, *How New York Stole the Idea of Modern Art: Abstract Expressionism, Freedom, and the Cold War*, trans. Arthur Goldhammer (Chicago: University of Chicago Press, 1983).
9. For a discussion, see Yves-Alain Bois, "Painting: The Task of Mourning," *Endgame* (Boston, 1990), p. 35.
10. Clement Greenberg, *Art and Culture: Critical Essays* (Boston, Beacon Press, 1961), p. 171. Greenberg went so far as to argue that even modern sculpture had lost its tactile associations to become almost purely visual (p. 142).

11. It also has often been compared with the defense of high modernism by Theodor W. Adorno. Adorno's "debate" with Walter Benjamin over the implications of mass culture became available for appropriation by Americans only in the early 1970s. Benjamin's sympathy for the emancipatory potential in mass culture was pitted against the apparent elitism of Adorno and used to reinforce the new anti-Greenbergian consensus. Here, too, differing attitudes towards Surrealism, which Benjamin generally supported and Adorno disdained, played a role. For a recent defense of Breton, which explicitly draws on Benjamin's debts to Surrealism, see Margaret Cohen, *Profane Illumination: Walter Benjamin and the Paris of Surrealist Revolution* (Berkeley: University of California Press, 1993).

12. In "After Abstract Expressionism," in *New York Painting and Sculpture: 1940–1970*, ed. Henry Geldzahler (New York: Dutton, 1969). See p. 369, in which Greenberg argued that the ultimate source of value in art is the artist's "conception" that dictates the essentializing reduction.

13. *Ibid.*, p. 7. More recently, the repressed debt of abstract expressionists like Jackson Pollock to the automatism of Surrealism has been recalled. See, for example, Peter Wollen, *Raiding the Icebox: Reflections on Twentieth-Century Culture* (Bloomington: Indiana University Press, 1993), p. 91.

14. For a comparison of Greenberg and Szarkowski, see Victor Burgin, *The End of Art Theory: Criticism and Postmodernity* (London: MacMillan, 1986), pp. 66f.

15. Michael Fried, "Art and Objecthood," *Artforum*, 5,10 (1967). This essay and Fried's other criticism of the 1960s have been republished with a long introductory essay as *Art and Objecthood: Essays and Reviews* (Chicago: University of Chicago Press, 1998).

16. See his "How Modernism Works: A Response to T.J. Clark," *Critical Inquiry*, 9, 1 (September 1982) and his interventions in the discussion "Theories of Art after Minimalism and Pop," in *Discussions in Contemporary Culture*, I, ed. Hal Foster (Seattle, Bay Press, 1987), p. 71f. In fact, in his series of later works on the dynamic of theatricality and absorption, Fried seems to privilege an almost tactile immersion of the painter's and the beholder's bodies in the canvas over the distance of a disinterested spectator. Or more precisely, he acknowledges an irreducible tension between the two impulses, which never allows one to triumph over the other for very long. For a reading of Fried that foregrounds his distance from an ahistorical attempt to find painting's optical essence and appreciates his debt to Derrida, see Stephen W. Melville, *Philosophy Beside Itself: On Deconstruction and Modernism* (Minneapolis, 1986).

17. There were, of course, other developments, such as the reintroduction of figural, often neoexpressionist painting by German artists like Baselitz, Kiefer, and Penck, which challenged the Greenbergian paradigm from another angle. For a debate over its significance, see Benjamin H.D. Buchloh, "Figures of Authority, Ciphers of Regression," and Donald B. Kuspit, "Flak from the 'Radicals': The American Case Against German Painting," in *Art After Modernism: Rethinking Representation*, ed. Brian Wallis (Boston: Godine, 1984).

18. Daniel Herwitz, *Making Theory/Constructing Art: On the Authority of the*

Avant-Garde (Chicago: University of Chicago Press, 1993).

19. Joseph Kosuth, "Art after Philosophy," in *Art after Philosophy and After: Collected Writings, 1966–1990*, ed. Gabriele Guercio (Cambridge, MA: MIT Press, 1991).

20. The celebrated attack on Minimalism as theatrical by Michael Fried in "Art and Objecthood" was directed precisely at the restoration of temporality. For a typical post-Greenbergian response to Fried on this issue, see Douglas Crimp, "Pictures," *October*, 8 (Spring 1979).

21. Burgin, *The End of Art Theory*, p. 21. The essay from which this citation comes, "Modernism in the Work of Art," was originally a talk given in 1976.

22. Rosalind E. Krauss, "Sculpture in the Expanded Field," *The Originality of the Avant-Garde and Other Modernist Myths* (Cambridge, MA: MIT Press, 1985); originally written in 1978.

23. *Ibid.*, p. 289.

24. Krauss herself was taken to task for being too beholden to an ahistorical structuralist logic and not sensitive enough to rhetorical, institutional, and ideological questions by Craig Owens in "Analysis Logical and Ideological" (1985), reprinted in his *Beyond Recognition: Representation, Power, and Culture*, eds. Scott Bryson et al. (Berkeley: University of California Press, 1992), pp. 268–83.

25. W.J.T. Mitchell, *Iconology: Image, Text, Ideology* (Chicago: University of Chicago, Press, 1986).

26. Michel Foucault, *This Is Not a Pipe*, trans. and ed. James Harkness (Berkeley: University of California Press, 1983).

27. Norman Bryson, *Vision and Painting: The Logic of the Gaze* (New Haven: Yale University Press, 1983). Bryson, to be sure, was skeptical of the earlier structuralist turn, sardonically commenting that "the misfortune of the French is not to have translated Wittgenstein; instead, they read Saussure" (p. 77). But he uses Derrida, Barthes, and Lacan to buttress his larger argument.

28. Norman Bryson, *Word and Image: French Painting of the Ancien Regime* (Cambridge, MA: Harvard University Press, 1981); *Tradition and Desire: From David to Delacroix* (Cambridge, MA: Harvard University Press, 1984).

29. Bryson, *Vision and Painting*, p. 94.

30. Krauss, "Richard Serra, A Translation," *The Originality of the Avant-Garde and Other Modernist Myths* (Cambridge, MA: MIT Press, 1985). Discussing Serra's 1970–72 sculpture *Shift*, Krauss interprets it as a tacit realization of the arguments of Merleau-Ponty's *Phenomenology of Perception*.

31. The absence of a strong psychoanalytic component in Merleau-Ponty's reflections on the body meant that he lacked an appreciation of the effects of desire in the visual field. His phenomenology could thus be important for Michael Fried as well as the minimalists. For a debate over who got him right, see "Theories of Art after Minimalism and Pop," p. 72–3. Denying that he ever privileged pure opticality, Fried argues that it was in fact minimalism that carried the Greenbergian reduction to an extreme of literalness rather than contesting it.

32. Laura Mulvey, "Visual Pleasure and Narrative Cinema," *Screen*, 16, 3 (1975).

33. Burgin, "Tea with Madeleine," *The End of Art Theory*, p. 106. This essay first

appeared in *Wedge* in 1984.

34. Mary Kelly, "Re-viewing Modernist Criticism," in Wallis, ed., *Art After Modernism*, p. 96. This essay first appeared in *Screen* in 1981. For a discussion of Kristeva's general importance for the recent interest in abject art, see my essay "Abjection Overruled," *Salmagundi*, 103 (Summer 1994).

35. Fried, for example, admitted, "Yes, I was aware of Duchamp; he just doesn't interest me a lot." "Theories of Art after Minimalism and Pop," p. 80.

36. Amelia Jones, *Postmodernism and the En-gendering of Marcel Duchamp* (Cambridge: Cambridge University Press, 1994); Jerrold Seigel, *The Private Worlds of Marcel Duchamp: Desire, Liberation and the Self in Modern Culture* (Berkeley: University of California Press, 1995); Dalia Judavitz, *Unpacking Duchamp: Art in Transit* (Berkeley: University of California Press, 1995), and "The Duchamp Effect," *October*, 70 (Fall 1994).

37. See in particular Andreas Huyssen's influential essay, "Mass Culture as Woman: Modernism's Other," in *After the Great Divide: Modernism, Mass Culture, Postmodernism* (Bloomington: Indiana University Press, 1986).

38. See, for example, Guy Debord's complaint in his 1956 "Methods of Detournement:" "Since the negation of the bourgeois conception of art and artistic genius has become pretty much old hat, [Duchamp's] drawing of a mustache on the *Mona Lisa* is no more interesting than the original version of the painting." *The Situationist International Anthology*, ed. and trans. Ken Knabb (Berkeley: Bureau of Public Secrets, 1981), p. 9.

39. Thierry de Duve, "Echoes of the Readymade: Critique of Pure Modernism," *October*, 70 (Fall 1994), p. 65f.

40. Fried, "Art and Objecthood," p. 142.

41. Krauss acknowledged in her 1990 essay "The Blink of an Eye," that "Lyotard has been alone, as far as I know, in pushing this notion of the carnality of vision deep into the heart of Duchamp's production, which is to say, onto the very surface, of the *Large Glass*." *The States of "Theory," History, Art, and Critical Discourse*, ed. David Carroll (New York: Columbia University Press, 1990), p. 182. Krauss's involvement with French theory and art criticism was deepened by her discussions with the group around the journal *Macula*, which published from 1976 to 1982, and included Yve-Alain Bois and Jean Clay. Along with Hubert Damisch, they are acknowledged in *The Originality of the Avant-Garde and Other Modernist Myths*.

42. Jones, *Postmodernism and the En-gendering of Marcel Duchamp*, p. 56.

43. Rosalind E. Krauss, *The Optical Unconscious* (Cambridge, MA: MIT Press, 1993), for example on p. 309.

44. *Ibid.*, p. 142.

45. Krauss, *Passages in Modern Sculpture*, p. 76.

46. *Ibid.*, p. 270.

47. Krauss, "The Blink of an Eye," p. 176.

48. Krauss, "The Im/pulse to See," in *Vision and Visuality*, ed., Hal Foster (Seattle: Bay Press, 1988), p. 63.

49. With Jane Livingstone, Krauss curated a very influential show of Surrealist art at the Corcoran Gallery of Art in Washington in 1985 entitled *L'Amour Fou:*

Photography and Surrealism (New York: Abbeville Press, 1985).

50. See in particular, "The Photographic Conditions of Surrealism" in *The Originality of the Avant-Garde and Other Modernist Myths*. For more recent evidence of the general impact of Derrida's ruminations on vision, see Peter Brunette and David Wills, eds. *Deconstruction and the Visual Arts: Art, Media, Architecture* (New York: Cambridge University Press, 1994).

51. Krauss, "Notes on the Index: Part 2," *The Originality of the Avant-Garde*, p. 219. Here she is referring specifically to a work of Marcia Hafif, but her point is a more general one.

52. Krauss had the advantage of a close relationship with the foremost Bataille scholar, Denis Hollier, who became a major figure at *October*.

53. Rosalind E. Krauss, "No More Play," *Primitivism in 20th Century Art: The Affinity of the Tribal and the Modern* (New York: The Museum of Modern Art, 1984); reprinted in her *The Originality of the Avant-Garde and Other Modernist Myths*, from which the following citations come.

54. *Ibid.*, p. 64.

55. Rosalind E. Krauss, "Antivision," *October*, 36 (Spring 1986).

56. *Ibid.*, p. 147.

57. *Ibid.*, p. 154.

58. Krauss notes that whereas Benjamin uses the term to imply the expansion of visual experience through new technologies like the camera, she wants to stress its implication of something that normally remains below the threshold of consciousness. "If it can be spoken of at all as externalized within the visual field," she writes, "this is because a group of disparate artists have so constructed it there, constructing it as a projection of the way that human vision can be thought to be less than a master of all it surveys, in conflict as it is with what is internal to the organism that houses it." *The Optical Unconscious*, p. 179–80.

59. Jonathan Crary, *Techniques of the Observer: On Vision and Modernity in the Nineteenth Century* (Cambridge, MA: MIT Press, 1990). His argument was already presented in his contribution to the *Vision and Visuality* conference at the Dia Art Foundation in 1988, "Modernizing Vision."

60. Other figures connected with *October*, most notably Benjamin H.D. Buchloh, also contributed to the political critique of Greenbergian high modernism. Buchloh championed artists like Michael Asher, Marcel Broodthaers, Hans Haacke, and Daniel Buren, who intensified the Duchampian subversion of the institutions of art. Issues of power, gender, and sexuality were also featured in the work of the one-time *October* collaborator Craig Owens, who acknowledged a strong debt to Foucault in particular. One of his major complaints against Michael Fried's mourning the end of modernism concerned in fact the absence of any discussion of power. See his 1982 *Art in America* essay "Representation, Appropriation, and Power," reprinted in *Beyond Recognition*.

61. *Ibid.*, p. 19.

62. *Ibid.*, p. 24.

63. Hal Foster, *Compulsive Beauty* (Cambridge, MA: MIT Press, 1993), chapter 8.

TEN

THE EPOCH OF THE BODY: NEED AND DEMAND IN KOJÈVE AND LACAN

CHARLES SHEPHERDSON

I. NATURE, CULTURE, AND PSYCHOANALYSIS

Psychoanalysis, as everyone knows, approaches the most concrete phenomena of the body in terms of representation, images, and language. The notorious point of departure for Freudian theory is, of course, the "symbolic" character of the bodily symptom. The entire field of psychoanalysis can be defined on this basis, isolated in its theoretical specificity, and distinguished from other forms of knowledge. And yet, the current arrangement of our knowledge makes this task less easy than it might appear, for one is perpetually tempted to displace the terminology of psychoanalysis onto a conceptual field that is fundamentally foreign to it.[1]

We are now familiar with debates between those who seek to demonstrate the biological foundations of sexuality and consciousness, and those who stress the radical contingency of human life, arguing that it has no essence, but is always decisively shaped by specific historical conditions. No theoretical alternative is more widely publicized than this, or more heavily invested today. It is therefore no surprise that contemporary psychoanalytic theory has been drawn into this debate, and understood by reference to its conceptual framework. But perhaps this debate, in which "nature" and "culture" are opposed to one another, is less the measure by which psychoanalysis should be judged, than a refusal of psychoanalysis, a distortion of its most basic vocabulary.

From his earliest work—in "A Comparative Study of Organic and Hysterical Motor Paralyses" (1888), for example—Freud insisted that, in the case of "hysterical" phenomena, the physical symptom is to be rigorously distinguished from its counterpart in organic disease (SE, 1: 160–72). Even when the hysteric is crippled by paralysis, or by some other bodily dysfunction (hallucination, dizziness, loss of speech or appetite, etc.), Freud maintains that "hysterics suffer mainly from reminiscences"

(SE, 2: 7), by which he means that the symptom has no biological cause, but is rather due in some way to "representation." Freud recognizes, moreover, that if the relation between language and the body is to be elaborated, a new vocabulary will be necessary: he writes of "a relation by means of what may be termed representative fibers," and even returns to hysterical paralysis, saying, "I propose the name of *representation paralysis*" (SE, 1: 161).[2]

The theoretical specificity of psychoanalysis would thus appear to be easily grasped: unlike the biomedical tradition, psychoanalysis would attend to the role played by representation, not only in the formation of the symptom, but in the very constitution of the body (as the famous mirror stage of Lacan suggests); and unlike the modes of sociohistorical analysis that dominate the human sciences, psychoanalysis would attend to the materiality of the body with a uniquely clinical attention, relying on modes of explanation (such as repression and the return of the repressed) and techniques of treatment (such as free association and transference) that the social sciences do not share.

And yet, these theoretical divisions separating biological, sociohistorical, and psychoanalytic knowledge are more elusive than one might expect, for the very effort to distinguish psychoanalysis from its disciplinary neighbors often entails a peculiar distortion, in which the distinctive orientation of psychoanalysis is quietly effaced. The secondary literature on Lacan repeatedly testifies to this effacement. On the one hand, it suggests that the great virtue of contemporary psychoanalytic theory is to have revealed the link between representation and the body, and that psychoanalysis can therefore be aligned with various arguments for the social construction of subjectivity. Even if its uniquely clinical orientation is considered, so that psychoanalysis is regarded as focusing, not on the history that provides us with so many varied *representations* of the body, but on the mechanisms which allow representation to affect *the body itself*, we are thereby encouraged to conclude that, for psychoanalysis, the body is not a biological entity, but a contingent historical formation, structured by the symbolic order. On the other hand, and at precisely the same time, we are warned that the principal deficiency of psychoanalysis lies in its unacknowledged biologism, its dependence on anatomy and sexual difference, all of which are said to contradict the historicist thesis, insofar as they refer to aspects of embodiment that seem to be noncontingent, universal, and beyond the possibility of change.

Thus, while it is commonly recognized that psychoanalysis departs in significant and obvious ways from both biological and sociohistorical modes of analysis, and attains its own conceptual autonomy, the very arguments which sketch this theoretical distinctiveness simultaneously assert that psychoanalysis is somehow *partly* historical and *partly* biological—as if, in the final analysis, it had no theoretical specificity at all, but were merely a confused combination of two incompatible traditions, both of which it claims to have transcended in the name of a new conceptual formation, but without in fact having done so. As a result, instead of forging a framework of its own, psychoanalytic theory would seem to remain uneasily suspended between a dubious and unacknowledged naturalism, and a hesitant respect for the contingent formation of subjectivity.

It is therefore no surprise that both of its disciplinary neighbors approach psychoanalysis with a skeptical and reluctant interest. For despite its alleged demonstration of the importance of the symbolic order, psychoanalysis would present cultural theory with an uneasy alliance, insofar as its sensitivity to the construction of the subject would be perpetually betrayed by its contradictory commitment to anatomical difference, or to some form of psychic essentialism that is not subject to historical transformation. This, at least, is the assessment commonly found in the literature that judges psychoanalysis from the standpoint of cultural studies.

The same judgment is rendered, in a very different way, from the standpoint of the scientific community. On the one hand, it is said that psychoanalysis was always intended by Freud to have a biological foundation. Since he did not have the tools of contemporary medicine at his disposal (especially recent developments in neurology), his notorious speculations are understandable, and we can even accept the fact that he aimed merely to "help the client to adjust," because he was not yet able actually to cure the mental disorders of his patients (as psychopharmacology and genetic engineering promise to do). But these deficiencies in the science of Freud's day cannot mask the fact that his aim was to found a scientific psychology, grounded in physiological data. On the other hand, we are simultaneously told that, given the many passages in his work that cannot be incorporated into the neurological picture of Freud, the serious scientist can only conclude that he was a "crank"—a genius, no doubt, who had many fascinating observations about human nature, but one whose theories bear only a superficial resemblance to "properly scientific" explanation. And because it continues to assert its possession of a distinct therapeutic technique, claiming a certain theoretical rigor, and drawing the attention of those who believe that some human phenomena fall outside the reach of the natural sciences, psychoanalysis cannot be left alone (as if it were merely history or literary criticism); on the contrary, it must be denounced, exposed as a pseudoscience, a speculative enterprise which cannot repeat its results in a predictable fashion, but relies on the charisma of its practitioners, who depend on vague analogies and metaphors in place of experimental proof. In short, given Freud's appreciation of the complexity of human life, and his sensitivity to the difficulties of cultural existence—what we might today call "the symbolic inscription of the subject"—we can only applaud his effort to account for neurosis, but in the final analysis, his claim to genuinely scientific knowledge must be regarded as fraudulent.

Here too, psychoanalysis would seem to be suspended between rigorously scientific knowledge, modeled on biochemistry (a discipline it admires but fails to emulate), and a form of sociohistorical analysis, attentive to the nuances of psychic life, but constantly hampered by its own scientific pretensions, and by the prejudices of Freud's day, which are wrongly asserted as eternal truths. Between biology and history, psychoanalysis would seem to have no theoretical orientation of its own. Instead, we are brought to an interpretive impasse which leaves psychoanalysis obscurely divided between the tradition of natural science (which it cannot properly attain) and the argument for social construction (which it perpetually betrays). On the basis of this impasse, we are constantly enjoined to enter the great debate as to whether Freud is a scientist *manqué*, a student of Helmholtz, Brücke, and Fechner who failed to provide the kind of causal mechanisms he sought (concealing that failure with the seductive power of his rhetoric), or whether he is to be read as a great moralist, and situated in the tradition of Voltaire, Kant, and Matthew Arnold.

It would be tempting to attribute this obscurity to Freud himself, pointing to the complex and overdetermined status of his writings (on the one hand, his grand meditations on culture, and on the other hand, his speculative remarks on neurons, cathexes, and energetic pathways). But the difficulties and contradictions are not always located on the side of the object (the notorious "text" of Freud). On the contrary: when the same "paradoxes" and "ambiguities" are encountered with such mechanical regularity, by critics whose disciplinary backgrounds and theoretical commitments are so drastically opposed, one can only suspect—particularly after Foucault—that a powerful interpretive chain is governing the conclusion in advance. From a genealogical point of view, the two competing traditions that organize our knowledge of psychoanalysis today, and give rise to such contradictory images of Freud, are profoundly linked to one another. However opposed they may seem to be, these two alternatives could be said to share a deeper commonality, a common history that has given rise to each, and bound them inexorably to one another. We should thus be prepared to consider that, if *our own accounts*—our speech and our truth—lead so predictably to the same repeated contradictions or confusions, which arise from the side of science and cultural studies alike, the problem may lie in the interpretive arrangement that we bring to Freud's thought, determining its possibilities in advance—an arrangement which *produces* the contradictions that are then conveniently attributed to Freud, or ascribed to his historical moment.

We therefore venture the following conclusion: the apparently urgent debate which compels us to situate Freud in relation to the natural and human sciences is the principal means by which his work is avoided today. Our task is therefore not to enter this debate, but rather to recognize its deleterious effect on our grasp of psychoanalytic theory. It is not a question of determining, once and for all, which of these two traditions finally characterizes Freud's work, or even of proving that his theory hovers ambiguously between them. It is rather a matter of demonstrating how, by virtue of this conceptual framework, the specific character of psychoanalysis is quietly eroded.

As Foucault would say, one is wrongly encouraged to avoid the emergence of a new discursive formation by the tendency to read every author in terms of a continuity, a tradition of recognizable ancestors, a tendency which allows us to eliminate all conceptual novelty by placing the object within a narrative that is already familiar. "Biologist of the mind" or "mind of the moralist"—these are the two available slogans. Thus, while some readers offer to situate Freud in the scientific tradition (where he can be easily denounced), others—in a narrative directly opposed to this, but in perfect keeping with it—regard Freud as a humanist, a discoverer of the social formation of sexuality, whose work echoes the wisdom of the ages, recalling Plato and Aristotle, who (although they did not speak of the id and the superego) understood very well the importance of the golden mean, and the respect that must be paid to the twin forces of eros and ethos, desire and morality. Such narratives make Freud familiar, but only at a cost, for they proceed by reducing what is most distinctive—and most historically momentous—about his thought.

Our difficulty can thus be put as follows: when we think of its particular features, or take up its technical vocabulary (the unconscious, repression, free association, etc.), it is perfectly clear that psychoanalysis is a unique conceptual formation, distinguished from both biomedical and sociohistorical modes of analysis; but when it comes to the difference between nature and culture, the conceptual place of Freudian thought remains profoundly obscure. Contemporary discussions of the body have brought this difficulty to light in a way that is especially pronounced, for although it is obvious that the psychoanalytic concept of embodiment is far removed from both biological and historical approaches to this topic, the theoretical specificity of psychoanalysis is constantly effaced, and we are offered two contradictory images—biological essentialism and social construction—even though it is acknowledged that psychoanalysis is distinct from both.

II. RETURNING TO LACAN

It is no surprise that the same difficulties and "paradoxes" (imposed rather than discovered) plague the reception of Lacanian theory today. The effort to maintain the conceptual particularity of Freudian thought was the hallmark of Lacan's work from the very beginning, and he was always vigilant about deviations—not so much because he wished to be the sole possessor of orthodox knowledge, but because he believed that Freud's discovery was constantly in danger of being lost, displaced by more familiar modes of thought. Such is his complaint against ego psychology and object-relations theory: the former avoids the Freudian "subject," replacing it with the familiar "self," while the latter ignores the peculiar logic of the symbolic order in favor of a pre-Freudian conception of the object. A return to Freud was therefore necessary. It is a historical irony that the same situation now obtains with respect to Lacan: although many basic introductions to Lacanian thought have been produced, and readers have turned their attention to more complex and enigmatic terms—such as the "object a" and *jouissance*—it could be shown that even the most elementary concepts have been distorted from the outset, and still remain in need of clarification. We will demonstrate this claim with respect to one of the most familiar points of Lacanian theory, the distinction between "need" and "demand"—terms which have oriented much of the secondary literature on Lacan, but which have been interpreted through a Kojèvean paradigm that distorts the very theory it promises to elucidate.

Let us recall the basic framework that distinguished Freudian theory from biomedical knowledge. Whereas medical science treats the body as an *organism*, a biological entity governed by natural laws, psychoanalysis begins with the observation that certain physical symptoms have an "Other" cause, and that the body is in some respects bound, not by the laws of nature, but by the laws of representation. This break with the natural sciences was characteristic of psychoanalysis from its very inception, as is evident from Freud's famous remark that "in its paralyses and other manifestations, hysteria behaves *as though anatomy did not exist*" (SE, 1: 169, emphasis added). Since Lacan, the tendency to read Freud in a non-biological way has been fairly well established.

In addition to being detached from biomedical models, however, psychoanalysis must also be distinguished from other theories that attend to what is (misleadingly) called the "symbolic order," the contingent network of conventions and institutions that form and deform the human animal, giving our existence its peculiarly unnatural mode of being. If the break between psychoanalysis and biological models has been clearly recognized today, the distinction between psychoanalysis and arguments for social construction has been less well established. And yet, in speaking of the "imaginary" and "real," as well as the "symbolic order," Lacan tried to insist upon the distinctive character of Freudian thought, giving weight not only to discourse or language (the symbolic), but also to *nondiscursive* aspects of human existence (which is not to say *prediscursive* or natural).[3] In this sense, and particularly in view of its clinical focus, psychoanalysis is clearly distinct, not only from biomedical models, but also from those forms of historicism that speak of subjectivity in sociohistorical terms as an effect or product of representation.

The difference between Lacanian theory and sociohistorical models is easily grasped if we note that psychoanalysis focuses on the *particularity* of the subject in a way that sociohistorical analyses do not. Even if every subject is profoundly affected by sociohistorical conditions, it is clear that we are not all "products of the symbolic order" *in the same way*. Thus, while it is perfectly possible to speak of "homosexuality in ancient Greece," or the "Renaissance experience of madness," not all subjects come out of the symbolic machinery in an identical form. Even Foucault, who is so often misconstrued as a historicist, saw clearly the philosophical need to theorize more adequately what one might call the exteriority of the subject, its capacity not to transcend history but nevertheless to stand in a critical relation to it.[4] This is particularly important if one wishes to understand how a subject, born into a specific cultural moment, can nevertheless contest the very conditions that supposedly constitute that subject.[5] Freud put the point rather differently, but touched on the same problem, in saying that the symptom is a form of protest, a bodily phenomenon that is irreducible to biology, and may even be a product of the social order in some sense (a "discontent of civilization"), but nevertheless indicates a problematic *relation between* the subject and the symbolic order.

The need to account in a theoretically adequate way for the specificity of the subject, beyond what sociohistorical analyses normally aim to do, is especially pressing in the clinical arena. In the case of anorexia, for example, it is crucial to stress the social domain of representation (the prevalent images of women in advertising and elsewhere), but one must also ask why a given subject is vulnerable to anorexia while others are not. Recent literature has argued convincingly that this "disorder" cannot simply be placed in the arena of medical science, or regarded as a purely biological disease, for even if it is accompanied by precise physiological features (amenorrhea, hormonal imbalance, adrenergic dysfunction, etc.), anorexia is profoundly shaped by the cultural horizons within which it appears: the forms of asceticism in the medieval monastic context, for example, differ greatly from the experience of the contemporary university student who is constantly confronted with images from Hollywood and the fashion industry.[6]

There are consequently good reasons to speak of the social construction of anorexia, and to refuse accounts that appeal only to biochemical explanations. From the standpoint of psychoanalysis, however, accounts of the general cultural space of representation do not explain why some individuals rather than others become anorexic. It therefore remains necessary to ask about the *subject*, whose specificity cannot be grasped by broad accounts of the sociohistorical milieu.

In constructing his "discourse theory" in *Seminar XVII: l'envers de la psychanalyse*, Lacan formalized the relation between the subject and the symbolic order not in sociological terms, but in terms of the link between the subject ($) and the signifying chain ($S_1 \rightarrow S_2$).[7] This formulation allowed him to distinguish (S_2), a body of knowledge or a given discursive practice (such as "medicine," for example) from (S_1), the master signifier that marks the subject's particular point of identification *in relation* to that body of knowledge (such as "rural family doctor" or "high-tech researcher"), distinguishing both of these in turn from ($), the subject who undertakes this identification, which always has a cost, in the sense that these two symbolic points of orientation do not capture the totality of the subject, whose full "being" is not contained by these organizing networks of "meaning." The subject ($) therefore remains lacking, repressed, outside representation (as the bar through the $ is intended to indicate). One can thus read this notation, as Robert Samuels has argued, in terms of the well-known Lacanian formula: the signifier (S_1—"rural family doctor") is what represents the subject ($) for another signifier (S_2—the knowledge and practice of "medicine").[8] The distinctive position of psychoanalysis is therefore evident, since it is clear that historical accounts of the contingent formation of medical knowledge (such as Canguilhem's famous book, *The Normal and the Pathological*) do not take as their task the elaboration of a particular subject's relation to the apparatus of medical knowledge, in the way that psychoanalysis does. The distinction between psychoanalysis and theories that focus on the symbolic order (understood sociologically, as referring to historical conditions) is even clearer if we recognize that, in addition to these three elements [the subject ($), the master-signifier (S_1), and knowledge (S_2)], Lacan took up a fourth element in forming a complete "discourse structure." For beyond the subject and the signifying chain, he was also concerned with an object, not as object-relations theory understands it, but as an "object of lack," the "*objet petit a.*" A complete discourse thus includes all these elements: $, S_1, S_2, and *a*, thereby providing us with a distinctive model—distinct not only from biomedical theories, but also from historicism.[9]

The term "symbolic order" is therefore misconstrued whenever it is equated with sociohistorical conditions, for in Lacan's usage, it concerns a logical or structural problematic, focused on the subject's constitution in language. Lacan's statement in "The Meaning of the Phallus" could not be clearer on this point:

> this advocacy of man's relation to the signifier as such has nothing to do with a "culturalist" position in the ordinary sense of the term. . . . It is not a question of the relation between man and language as a social phenomenon . . . something resembling the ideological psychogenesis with which we are familiar (E, 689/284–85).

This explains Lacan's remark, in "The Agency of the Letter," that psychoanalysis has brought about a reorganization of the sciences, by challenging the familiar distinction between nature and culture:

> the ethnographic duality of nature and culture is giving way to a ternary conception of the human condition—nature, society [that is, historical conditions], and culture—the last term of which could well be reduced to language (E, 496/148).

The symbolic order ("language") thus defines a field that falls outside the usual opposition between nature and history. Here too, we should note the clinical aspect of this claim, its bearing on the question of the body, for if one appeals to sociohistorical arguments in place of the logic of the subject, Lacan says, "one soon realizes that it is impossible to note the structure of a symptom in the analytic sense of the term" (E, 689/285).

In spite of this obvious difference between psychoanalysis and both medical and sociohistorical analysis, however, the theoretical specificity of psychoanalysis is constantly effaced in the course of its reception. For whenever a debate is formed between biological paradigms and analyses that focus on the social construction of subjectivity, the basic vocabulary of psychoanalysis has already been avoided, displaced by a more familiar terminology. In such circumstances, it is best to return to essentials, and seek clarity on the most foundational points. For perhaps this debate, this forced choice between the biological and the symbolic, should not serve as a paradigm for the evaluation of psychoanalysis. On the contrary, this debate could be seen as strictly symptomatic: it manifests the degree to which the theory has not been clearly articulated, but forced instead to coincide with a more familiar terminology, an inherited conceptual arrangement that translates the very concepts it is intended to explain.

III. SEX AND GENDER

A number of theoretical distortions follow from the displacement of psychoanalytic terminology into a more familiar framework. Consider the term "sexual difference," which so often appears in French psychoanalytic literature. Current discussions of psychoanalysis are largely organized by the distinction between "sex" and "gender."[10] This distinction has been very useful in allowing us to separate the biological aspects of sex from the historical conventions governing gender. In perfect keeping with this conceptual arrangement, one finds numerous books that offer to explain the difference between the sexes on biological grounds (Simon Levay's *The Sexual Brain*, for example, or the more popular *Brain Sex*), while others insist upon the contingency of human conventions, including conventions of knowledge about sex (Thomas Laqueur's *Making Sex*, for example, or John Winkler's *The Constraints of Desire: The Anthropology of Sex and Gender in Ancient Greece*).[11] And yet, on the basis of this alternative between biology and culture, the very terminology of psychoanalysis is dropped, and readers are forced to decide whether the term "sexual difference" refers to biological matters (sex), to social effects (gender), or to some obscure combination of both.

This problem has an impact on a number of basic terms, and is especially evident in discussions of the phallus, which is said to be a signifier (and thereby placed in the symbolic order, the domain of the "arbitrary" and "conventional," as Saussure says), while at the same time it apparently remains bound to anatomical difference (and thereby tied to biology). In this way, one of the most elementary concepts of psychoanalysis is regarded as ambiguous or unclear, or—to give a less charitable account—as precisely designed to give the appearance that psychoanalysis is sensitive to "symbolic" issues, while in fact "enforcing the law" all the more decisively, perpetuating an essentialist model that does not do justice to the historical formation of the subject. Indeed, the entire debate is configured in such a way that the "truth" of psychoanalysis is thought to emerge only when its theoretical terminology has finally been forced to confess itself in terms of a more recognizable paradigm: just as sexual difference is translated into the vocabulary of sex and gender, so also the phallus is read in terms of the opposition between the symbolic and the biological, and thus in terms of an inherited debate between nature and nurture—a debate which has a specific historical determination, and should not be taken for granted as the only possible framework for posing questions of sexuality and embodiment.

Freud's work is prey to exactly the same difficulties, such that one is forced to weigh two different and even contradictory lines of thought against one another. On the one hand, we are asked to recognize his claim that femininity and masculinity are matters of identification, and therefore highly variable (thus, in his treatment of the Oedipal complex, Freud speaks of boys with a maternal identification and girls with a paternal identification); and yet, we are also asked to acknowledge his notorious remark that "anatomy is destiny," a remark that would seem to be grounded in biology and a doctrine of natural differences (thus, in his treatment of the Oedipal complex, Freud insists that the little boy and girl have a different relation to castration, a different "destiny," based on physiological differences). Here again, one seems forced to decide whether Freud has discovered the cultural construction of gender, or whether he remains entrenched in the Darwinian century, and committed to a biological account of sexual difference. Readings which conclude that Freud's work entails "a little of each" do not fundamentally change the horizon of this debate.

But perhaps the distinction between sex and gender is a discursive formation that is foreign to Freud's thought. In that case, it would be a mistake to try to determine which of these categories Freud really wishes to endorse. The very distinction between sex and gender would be inadequate as a way of situating Freud, just as the debate between biological and social models is insufficient to grasp what Lacan speaks of as the "knot" that holds together the imaginary, symbolic, and real. It is this knot—the Borromean knot of the late work, but also the "knot of imaginary servitude" of the early work—that leads Lacan to rethink the entire conceptual division between nature and culture. This issue was already present in "The Mirror Stage," in the reference to transference love:

> At this junction of nature and culture, so persistently examined by modern anthropology, psychoanalysis alone recognizes this knot of imaginary servitude that love must always undo again, or sever (E, 100/7).

In short, just as the phallus cannot be understood in terms of the debate between biological and symbolic (i.e. sociohistorical) models, but must be situated in terms of the imaginary, symbolic and real, so also sexual difference cannot easily be situated in terms of the distinction between the cultural category of gender and the natural category of sex. As Mannoni says in *Seminar II*, "after Lévi-Strauss, one has the impression that we can no longer use the notions of culture and nature" (SII, 39).

In short, if it is true that psychoanalysis is a distinct theoretical formation, and not a confused mixture of social theory and biomedical pretention, then we would have to consider that the term "sexual difference," far from being an ambiguous reference that is partly biological and partly social, functions in fact as *neither*. The point is not that biological accounts of health and disease, or sociohistorical accounts of embodied life, are irrelevant or incorrect, but simply that the theoretical orientation of psychoanalysis cannot be grasped in terms of these two approaches. This is the great enigma, but also the theoretical importance, of psychoanalysis: *sexual difference is neither "sex" nor "gender."* "It is perhaps there," Lacan says, "that psychoanalysis represents an earthquake yet to come" (E, 797/296).

Freud's own work appears to confirm this peculiar formulation in which the vocabulary of sex and gender proves insufficient. In his *New Introductory Lectures on Psychoanalysis*, Freud opened every session with the same familiar and obvious formula: "Ladies and Gentlemen." (One is obviously reminded of the apologue of the two doors marked "Ladies" and "Gentlemen" in Lacan's "Agency of the Letter" [E, 499–500/151–52].) And yet, when he arrives at the particular lecture called "Femininity" (SE, 22: 112–35), Freud pauses on this obvious and familiar formula, weighing things further:

> When you meet a human being, the first distinction you make is "male or female?" and you are accustomed to make the distinction with *unhesitating certainty* (SE, 22: 113, emphasis added).

Irigaray has criticized Freud for relying so quickly upon *the visual order*, for giving such a privilege to sight, and indeed for "keeping up appearances." But as the late Sarah Kofman points out, Freud proceeds in this passage in a quasi-Cartesian fashion, not insisting upon the truth of this imaginary distinction, but rather subjecting it to the method of doubt.[12] We may be "accustomed" to making this distinction with "unhesitating certainty," on the immediate evidence of the senses, but things are not always so clear. Appearances are deceiving, and if we turn from custom and first appearances to the more rigorous procedures of "science," things are no better, no more clear and distinct: "Science next tells you something that runs counter to your expectations," so that eventually "you are bound to have doubts" (114). Thus, even "anatomical science," Freud says, "shares your certainty at one point and not much further" (113). What is more, this "one point" does not reside, for "anatomical science," where one might expect, for Freud appears to be speaking here of the difference between the egg and sperm—the only scientific measure of sexual difference, and one which cannot automatically be extended to the difference between men and women. Thus, when it comes to sexual difference, Freud proceeds to doubt, to wonder in the face of this *unhesitating certainty*, asking whether this apparent knowledge gives us the truth, or merely amounts to *a form of belief*. He concludes that we are faced with "an unknown characteristic which anatomy cannot lay hold of" (114).

Having deprived his audience of recourse to the empirical facts of biology, he now imagines them taking refuge in *the conventions of culture*. If biology cannot provide the ground of our customary certainty, "Can psychology do so perhaps?" (114). Freud thus turns from anatomical certainty to another customary answer:

> *We are accustomed* to employ the terms "masculine" and "feminine". . . . Thus, we speak of a person, whether male or female, as behaving in a masculine way in one connection and in a feminine way in another. But you will soon perceive that this *is only giving way to anatomy or to convention* (114, emphasis added).

Freud thus refuses to accept both nature and culture, both anatomy and convention. Recourse to either amounts to what we might call *taking refuge from the question*, displacing sexual difference into the framework of sex and gender.

The theoretical specificity of psychoanalysis, but also its peculiar historical position in the arrangement of our knowledge, is thereby clarified: when contemporary accounts of Lacan debate the question as to whether his theory amounts to another form of biological essentialism or shows that sexuality is a cultural construction, the entire field of psychoanalysis has already been forgotten. This is one reason why French psychoanalytic feminism has had such a difficult reception in the United States, where the discussion of "sexual difference" is either collapsed into the historicist argument, and regarded as an account of gendered subjectivity, or else rejected for its purportedly biological determinism.[13] As a result, whether psychoanalysis is celebrated for demonstrating the contingent formation of gender, or denounced as a return to pre-linguistic anatomical reality, the entire orientation of psychoanalysis has been lost from the beginning, collapsed into the very framework that Freud's theory was meant to displace.

IV. NEED AND DEMAND

Let us now narrow our focus, and try to situate the terminology of psychoanalysis within its own particular horizon, taking up one of the most familiar points of Lacanian theory, the distinction between "need" and "demand." Here too, where our grasp of psychoanalysis might seem to be most secure and unproblematic, it can be shown that the basic terminology still remains obscure.

Taken from Kojève, the distinction between need and demand has served to orient many accounts of Lacanian theory.[14] It allows us to separate the biological aspects of embodiment (the "need for food," for example) from the uniquely human arena, the sphere of intersubjectivity, where the great Kojèvean themes—the master-slave relation and the desire for recognition—are situated. Kojève puts the essential point in terms of "animal" and "anthropogenetic" desire:

> anthropogenetic Desire is different from animal Desire (which produces a natural being, merely living and having only a sentiment of its life) in that it is directed, not toward a real, "positive," given object, but toward another. Thus, in the relationship between man and woman, for example, Desire is human only if the one desires, not the body, but the Desire of the other; if he wants "to possess" or "to assimilate" the Desire taken as Desire—that is to say, if he wants to be "desired" or "loved," or, rather, "recognized" in his human value.[15]

The psychoanalytic vocabulary is of course slightly different, but Kojève's distinction has an obvious impact on Lacan's thought. In "The Direction of the Treatment," for example, Lacan speaks of "the demand for love, which is not a demand arising from any need" (E, 635/270). On this view, Lacan would distinguish "need," understood as a "biological" phenomenon, an organic, bodily *relation to the object*, from "demand," which refers to the world of speech and "intersubjectivity" where we find the *relation to the other*.

The division separating the (natural) relation to the object from the (intersubjective) relation to the other is clear, but it is not as simple as this first indication would suggest. Indeed, the link between Kojève's account and psychoanalysis can be made still more precise if we note that, for Kojève, "anthropogenetic Desire" not only involves the *relation to the other*, but also has effects on the *object-relation*. Kojève continues:

> Likewise, Desire directed towards a natural object is human only to the extent that it is "mediated" by the Desire of another directed toward the same object: it is human to desire what others desire, because they desire it (6).

"Anthropogenetic Desire" is therefore not merely concerned with a disembodied domain of intersubjectivity and recognition, for it also has a bearing on the most concrete domain of human life, detaching the object from its natural or immediate being, and placing it in the symbolic arena, where it is mediated by the relation to the other. Such, at least, is the usual understanding of need and demand, explained by way of Kojève's thought.

Kojève's distinction has been crucial to much of the secondary literature on Lacan. Jonathan Scott Lee explains the essential point quite clearly when he writes of the first emergence of the "subject," the moment when the biological order of need is transposed into the domain of language:

> What the child would appear to ask for, in her first attempts at speech, is the satisfaction of her bodily *needs*. But what Lacan emphasizes is that the linguistic translation of these needs—what he calls *demand*—is inherently interpersonal: demand is always addressed to another person, at first a parent or caretaker. Indeed, the child is not simply asking for food when she demands this of her parent; rather, she is using the demand for food to provoke the parent, the other, into recognizing her.[16]

Following Kojève, Lacan would thus insist on a uniquely human dependence on recognition that is radically distinct from organic dependence, or any natural need. In his essay on psychosis, Lacan stresses the importance of this point for our understanding of the relation to the mother. Popular literature may speak of the "maternal" in terms of a quasi-biological nurturing, but Lacan insists that the child's relation to the mother is "a relation constituted in analysis not by his vital dependence on her, but by his dependence on her love, that is to say, by his desire for her desire" (E, 554/198).

As with Kojève, moreover, so also with Lacan, it is not simply a question of intersubjectivity, for the relation to the object will also be affected by this uniquely anthropogenetic dimension. As Lacan says in "The Meaning of the Phallus," we are faced not simply with the *elimination* of needs, but with a "*deviation* in man's needs . . . insofar as his needs are subjected to demand" (E, 690/286, emphasis added). Even the most natural aspects of human life are thus reorganized and profoundly altered when they are obliged to pass through the mediation of language—what Lee calls "the linguistic translation of these needs."

This passage through the domain of the signifier is nothing other than the law of language, which will henceforth be understood, not simply as *representing* needs, but as actually transforming or "translating" them, so that we are no longer in the order of natural life. As Lacan says in "The Direction of the Treatment": "[I]n articulating the life of the subject according to its conditions, demand cuts off the need from that life" (E, 629/265). Lacan is not alone in making this distinction. Deprived of his retainers, cast out by his daughters, and exposed to the fury of the elements, King Lear explains the peculiar character of even the most basic human need, which is separated from nature and marked by a strange "superfluousness":

> O! reason not the need; our basest beggars
> Are in the poorest things superfluous:
> Allow not nature more than nature needs,
> Man's life is cheap as beast's.[17]

Thus understood, the distinction between need and demand separates the domain of recognition, intersubjectivity, and symbolic exchange from the domain of biological life and death: it explains why Lacan refuses all biological readings of Freud, while suggesting a certain correlation between the field of demand and current forms of historicism, which would account for the symbolic aspect of demand in terms of the contingent, socio-historical formation of subjectivity. Such an account also suggests a correspondence between "demand" in psychoanalysis and more or less Marxist accounts of exchange, in which natural relations of need are disrupted by an economy of "supply and demand," such that objects are desired not simply to satisfy needs, but also for the recognition they confer. On this account, the distinction between need and demand would even provide a link between psychoanalysis and certain motifs of existentialism, where the "subject" appears in its non-natural mode of being—characterized by a fundamental "alienation," "thrownness," and "negativity" that are irreducible to natural existence. This account is now virtually canonical in the secondary literature.

In spite of this familiar starting point, however, it still remains necessary to ask (a) just what this distinction means in psychoanalysis, and (b) whether it allows us an adequate clarification of the body in Lacanian theory. For the distinction between need and demand, construed as a distinction between the domain of nature and the domain of intersubjectivity and symbolic exchange, does not allow us to grasp the *bodily* aspect of psychoanalysis. Let us put the problem in a preliminary way: if need can be placed at the level of the *organism* and its biological life, and demand concerns the *subject* (or perhaps the *ego*) in its search for recognition, then where are we to situate the body? The body is not reducible to the biological organism, but neither is it simply to be equated with subjectivity, representation, or the symbolic order. Is the body an obscure combination of these two, or perhaps a domain that falls outside the distinction between need and demand? We are thus left with a very basic problem: either the distinction between need and demand is insufficient to clarify the status of the body (in which case these two terms, which have been so fundamental to the secondary literature, tell us nothing about one of the most elementary issues of psychoanalysis), or else need and demand are fundamentally distorted when they are construed in terms of the distinction between "animal Desire" and "anthropogenetic Desire"—understood, that is, by way of the well-known dichotomy between the biological domain and the world of symbolic exchange. Is it possible to reconsider this famous distinction in such a way as to cast light on the problem of embodiment?

Two questions can guide us here: first, although we must note that the distinction between need and demand is taken from Kojève, we may ask whether the Lacanian use of these terms remains within the horizon of Kojève's thought, or whether they are transformed by the specific theoretical framework of psychoanalysis; and second, we may ask how the concept of demand in psychoanalysis is linked to the drive—a concept which does not appear in Kojève, but is central to Freudian theory. These two issues will guide the rest of our remarks.

V. THE CONCEPT OF DEMAND

Let us grasp the basic difficulties more precisely. A first indication that Kojève's account does not correspond to Lacan's is that Kojève does not distinguish between the "other" and the "Other." Kojève does indeed provide us with a distinction between biological need (what Kojève calls "appetite") and intersubjective desire. The latter is specifically human, and allows Kojève to say that "man's desire is the desire of the other," a phrase Lacan will repeat. But repetition is not always sameness, for with Kojève, this claim means that the subject desires what the other subject desires (we recall the quotation: "Desire directed towards a natural object is human only to the extent that it is 'mediated' by *the Desire of another* directed toward the same object" [6], emphasis added). For Lacan, by contrast, the claim that "man's desire is *the desire of the Other*" (with a capital O) takes the entire analysis out of the domain of intersubjective rivalry and places it in a triangulated structure, governed by the logic of the symbolic order (the Other).[18] As Lacan says in "The Agency of the Letter":

> [W]ho then is this other to whom I am more attached than to myself, since at the heart of my most accepted identity with myself, it is he who agitates me? (E, 524/172).[19]

He continues, adding that this other (the "Other") cannot be understood in intersubjective terms:

> His presence can only be understood at *a second degree of otherness*, which situates him from the very start in the position of *mediating between me and the double of myself* (E, 524/172, emphasis added).

As a result, we misconstrue the psychoanalytic field as long as we remain within the domain of intersubjective recognition as Kojève understands it, for "here the problems are of an order the heteronomy of which is completely misconstrued if reduced to an 'awareness of others,' or whatever we choose to call it" (E, 525/173).[20]

It is crucial to grasp this third dimension, the "beyond" *in which* the much-discussed "relation to the other" is constituted, for it will lead from intersubjectivity to the concept of the unconscious:

> If I have said that the unconscious is the discourse of the Other (with a capital O), it is in order to indicate the beyond in which the recognition of desire is bound up with the desire for recognition (E, 524/172).

In fact, this passage not only distinguishes the Other and the other, but also suggests that if we wish to speak of "desire" in Lacanian terms, we must distinguish the familiar Kojèvean *"desire for recognition"* from the psychoanalytic *"recognition of desire,"* for whereas the former concerns the master-slave relation and the struggle for prestige, the latter takes us beyond intersubjectivity to the unconscious. In "The Freudian Thing," this same distinction is given a clinical bearing, showing us instances in which "the desire of recognition dominates . . . the desire that is to be recognized" (E, 431/141). With this formulation, Lacan points out that the *ego's* struggle for prestige may be at odds with the *subject's* desire, and that there is, to put it simply, more than one form of recognition, and more than one level of "subjectivity" when it comes to the problem of desire. Thus, failure to distinguish between the other and the Other (or between the ego and the subject) explains why Kojève does not speak of the unconscious, or indeed of the drive, or the body, or sexual difference, or any number of concerns that are central to Freud. Readings of Lacan that are guided by Kojève are also likely to avoid these topics, or to approach them through a framework that misconstrues them from the start. The vocabulary of Kojève thus cannot neatly be mapped onto the psychoanalytic terrain as if the one could automatically be translated into the other. And yet this translation machine continues to operate in the reception of Lacanian theory, as if Lacan stole his ideas from Kojève, or merely repeated what he had learned from the master.

A second indication that Lacan's thought goes beyond the Kojèvean framework can be found in another simple fact of terminology, one that is even more central to our concerns: where Kojève distinguishes between "animal Desire" and "anthropogenetic Desire," Lacan gives us three terms: need, demand and desire. For Kojève, the crucial point is to separate animal life from the domain of human existence, which is characterized by a number of peculiar features (mimetic desire, the master-slave relation, a denaturalized relation to the object, and so on). For Lacan too, the human being is separated from the order of need, but where Kojève speaks of "Anthropogenetic Desire," Lacan insists on a further distinction between demand and desire. We know that Lacan, who attended Kojève's lectures, was profoundly influenced by them, and that he takes over the analysis of "anthropogenetic Desire" in seeking to articulate the peculiarly denatured character of human existence. How much difference does this additional terminology really make? To what extent does the distinction between demand and desire take us beyond the horizon of Kojève's thought?

The obvious solution to this problem is simply to note that Lacan generally uses the term "desire" to refer to the *unconscious*—a concept that Kojève does not develop. (Indeed, Lacan does not usually speak of the "desire for recognition," unless, as in the passages above [E, 524/172; 554/198], he is implicitly giving voice to someone else's doctrines.) In this sense, the problems Kojève addresses under "anthropogenetic Desire" correspond more closely to what Lacan calls "demand," which always amounts to a "demand for recognition." Accordingly, Lacan usually speaks of demand (and not desire) when he takes up the theme of intersubjectivity and the famous master-slave relation. In "The Meaning of the Phallus," for instance, Lacan can indeed be said to follow Kojève when he distinguishes "the appetite for satisfaction" from "the demand for love" (E, 691/287). It would therefore be tempting to believe that the further refinement of Lacanian theory can be grasped by this simple division of terminological labor: "demand" articulates the Kojèvean themes, while "desire" elaborates the Freudian unconscious.

This would make sense of a fundamental Lacanian claim about the relation between demand and desire, namely, that all speech is essentially a demand, a quest for recognition, a product of the conscious ego, while desire is essentially unspeakable, the "unsaid" or "half-said" ("*le mit-dit*") that haunts the discourse of the *ego*, appearing in speech as a disruptive unconscious material—the forgotten word or lapsus that designates the place of the *subject* beyond the discourse of the *ego*. Hence the formulation in "The Direction of the Treatment": "Desire is produced in the beyond of demand," or "hollowed within the demand" (E, 629/265). Attention to the unsaid or unsayable aspect of the unconscious would also explain why Lacan insists that in spite of his emphasis on speech and verbalization, it is not a matter of "making the unconscious conscious," or reducing everything to discourse—claiming that everything can be hermeneutically resolved at the level of meaning:

> I can already hear the apprentices murmuring that I intellectualize analysis: though I am in the very act, I believe, of preserving the unsayable aspect of it (E, 616/253).

The unconscious thus appears in speech, within the articulation of demand, but as a perpetually alien element (a slip of the tongue, or some unexpected verbal association that emerges in the chain of signifiers). As he says in "Subversion of the Subject," "[I]t is precisely because desire is *articulated* that it is not *articulable*" (E, 804/302, emphasis added).

Such would be the solution: the unconscious is the unspeakable dimension of desire, manifested in the symbolic debris that disrupts the narrative of the ego. Unconscious desire appears as the famous "discourse of the Other"—a dimension of alterity which is irreducible to the "other" of Kojèvean intersubjectivity, and which the Freudian unconscious would add to Lacan's system. In different language, one could say that Kojève's theme of "anthropogenetic Desire"—intersubjective rivalry and mimetic identification—is developed by Lacan in terms of the *imaginary*, whereas the Freudian component of Lacan refers to the *symbolic* order (unconscious desire). The elegance of this solution is that it would allow us to see the link between Kojève's dichotomy and Lacan's distinction between need and demand, while also grasping the further alterity that is introduced by desire, understood as the "discourse of the Other," the unconscious material that disrupts the discourse of the ego.

But this solution is not sufficient, for even if we reserve "desire" in the Lacanian sense for a properly Freudian problematic, and stress—with a good deal of legitimacy—the link between Kojève's anthropogenetic Desire and Lacan's demand, it cannot be a matter of indifference that where Kojève gives us one term, "anthropogenetic Desire," to designate a set of uniquely human relations, Lacan divides this domain, insisting upon a further distinction. If this distinction is serious, it cannot be simply "desire" that refers to matters we do not find in Kojève: "demand" must also have a more precise and technical meaning for Lacan than we find in Kojève, a meaning that Kojève's anthropogenetic Desire does not entail. This is not a merely academic point, for in fact Lacan claims that the failure to distinguish adequately between demand and desire will lead to such confusion that one will no longer see clearly what distinguishes either of these terms from need. As he says in "Subversion of the Subject": "where it is a question of desire, I find its irreducibility to demand the very source of that which also prevents it from being reduced to need" (E, 804/302). Thus, it is insufficient to say that "desire" in Lacan has a specific reference to the unconscious that we do not find in Kojève. We must also grasp the specific sense that "demand" has in Lacan, beyond its general resemblance to Kojève's "dualistic ontology."[21]

We can now take an additional step. For if demand acquires a meaning in psychoanalysis that "anthropogenetic Desire" does not entail, it is because demand has a crucial bearing on the concept of the body. This is the decisive point: when Kojève distinguishes animality (the "need for food") from the human sphere of intersubjectivity (the "demand for love"), *the question of the body tends to be avoided*. For Kojève, the body is situated at the level of biological need, a domain of animality that—in keeping with a long philosophical tradition—is contrasted with the properly human arena of subjectivity and recognition. For Lacan, by contrast, the concept of demand is bound up with the problem of the *somatic symptom*, that material dimension of embodiment that goes beyond organic life, but yet cannot be grasped at the level of speech and intersubjectivity.

These remarks allow us to refine our understanding of Lacan's terminology. It is true that "demand" for Lacan is often used to designate speech, and that he regards all speech as demand. This discursive and intersubjective aspect of demand has often been stressed in the secondary literature. But Lacan also uses the term in a different way. It is this development that will take the concept of demand beyond intersubjective speech, leading us to the drive, and thus to the psychoanalytic concept of the body. It should already be clear, however, that if we wish to understand how Lacan's thought diverges from Kojève's, we cannot simply point out that desire in Lacan introduces a specifically Freudian problematic (the unconscious, the "discourse of the Other"), while equating "demand" with the Kojèvean quest for recognition; we must also come to understand how demand goes beyond the Kojèvean framework, precisely insofar as it bears on the concept of the body.

VI. THE CONCEPT OF THE DRIVE

We are now at the heart of the matter. We have seen that if demand is understood from the perspective of Kojève, as a demand for recognition, the status of the body tends to remain obscure. There is, however, another term, namely the drive, which would seem to correct this deficiency. Is not the drive the most obviously corporeal of psychoanalytic concepts, being directly linked to the bodily orifices (oral, anal, scopic, etc.)? If the concept of the body is not sufficiently clarified by the Kojèvean interpretation of need and demand—that is, if the "body" is neither reducible to the order of biological need nor adequately grasped by the analysis of recognition and intersubjective demand—how does it stand with the drive, which is more directly tied to embodiment?

Here too the basic concepts still remain obscure. In fact, the usual triad addressed in the secondary literature on Lacan, the triumvirate of need, demand, and desire, has tended to circumvent the question of the drive, in favor of a discussion of recognition and symbolic exchange that fits well with certain aspects of the existentialist tradition, and with historicist accounts of the shifting construction of subjectivity, but thereby avoids one of the most fundamental features of psychoanalytic theory, its notorious somatic aspect. We are told that need refers to the biological domain, while demand and desire refer to the subject and the symbolic order. In this way, the drive is omitted, and Kojève's "dualistic ontology" is maintained. Again, lack of clarity about the status of the body in psychoanalysis is the conspicuous result. In fact, the concept of the drive has been so neglected in the secondary literature that some have spoken of a "return to the drive" as though this would correct a deficiency in Lacan's work. As Kelly Oliver writes, "It is this realm of bodily drives that Kristeva wants to bring back into Lacanian theory."[22]

It is difficult to see how Lacan's remarks on the drive could have been ignored for so long, in favor of a more or less social and psychological account of demand and desire, since he developed a "matheme" for the drive as early as *Seminar V: Les formations de l'inconscient* (1957–58), devoted a substantial portion of *Seminar XI* to Freud's account of the drive, gave attention to the drive by placing it on the graph of desire in "Subversion of the Subject," and is often considered the main force in bringing to attention Freud's remarks on the death drive.[23] What is more, the most elementary attention to the drive would have stressed *the somatic aspect of demand* from the very outset, and revealed the limits of the Kojèvean interpretation, in which demand is tied to subjectivity and recognition. For Lacan's matheme for the drive ($ \lozenge D$) is written with demand as one of its components—the formula indicating that in the drive, the subject ($) is in some way "bound" to symbolic demand (D). If the subject refuses to eat, or eats only to regurgitate immediately afterward, with a compulsiveness that is beyond the subject's control, as though following its own repetitive course with a commanding power that the subject does not entirely understand or even choose, this is an instance of the oral drive, a corporeal symptom that indicates that the subject's desire has been closed down, and replaced by a somatic formation, which Lacan speaks of in terms of "symbolic demand." The drive is precisely *a bodily inscription of demand*, in which the flesh is no longer animated, no longer carried by desire, but loses its temporal fluidity, its capacity for historical life, and is condemned to repetition, as if "haunted by the form of a bloody scrap—the pound of flesh that life pays" when the subject refuses the debt of symbolic castration (E, 629-30/265). The somatic aspect of demand, as well as the link between demand and the drive, should therefore be evident.

In fact, as Slavoj Žižek points out, the formula for the drive may be seen as taking up the classical question of hysterical symptoms:

> Why is the Lacanian matheme for the drive $ \lozenge D$? The first answer is that the drives are by definition "partial," they are always tied to specific parts of the body's surface—the so-called "erogenous zones"—which,

contrary to the superficial view, are not biologically determined but result instead from the signifying parceling of the body. Certain parts of the body's surface are privileged not because of their anatomical position but because of the way the body is caught up in the symbolic network. This symbolic dimension is designated in the matheme by D, i.e., symbolic demand.[24]

The bodily inscription of demand should therefore be evident, and yet, when demand is regarded as a matter of intersubjectivity or understood as the demand for recognition, the bodily aspect of demand is lost, and its relation to the drive (a term Kojève does not use) disappears entirely. As a result, Lacan is criticized for his "excessive interest in language" or his "neglect of affect" or his "disembodied theorizing," and we are encouraged to return to the body, as if this might take us "beyond Lacan."

One thus begins to see how, on the basis of the popular distinction between the biological and the symbolic, many basic psychoanalytic concepts have been interpreted in such a way that its corporeal dimension remains obscure. And one begins to wonder what it might mean to give these concepts the theoretical precision they require. For an account of the drive would not simply introduce one more cumbersome term into the theoretical apparatus, adding to the list of need, demand, and desire; on the contrary, it would oblige us to reformulate our account of many concepts that have long seemed familiar, beginning with demand.

VII. THE EPOCH OF THE BODY

The broader historical and theoretical stakes of these remarks should now be clear. The reception of contemporary psychoanalytic theory has been subject to a peculiar instability, one that bears decisively on the problem of the body. For the horizon of our thinking is such that the opposition between nature and culture distorts the very concepts it promises to elucidate. But if the reception of psychoanalysis is profoundly unstable today, this is not only due to its ambiguous *theoretical* position. It is therefore insufficient to point to a conceptual difficulty, noting that readers are constantly tempted to translate psychoanalysis, interpreting it by trying to decide whether psychoanalysis regards the body as a natural fact or a cultural construction. If the reception of psychoanalysis is ambiguous and unstable, it is not simply for conceptual reasons, but also because of the *historical* position of psychoanalytic theory, the peculiar challenge it represents in relation to the inherited configuration of our knowledge, by exceeding the alternative between biological and symbolic models.

This genealogical claim should help to clarify the peculiar deformations in the reception of psychoanalysis today. But it should also allow us to see why the body has come to play such a decisive role in contemporary cultural theory. For if the body has acquired an unprecedented degree of attention today, drawing scholars in virtually every field to discuss it, this is not simply because the body is suddenly "in fashion." On the contrary, it is only in fashion today because it must be discussed, because it represents an impasse in the very arrangement of our knowledge, obliging research in a great diversity of fields to come to grips with it. The question of embodiment is thus not simply a *theoretical* problem, but a problem that has emerged for strictly *historical* reasons. This also means, however, that while a certain historical necessity has led the body to require attention in a great variety of disciplines, the body simultaneously remains obscure, and for precisely the same reason, insofar as our ways of addressing it remain attached to forms of thought that are inadequate to the very phenomenon they seek to address.

This is what it means to speak of the "epoch of the body": if we take seriously the historical necessity of the contemporary interest in the body, and do not simply dismiss it as a fashion, we would have to regard it not only as an enigma that poses a *conceptual* challenge, but also as an epochal matter—a problem that arises from within the history of our thought, as a rupture within that history. As an "intersection" between nature and culture, the body can indeed become a phenomenon for both natural and historical sciences; and yet it simultaneously marks a point of excess that calls into question the very techniques that seek to address it, exceeding the alternative between biological and symbolic models. In this sense, it may no longer be a matter of asking whether the body belongs to biology or history, but of considering that the body may mark the very limit of this alternative, the point at which this debate between nature and nurture has reached an impasse. We have tried to suggest how this difficulty bears on the reception of contemporary psychoanalytic theory, which is, in many respects, a theory that is still waiting to be read.

ABBREVIATIONS

Lacan

E   *Écrits* (Paris: Seuil, 1966). A portion of this volume has appeared in English as *Écrits: A Selection*, trans. Alan Sheridan (New York: Norton, 1977). References will be given to both volumes, whenever possible, French pagination first, English second. Translations are occasionally modified.

FS	*Feminine Sexuality: Jacques Lacan and the école freudienne*, eds. Juliet Mitchell and Jacqueline Rose, trans. Jacqueline Rose (New York: Norton, 1985).

SII	*The Seminar of Jacques Lacan, Book II: The Ego in Freud's Theory and in the Technique of Psychoanalysis, 1954–55*, ed. Jacques-Alain Miller, trans. Sylvana Tomaselli, with notes by John Forrester (New York: Norton, 1988).

SXI	*Le Séminaire, livre XI: Les quatres concepts fondamentaux de la psychanalyse*, ed. Jacques-Alain Miller (Paris: Seuil, 1973). *The Four Fundamental Concepts of Psychoanalysis*, trans. Alan Sheridan (New York: Norton, 1978). References will be given to both volumes, French pagination first, English second; translations are occasionally modified.

SXVII	*Le Séminaire, livre XVII: L'envers de la psychanalyse (1969–70)*, ed. Jacques-Alain Miller (Paris: Seuil, 1991).

T	"Television," trans. Denis Hollier, Rosalind Krauss, and Annette Michelson in *Television: A Challenge to the Psychoanalytic Establishment*, ed. Joan Copjec (New York: Norton, 1990).

Freud

SE	*The Standard Edition of the Complete Psychological Works of Sigmund Freud*, trans. James Strachey, ed. James Strachey et al. (London: The Hogarth Press, 1953). 24 volumes. Works will be cited by volume and page number.

NOTES

1. I first began to consider the position of psychoanalysis in relation to current debates over nature and culture during a postdoctoral fellowship at the Commonwealth Center for Literary and Cultural Change, at the University of Virginia. I am indebted to Dell Hymes and Ralph Cohen, for running a seminar on "Cultural Evolution" which helped me to see the complexity of the arguments on both sides of this debate, but particularly among those scholars who are trying to elaborate more satisfactory biological models of cultural evolution. These are models that Freud would certainly reject, but they are more careful and sophisticated than their critics sometimes imply. I also thank Hubert Dreyfus, David Hoy, and the National Endowment for the Humanities, for the Institute on Embodiment at Santa Cruz that allowed me to develop this work.
2. I have discussed this text in more detail in "Adaequatio Sexualis: Is There a Measure of Sexual Difference?" *From Phenomenology to*

Thought, Errancy, and Desire, ed. Babette Babich (Dordrecht: Kluwer, 1995), pp. 445–71.

3. As Lacan's use of the Borromean knot suggests, the three orders of imaginary, symbolic and real are mutually constitutive, such that the "real," while not being simply an effect or product of language (in which case it would be reducible to the symbolic), is nevertheless constituted *through* and *in relation* to the imaginary and symbolic orders. The "real" therefore cannot be properly regarded as equivalent to a "prediscursive reality." See Tim Dean, "Transsexual Identification, Gender Performance Theory, and the Politics of the Real," *literature and psychology*, 39:4 (1993), pp. 1–27.

4. For an argument contesting the link between Foucault and historicism, see Charles Shepherdson, "History and the Real: Foucault with Lacan," *Postmodern Culture* [an electronic journal published by Johns Hopkins University Press], 5:2 (January 1995).

5. This point often arises in Marxist and Habermasian readings of Foucault, which ask how Foucault can provide a form of critique if he regards the subject as a "product" of history, subject to historical formation, and apparently unable to reflect upon that history in a rational way. For his response to these objections, see Michel Foucault, "What is Enlightenment?" *The Foucault Reader*, ed. Paul Rabinow (New York: Pantheon, 1984), pp. 32–50, and "The Concern for Truth," *Michel Foucault: Politics, Philosophy, Culture*, ed. Lawrence Kritzman (New York: Routledge, 1988), pp. 255–67.

6. In *Unbearable Weight: Feminism, Western Culture, and the Body* (Berkeley: University of California Press, 1993), Susan Bordo provides an excellent account of the social dimension of anorexia. From the perspective of psychoanalysis, however, she tends to avoid the task of determining why some women rather than others become anorexic, a task that requires a more precise account of the subject's *relation* to the social order. I discuss the Lacanian perspective on anorexia and orality in more detail in "The Gift of Love and the Debt of Desire," forthcoming in *Differences: A Journal of Feminist Cultural Studies.*

7. This seminar contains the "four discourses" (of the "master," the "university," the "hysteric," and the "analyst"). It is briefly described by Juliet Mitchell and Jacqueline Rose in *Feminine Sexuality*, in their notes to "A Love Letter" (pp. 160–61), though the seminar is incorrectly identified as seminar 18.

8. Robert Samuels, *Between Philosophy and Psychoanalysis: Lacan's Reconstruction of Freud* (New York: Routledge, 1993), p. 83. See also the discussion of this Lacanian formula in Slavoj Žižek, *For they know not what they do: Enjoyment as a political factor* (New York: Verso, 1991), pp. 21–7.

9. Several useful accounts of Lacan's four discourses have appeared. See Sylvia A. Rodríguez and Leonardo S. Rodríguez, "On the Transference," *Analysis*, no. 1 (1989), 165–85; Robert Samuels, *Between Philosophy and Psychoanalysis*; and Mark Bracher, *Lacan, Discourse, and Social Change: A Psychoanalytic Cultural Criticism* (Ithaca: Cornell University Press, 1993). Patricia Elliot has suggested that the four discourses may be used to distinguish the theoretical positions of various movements within psychoanalytic feminism itself, in *From Mastery to Analysis: Theories of Gender in Psychoanalytic Feminism* (Ithaca: Cornell University Press, 1991). See also Eric Laurent, "Alienation and Separation," *Reading Seminar XI: Lacan's Four Fundamental Concepts of Psychoanalysis*, eds. Richard Feldstein, Bruce Fink, Maire Jaanus (Albany: State University of New York Press, 1995), pp. 19–38.

10. For an excellent account of the way the distinction between "sex" and "gender" has functioned in the recent history of feminist theory, and of certain impasses or complications that have arisen from the use of these terms, particularly in the reception of continental feminism, see Tina Chanter, *Ethics of Eros: Irigaray's Rewriting of the Philosophers* (New York: Routledge, 1995), pp. 21–46.

11. Simon Levay, *The Sexual Brain* (Cambridge: MIT Press, 1993); Anne Moir and David Jessel, *Brain Sex: The Real Difference Between Men and Women* (New York: Dell, 1989); Thomas Laqueur, *Making Sex: Body and Gender from the Greeks to Freud* (Cambridge: Harvard, 1990); John Winkler, *The Constraints of Desire: The Anthropology of Sex and Gender in Ancient Greece* (New York: Routledge, 1990). As the latter two examples suggest, it is possible for historians of science to argue for historical construction in the case of sex, just as much as in the case of gender, since biological theories have a history as much as social practices governing gender do. This complication, however, does not alter the framework in which nature and history are opposed as two alternatives; it merely puts sex on the historical side, like gender.

12. See Sarah Kofman, *L'énigme de la femme: La Femme dans les textes de Freud* (Paris: Galilée, 1980), pp. 43 and 125–27; *The Enigma of Woman: Woman in Freud's Writings*, trans. Catherine Porter (Ithaca: Cornell University Press, 1985), pp. 36 and 106–08.

13. As Constance Penley says, the effacement of the term "sexual difference" in favor of sociohistorical accounts of gender can be seen in "the recently renewed will to purge feminism of psychoanalysis [which] takes the form of a call to substitute 'gender' for 'sexual difference' as an analytic category for feminist theory—thus displacing the role of the unconscious in the formation of subjectivity and sexuality—or to substitute a theory of a *socially* divided and contradictory subject for one that is psy-

chically split." Constance Penley, "Missing *m/f*," *The Woman in Question*, ed. P. Adams and E. Cowie (Cambridge: MIT Press, 1990), p. 7.

14. See, for example, Mikkel Borch–Jacobsen, *Lacan: The Absolute Master*, trans. Douglas Brick (Stanford: Stanford University Press, 1991); Jonathan Scott Lee, *Jacques Lacan* (Boston: Twayne, 1990 [Amherst: University of Massachusetts, 1991]); Peter Dews, *The Logics of Disintegration: post–structuralist thought and the claims of critical theory* (London: Verso, 1987); and David Macey, *Lacan in Contexts* (London: Verso, 1988).

15. Alexandre Kojève, *Introduction to the Reading of Hegel: Lectures on the Phenomenology of Spirit*, assembled by Raymond Queneau, ed. Allan Bloom, trans. James H. Nichols, Jr. (Ithaca: Cornell University Press, 1980 [Basic Books, 1969]), p. 6. Citations will henceforth appear in the text.

16. Jonathan Scott Lee, *Jacques Lacan*, p. 58–59. Citations will henceforth appear in the text.

17. *King Lear*, Act II, scene iv.

18. As Richard Boothby notes, "Desire is articulated in that Other beyond the imaginary other." See *Death and Desire: Psychoanalytic Theory in Lacan's Return to Freud* (New York: Routledge, 1991), p. 164. On the same page Boothby also cites the unpublished *Seminar V*: "at the level of this intersection of desire and the signifying line, it encounters what? It encounters the other . . . It encounters the other, I did not say as a person—it encounters the other as the treasury of the signifier" (SV, 1/8/58).

19. This passage seems to have been virtually quoted by Michel Foucault in *The Order of Things*, in the section titled "The Cogito and the Unthought." See Michel Foucault, *Les mots et les choses: une archéologie des sciences humaines* (Paris: Gallimard, 1966), pp. 333–39; *The Order of Things: An Archaeology of the Human Sciences*, trans. Alan Sheridan (New York: Vintage, 1970), pp. 322–28. Although Lacan's *Écrits* was only published in 1966 (the same year as *The Order of Things*), this lecture, "The Agency of the Letter," was given to a group of philosophers at the Sorbonne in 1957, and was published in a special issue of *La Psychanalyse* (volume 3) entitled *Psychanalyse et sciences de l'homme*.

20. It would be possible to argue that Kojève's argument already presents intersubjectivity within a quasi-linguistic network of exchange, such that the relation between two partners or rivals would only be conceivable on the basis of a symbolic medium that transcends them both. Jean Hyppolite, at least, has made this argument with reference to Hegel (rather than to Kojéve). See Jean Hyppolite, "The Structure of Philosophic Language According to the 'Preface' to Hegel's

Phenomenology of the Mind," *The Structuralist Controversy: The Languages of Criticism and the Sciences of Man,* eds. Richard Macksey and Eugenio Donato (Baltimore: The Johns Hopkins University Press, 1970), pp. 157–69.

21. I take the phrase "dualistic ontology" from Mikkel Borch-Jacobsen, who uses it in *Lacan: The Absolute Master,* where he argues that Lacan remains trapped within a Kojèvean model.

22. Kelly Oliver, *Reading Kristeva: Unraveling the Double-Bind* (Bloomington: Indiana University Press, 1993), p. 32. Oliver goes on to note, however, that "Kristeva may be oversimplifying Lacan's theory of drives" (p. 33).

23. For a useful account of the unpublished *Seminar V,* and a commentary on the "graph of desire," see Joël Dor, *Introduction la lecture de Lacan: l'inconscient structuré comme un langage* (Paris: Denoël, 1985), esp. pp. 97–113. Especially relevant sections of *Seminar XI* include pp. 185–208 (English pp. 203–229). For the graph of desire see Jacques Lacan, "Subversion du sujet et dialectique du désir dans l'inconscient freudien" (E, 793–827/292–325).

24. Slavoj Žižek, *Looking Awry: An Introduction to Jacques Lacan through Popular Culture* (Cambridge: MIT, 1991), p. 21.

ELEVEN

DISCIPLINING THE DEAD

KEVIN O'NEILL

During much of the nineteenth century the
boundary between life and death was unclear. [1]

For Americans of the twentieth century, connections
between the world of the dead and that of the living
have been largely severed. [2]

INTRODUCTION:
FROM THE ANNEXATION OF HEAVEN TO THE DYING OF DEATH

Death seems so irreducible a reality that sketching its history might seem foolish. How much can death change? Yet death does change, and its changes tell us much about how the culture in which this happens is faring. Death in America changed radically from the mid-nineteenth to the early twentieth centuries. At mid-century, before the spiritual and material changes occasioned by the Civil War, and as industrialization, urban life, and immigration from Europe were altering the texture of life, death was widely regarded as a simple transition. Dying did not mean an unbridgeable separation from the living, and representations of the dead—in memorial photography, cemeteries, and popular literature—all suggested continuity between the living and the dead. By the end of the century the dead had been relegated to a marginal position in culture, and the sense of connection between the living and the dead had been lost. If Americans of 1850 were guilty of "annexing Heaven," [3] those of the turn of the century were exulting in the "dying of death," [4] and celebrating death's disappearance from their lives. Representations of the dead in this later period—in photographs, funeral practices, and cemetery designs—illustrate this alienation between living and dead, and furnish images through which we can think of our current distance from the dead.

PART ONE:
THE ANNEXATION OF HEAVEN:
MEMORIAL PORTRAITS, RURAL CEMETERIES,
AND LITERARY HEAVENS

> *"There is no death", what seems so is transition;*
> *This life of mortal breath*
> *Is but the suburb of the life elysian*
> *Whose portal we call Death.*

Poem inscribed on gravemarker of James Pilling [5]

In 1850 people died at home, often without a doctor in attendance. The body was washed, dressed, and laid out by family members. Local carpenters were called in to make a simple coffin.

The middle-class home in which death occurred had special importance, as well as a special fragility. America was urbanizing and changing more rapidly than at any other time in its history: ". . . the proportion of people living in cities (between 1820 and 1860) rose by 797 per cent."[6] As cities grew, relationships among people changed. The changing scale of the city forced all residents to confront new, even alien work and interpersonal relationships,

> to confront the sights and sounds of an accelerated urban economy. . . .
> This shift from country to city, from farm to factory, was perhaps the
> most fundamentally dislocating experience in all of American history.[7]

And "most devastating was the break in the ways individuals associated with each other."[8] The network of households linked together by blood ties in the rural world was under pressure as more people moved to cities in which the nuclear family was isolated in its single home. Since work was moving out of the home as industrialization led to the specialization of labor, the home was a nonproductive haven in which wives and mothers offered moral instruction to children and provided a respite from commerce for their entrepreneurial mates:

> Because the home defied economic rationalization and eluded the cash
> nexus, it came to be seen as a separate social sphere, a retirement or retreat
> from the larger world . . . . "The central convention of domesticity . . . was
> the contrast between the home and the world."[9]

The center of this home was the parlor, in which weddings and funerals took place, in which the private life of the family intersected with the world of commerce, the realm of strangers.

> The parlor was the front room of the middle-class home where friends, acquaintances, and carefully screened strangers met formally "in society". Geographically, it lay between the urban street where strangers freely mingled and the back regions of the house where only family members were permitted to enter uninvited. . . . The parlor provided the woman of the house with a "cultural podium" from which she was to exert her moral influence over American society. [10]

This middle-class home, freighted with its new moral significance, was also the site of death. In 1850 young people died, proportionally more frequently, more quickly, and with less effect on their vigorous appearance and youthful beauty. Viral and bacterial infections that acted on major systems—respiratory, gastrointestinal, circulatory—killed young people who had not had time to build up immunity and older people with weak systems.

Wives died in childbirth or from infections and hemorrhages that followed it. Men died of heart attacks, strokes and embolisms, because of a fat-rich diet and the stress of a commercially-driven life.

Others, fewer, died after prolonged suffering. Cancer, which was less common but also less subject to surgical intervention, was the cause of prolonged, tortured deaths, as were tubercular and other infections.

Virtually all of these people died at home in their beds. Hospitals were reserved for the indigent or those without friends or family and were sites of death rather than of cure.

Death at home in the urbanizing nineteenth-century home was somewhat different from death in earlier rural homes because the new urban home was more isolated from a traditional social network and from extended family, and the urban home was a center for moral training and for respite from the stresses of commercial activity.

The meeting of the new urban middle-class home and its moral idealism with the dead, especially the young dead, produced representations of the dead that inscribed the dead in a "cult of domesticity," and kept them alive within the family. Memorial portraits, the monuments in rural cemeteries, as well as the design of such cemeteries and the descriptions of the dead in Heaven in consolation literature, all placed the dead, as if still alive, in the protective bosom of the family—as if, in a world in which traditional kinship and community ties were breaking down, every family member, dead or alive, were vitally important and not to be surrendered, and as if that person were still a subject for moral training and protection from the larger world.

The home as the site of moral instruction and of death, and the home as centered in the parlor, all played a role in the new photographic representations of the dead. The middle-class dead were routinely photographed in the home in which they had died and they were routinely depicted using the conventions of the miniature portrait. The subject, if depicted alone, was usually standing or sitting, either facing the camera directly or looking off slightly to one side. If the portrait was a family portrait, the scene was often of a parent and a small child, the parent seated and the child perched on the father's or mother's knee. If the portrait was of a very small child, or an infant, the subject was usually pictured as if asleep, stiller than a living baby could ever be.

These three styles of portrait were transferred directly to the dead, with no alterations in pose or composition. There was no concession made to the fact that the subject was not alive. He or she was pictured in everyday clothing, sitting on a love seat or sofa in the family parlor, or standing by a small table, or sleeping in her crib. Most often the subject's eyes were closed, as if they might be in a light sleep. There were sometimes tell-tale symbols, like roses held in the hand, that indicated that the subject was dead. At other times the subject's eyes were open and it was difficult to tell whether the subject was alive or dead .

One effect of these portrait-like images of the dead, who looked as if they were alive, was to keep the dead family member among the living. This "living" member, or her representation, would remain with the family, displayed in its case in the parlor, to be looked at and mourned over as the years passed. These images were often a consolation to the living, especially if they were of young children, because they represented people who would never be sullied by commerce, and who were therefore innocent and pure, thus instantiating the central values of the middle-class home. If the dead were kept safe, as images, in the bosom of a home seen as a haven, they also made the home safe by representing the sort of moral innocence that homes promoted.

Furthermore, in an age when Americans believed strongly in an afterlife, memorial photographs represented a family member who was gone, but also a family member whom one could look forward to seeing again in Heaven.

I want to suggest, in addition, that the dead were kept "alive" in the home, and especially in the parlor, as portraits, because in portraits one's character gets revealed. The history of portraiture in the West strongly suggests, as Brilliant among others argues,[11] that being the subject of a portrait indicates a certain pre-eminence in the one portrayed. It meant that one was either sufficiently powerful or notorious or good to warrant such a depiction.

Ordinary individuals became fit subjects for portraits during the late Renaissance because, with the increased secularization of life and the emergence of a middle class, successful patriarchs of this class were considered men of sufficient probity to warrant portraitic memorialization. Later, the wives and children of such individuals also became subjects of portraits, because they too were felt to be of sufficient moral presence to justify such memorials. Their wealth was evidence of worthiness, based, as it was believed to be, on hard work, prudence, and good personal habits.

This turn to portraits of private citizens was encouraged by the republican ideologies that prevailed in the United States, though the practice was discouraged by Puritan theology. If most of the dead were believed to be condemned to Hell, making and showing portraits of deceased people was in highly questionable taste.

However, a new religious optimism mitigated this diffidence. Most Americans by the 1850s believed that nearly all of the dead were saved. Depictions of the deceased were representations of the saved, as well as of the morally upright, and thus pictures of the dead could reveal the saved condition and high moral character, or innocence, of the deceased.

Photographic representations were believed to be even better means for representing moral probity and innocence than were painted portraits, because of their greater verisimilitude. If, as was commonly believed, "outer physical features could be clues to inner character,"[12] and portraits "could express the essence of the subject, the true moral character,"[13] then daguerreotypes, with their almost preternatural clarity, could be seen as "the completely true depiction of nature."[14] Holgrave, Hawthorne's daguerreotypist protagonist in *House of the Seven Gables*, summarizes the age's typical response to photographic representations: "While we give it credit only for depicting the merest surface, it actually brings out the secret character with a truth no painter would ever venture upon, could he detect it."[15] Thoreau concurs. He believes that ". . . the daguerreotype reveals how an exact and accurate description of facts can release symbolic resonances and implications."[16]

Thus, the post-mortem photograph became a precious and accurate record of the worth of the deceased, and it entered the parlor as a part of the family's self-representation to the outer world. Daguerreotype portraits were photographic substitutes for the "missing" family members; when one met and visited the family in its parlor, one also met and visited its worthy dead.

The young dead, considered innocent, instantiated in their photographs the virtues that the home existed to inculcate and protect. And the older dead stood for the fact that even those who had engaged in commerce outside the home were, finally, defined by their membership in the family and, in death, reintegrated in their recaptured moral innocence (for death was seen as a great cleanser) into the pure family life from which they had emerged into the world.

The family-based retreat from the urban world offered by the middle class home and its gallery of post-mortem portraits was mimicked almost exactly in the rural cemeteries that flourished during this period, where one could find monuments carved in the shape of children sleeping in their cribs that, as Snyder writes, ". . . establish clear visual correlations between the child and the home."[17]

The first rural cemetery, Mount Auburn in Cambridge, was planned by horticulturists to recall a simpler rural past in which Americans lived closer to innocent and pure Nature and to each other. Rural cemeteries were laid out in hilly terrain, and were laced with broad, winding "streets" that gave onto unexpected vistas and hidden glades and dells. They were heavily planted with trees, shrubs, and flowers, and dotted with a wide variety of monuments, mausoleums, chapels, and crypts.

They were like the middle-class home, and the middle-class neighborhood, in two respects. First, rural cemeteries were planned around the nuclear family. Every cemetery lot was sold to individual families, who were free to design its monuments and plantings without asking permission from the cemetery administration so that "the family dominated the landscape of the dead."[18] Americans saw the rural cemetery "grave as a home in which the deceased rested with family and friends. Just as the family was the central unit of civil society, so also would it be the organizational unit of the rural cemetery."[19] As Sloane puts it, "Within these picturesque grounds, lot-holders wished to celebrate their heritage and success. Family lots became means through which middle class Americans could commemorate their families."[20] And families took such a hand in designing and separating their plots that later cemetery managers complained: they "decried the tendency in . . . people to be as exclusive and private in their lots as in their dwellings."[21]

This leads to the second tie between rural cemeteries and the home and neighborhood. Both were retreats from the world of commerce and both privileged moral training and reflection: "Conceptions of home, suburb, and the rural cemetery as utopian retreats served as a safety valve"[22] and "Like the home the grave was portrayed as a haven in the heartless world"[23] where people found "an asylum from their industrialized work place."[24]

In rural cemeteries, "Those yearning for a sense of community lost found gratification."[25] and "Rural cemeteries were promoted as an answer to the confusion and complexity of urban life,"[26] because "Americans identified domestic tranquillity with . . . horticulture."[27] "Supporters had designed them to fulfill the same sanctuary functions as the home was traditionally supposed to serve."[28] Just as the tranquillity of the bourgeois home made it a site of moral education, so in the tranquillity of the rural cemetery people found instruction: as Justice Story looked out on Boston, and into Mount Auburn, standing on one of its heights, he was moved to reflect: ". . . we stand on the borders of two worlds, and . . . we may gather lessons of profound wisdom by contrasting the one with the other."[29] Religious worthies like William Ellery Channing and John Pierpont "argued that pastoral cemeteries served as schools of moral philosophy and catalysts for civic virtue," because their natural tranquillity offered the chance, among the memorials to the dead, to "contemplate the meaning and management of their lives."[30] As Alexander Everett of Boston wrote: "How salutary is the effect which a visit to its calm and sacred shades will produce on souls too much agitated by the storms of the world."[31]

If rural cemeteries, and their family lots, were analogous to the bourgeois home in the ways cited above, the dead in rural cemeteries were also characterized very much as they were in memorial portraiture. In the rural cemetery the dead under the ground were most often represented above the ground either by monuments that gestured toward home or by forms like obelisks and urns that gestured toward Egyptian and classical symbols of immortality. Thus, as in the case of post-mortem portraiture, the dead were represented as in some sense living: "The rural cemetery became home to monuments that were stonework versions of mourning paintings."[32]

This theme of death-in-life in the context of membership in the family was strikingly evidenced in the common children's gravemarkers , small beds or chairs in which children were gently sleeping. These monuments "establish(ed) clear visual correlations between the child and the home, the purity of nature, and symbols of childhood."[33] Thus, the bed sculptures refer to the nursery, seen as "a moral incubator."[34]

And in all these references from monument to child to home, "Euphuistic sepulchral inscriptions like 'asleep in Jesus', a favorite for children's graves, poetically stressed the continuing presence of the deceased,"[35] because in the economy of the sentimental American middle class family at mid-century,

> It is absolutely essential that the deceased not truly die. The planned and picturesque new "rural cemeteries" promoted and rapturously described by the same groups who produced consolation literature . . . were dedicated to the idea that the living and the dead still cared.[36]

As Miss Martineau, an English visitor, remarked, "A visitor from a strange planet . . . would take this place (a rural cemetery) to be the sanctum of creation. Every step teems with the promise of life.'" [37]

The rural cemetery was thus seen as an analog of home, as a site of life, and the monuments gestured toward a reaffirmation of the immortality of the dead, and toward home. These monuments in their size and serious-ness, and in the fact that they recorded the life and death of the beloved deceased, in incised inscriptions on the stone, also reaffirmed, as did the photographic portraits, the innocence and moral probity of the dead, their worthiness to be included in these cemetery analogs of home.

This reflection offers a transition to the third site of representation of the dead, the descriptions of Heaven offered in consolation literature. If middle-class homes and rural cemeteries were family-centered havens in a heartless world, "oases of safety," within which the beloved dead were kept "alive," these same themes are even more clearly presented in the descrip-tions of Heaven offered in consolation literature. Consolation literature, as defined by Ann Douglas in her essay "Heaven Our Home," consisted of "openly fictionalized and avowedly factual accounts of deathbed scenes and celestial communication . . . whose purpose is clearly consolatory, whose authors, in other words, are writing to reach and comfort those suf-fering bereavement and loss." This literature, which "crowded the book-stalls in the decades before the Civil War," crossed many genres, including "prayer manuals, poetry, hymns, fiction and biographies."[38]

I will restrict most of my attention to the work of Elizabeth Stuart Phelps, the most popular consolation novelist, who wrote a series of books about Heaven and edited a book containing poems that she claimed were written by dead people and transmitted to this world through spiritualist mediums. The novels that will be the focus of my special attention are *The Gates Ajar* and *Beyond the Gates*.[39]

In both novels the protagonist—in each case named Mary—lives and dies, or appears to die in a middle class home occupied primarily by women. The themes that dominate both works are familiar ones. First, the novels argue forcefully and at length that when a loved one dies, she is not lost or changed, save to be improved. The familial dead are still interested in the living, still care about the living, and are even physically close to the living. In *The Gates Ajar*, Mary is talking to her aunt Winifred about whether her brother, who was killed in the Civil War, still loves her, and whether there can be contact between them.

> "Roy loved you. Our Father, for some tender hidden reason, took him out of your sight for a while. Though changed much, he can have for-gotten nothing. Being only out of sight . . . not lost, nor asleep . . . he goes on loving. To love must mean to think of, to care for, to hope and pray for."

> "But that must mean—why, that must mean—"

> "That he is near you. I don't doubt it."[40]

Family ties survive death. Roy "is near." This theme is repeated in *Beyond the Gates* when the other Mary returns to witness her funeral and by her unseen presence soothes grieving family members.

Not only can we love and care beyond death; in Heaven, families will be reunited, and live in homes that resemble the idealized havens described in this essay.

> Do you think you'll see him again? You might as well ask me if I thought God made you and made Roy, and gave you to each other. See him! Of course you'll see him as you saw him here . . . (and) . . . he will still love his sister as himself . . . (because) . . . He is not any the less Roy, who will love you . . . and be very glad to see you.[41]

This family reunion theme is played out more literally in *Beyond the Gates*, when Mary notes that Heaven is made up of homes that are perfected versions of middle-class American homes:

> Was Heaven an aggregate of homes like this? Did everlasting life move on in the same dear ordered channel—the dearest that human experiment has ever formed—the channel of family love? Was there always in the eternal world "somebody to come home to?" And was there always the knowledge that it could not be the wrong person? Was all that eliminated from celestial domestic life?[42]

If family love and the home are important, so is the idea that Heaven itself, like a capacious home, is the perfect haven from a heartless world. Heaven has beautiful landscapes like a rural cemetery, and, like such a cemetery, cities in which there is no poverty, violence, or drunkenness— and no commerce.

> Chiefly, I think, I had a consciousness of safety—infinite safety. All my soul drew a long breath—"Nothing more can happen to me."[43]

Thus, as safe haven, Heaven is a "continuation of the domestic sphere", and is also a continuation because in Heaven, the moral values praised in the home are exalted as they are not on earth. In Phelps's Heaven the highest honor was given to women who had sacrificed for others or endured pain without complaint.

Finally, Phelps's Heaven surpasses the middle-class home and the rural cemetery in denying death to its dead inhabitants. The dead in Heaven, unlike the dead in rural cemeteries, are not asleep; nor are they, like the dead in portraits, immobile. The dead have "lives" that are more vital than their earthly lives, and have bodies that are improved versions of their earthly ones:

I saw that I myself was not . . . greatly changed. I had form and dress, and moved at will, and experienced sensations of great pleasure and, above all, of magnificent health.

Beautiful, too, I suppose we shall be, every one. We shall find them (our bodies) vastly convenient.

Given: a pure heart, perfect health . . . the elimination from . . . life of anxiety and separation.[44]

Phelps's Heaven serves as the third site of the representation of the dead in antebellum America. In all three the dead appear in a family/home setting, and in each the dead are defined by the moral values of innocence, purity, and sincerity that were dear to the middle-class home. In each case the dead, as represented, are kept alive in the home/cemetery/Heaven, as if the beleaguered middle-class home at mid-century, isolated from its rural roots and separated from the world of commerce, could not afford to let any of its members, and especially the young innocent dead, go, lest the home become more vulnerable to the amoral world of commerce that lurked just beyond the parlor door, and which had already, perhaps surreptitiously, penetrated the parlor and begun the long process of wresting control of the domesticated dead from their various morally protected havens.

PART TWO:
THE DYING OF DEATH:
CASKETS, EMBALMING, AND THE LAWN PARK CEMETERIES

The exile of the dead began when the family began to put the dead under the control of the world of commerce, which had been barred from the middle-class home. As soon as a daguerreotypist entered the parlor of the bourgeois home to "shoot" a dead person, a contest for control of the dead body and how it would be represented, between the home and the world of commerce, had begun. It was a contest that the home and family could not win.

Over the last four decades of the nineteenth century funeral professionals took increasing control of the body and the ways in which it could be shown. Funeral directors and cemetery managers as well as casket manufacturers and florists, symbolically or literally entered the parlor of the bourgeois home and transformed the scene of death, increasing the distance between the living and the dead, rendering memorial portraits, rural cemeteries, and consolation literature obsolete. These professionals took control of the rural cemetery and "rationalized" it, wresting control from families, turning an unprofitable if lovely site of mourning into an orderly and profitable, if less appealing, abode for the dead. The professionalization of death also led to a lessening of sentimentality. The object that had been a beloved family member worthy to be kept safe in the parlor in a photographic image, and which had had a post-mortem career in Heaven, was now taken away by professionals, embalmed and made up, and placed in a huge casket, immobilized rather than invigorated by death, prised loose entirely from its homely setting and reinserted in a funerary scene from which it could no longer emerge into a new life.

The Civil War marked a watershed in the contest over who would control representations of death. For the first time a major war was photographed. Matthew Brady and his assistants pictured camps, supply trains, arms depots, and battlefields. In the last category of images were pictures of what battles left behind—the corpses of the dead.

Hegel, in his *Lectures on Aesthetics*, wrote that Greek classical art was foreclosed as an aesthetic option by the crucifixion of Jesus.[45] The image of his once-beautiful, near-naked body twisted and bloody on the Cross redefined the simple appeal of the classical male nude, and indicated that Jesus's tortured body was trying to express a meaning too grand for any body in classical repose to express. Classical bodies, Hegel argued, are the last Western example of beauty in art in which there is a fit between the body represented and the idea it is required to express because in classical art the body perfectly and fully expressed what the ancients understood about the human soul and how it can inhabit bodies.

Something analogous to the death of classical art happened to post-mortem photographic portraits after the Civil War. The terrible images of battlefield death, in which the bodies of men were depicted sprawled in public, possibly rendered memorial portraits a cultural impossibility, as the twisted body of Christ rendered serene classical representations of the body impossible. Memorial photography survived the war, but after 1860 photographs of the dead were no longer portraits.

The second effect of the Civil War on representations of the dead had to do with how the war dead were deployed in graveyards. In 1855 the Cincinnati rural cemetery, Spring Grove, had hired Adolph Strauch, a German landscape architect, as its new director. Strauch found the rural cemetery far too disorderly a place. The variety of monuments, whose size and shape each family controlled, the plethora of different chapels and crypts and statues, sprawled across a landscape heavily planted with any number of different trees and shrubs, suggested to Strauch both a lack of planning and an economic mistake. Rural cemeteries were expensive to maintain because of their twisting pathways, their cluttered grounds, their lot fences, and the large areas devoted to nonproductive "scenery." It was very difficult to do effective gardening and lawn care in such places, and the large lots were not good money-makers. Strauch proposed a different form of cemetery, the lawn park type, in which central cemetery management would have much more control over the size and types of monuments and plantings, and the deployment of headstones across open, unobstructed lawns. Far from being a complex picturesque geography for quiet retreat and contemplation, the newer cemeteries were open lawns on which smaller, more uniform headstones were arranged in orderly rows. There were still plantings but these were far fewer and less dense. Cemetery management chose what to plant, and where. Monuments and mausoleums and chapels were fewer in number, and they were separated from the ordinary grave sites.

The changes in how cemeteries looked were a mirror of changes in the way they were being run. Postwar cemeteries were in the control of professional managers who sought to make a profit: "'Our modern cemeteries are modern because they are established and managed on business principles.'"[46] And "business principles" included getting control of individual plots and imposing a rigid order on them.

The newly formed AACS (American Association of Cemetery Superintendents) worked from a widespread cultural assumption that "'this is an age of organization. . . . We must cease our individual activities. No man liveth unto himself alone, and no man dieth to himself alone. This is an age of social life, and the social point of view.'"[47] In cemeteries, "'Individual rights must be subordinated to the general plan. . . . Civilization consists in subordinating the will of the individual to the comfort and well-being of all.'"[48] This meant that the superintendent must "'assert . . . complete control over the landscape. The first and most important thing is to get control of the ground.'"[49]

This rationalization of the cemetery was mimicked in the large cemeteries the government created for war dead. These military cemeteries, of which Arlington Cemetery is a prime example, followed an aesthetic similar to that embraced by Adolph Strauch. Row after row of identical, small, simple white markers represent the war dead. Rather than being individual members of specific nuclear families, the war dead were incorporated into a larger, fictional national "family" to which each equally belonged. Members of a great national army whose purposes were greater than the individual concerns of any soldier or family, these dead had been homogenized. This blank uniformity, which tends to separate the living from the dead by rendering all the dead alike, was a compensation for the grotesque chaos of the battlefield. That field of chance and unlooked-for death, that field of corpses, was replaced by the perfectly orderly field of clean white stones and lush green grass, undisturbed by the detritus, human and otherwise, of war.

The effect of lawn park and military cemeteries was a greater unity in the cemetery but a greater distance between the living and dead. Sloane gestures toward both tendencies:

> Cemeteries would become more parklike. Monuments would be more formalized and standardized. The artfulness of the landscape would become more obvious and more celebrated.

But:

> This formality . . . represented the distancing of the living from the dead.[50]

Farrell sums up the distancing effect of the new cemeteries in his discussion of the "pictorial ideal":

> The pictorial ideal . . . betrayed a psychological change in cemetery work, as nature became landscape, as panorama became picture, sight supplanted the other senses in experiencing the cemetery . . . the observer took up a mediated relationship with nature. The pictorial ideal presupposed a frame for the picture, and a spatial and psychological distance between the viewer and the view. Rural cemeteries had promoted a complete communion between people and nature, but park cemeteries reduced the connection to a point of visual contact.[51]

By the end of the nineteenth century the cemetery was no longer a surrogate home, the plot no longer a parlor.

The third effect of the war was to install the practice of embalming into the scene of death, a development that would radically change the way the dead looked, and the way in which they were displayed. The ramshackle buildings and the crude signs photographed immediately adjacent to battlefields as the dead were being collected and identified show that embalming was done on a rough and ready basis during the war. It is not entirely clear from the existing records whether the government subsidized such a practice, but the photographs indicate that it was a common practice, perhaps paid for by the families of the deceased.[52]

Embalming occurred because, first, there was a transportation infrastructure, the railroads, capable of moving the dead from the battlefields to their homes in other states. Second, the railroads could deliver bodies but could not do so quickly enough for them to be in any condition to be viewed or handled by family members, especially during the warmer months. The combination of a transportation system that was good enough to get bodies home but not good enough to get them home rapidly, made some form of preservation of the bodies of the war dead desirable. This is where embalmers entered the picture, a picture from which they have not been removed. As Habenstein and Lamers write: "by the time the last shot had been fired, this mode of preservation had secured for itself a permanent place in American funeral customs."[53]

Embalming the dead, which has never become the custom in other industrialized nations, became more popular in the United States until by the turn of the century it was more common than not. Americans grew accustomed to dealing with the embalmed dead during the Civil War. Second, Americans were more mobile than most other peoples, and families tended to disperse themselves over wide ranges of a large country. Relatives might have to travel from several distant states to participate in the funeral. Embalming made it possible to keep the dead body in an acceptable condition until such relatives could arrive.

But there is a subtext here. As the details of handling the dead body passed more and more, in the urban setting, from the control of the family and into the hands of professionals who would supply specially made coffins and caskets, grave clothes, carriages, and pallbearers, the practice of embalming became a critically important extra service offered by such professionals. This service added substantially to their income and placed the body much more firmly under the control of the funeral director, because embalming itself was a way of controlling the body and, once embalmed, the body must then be made up and laid out in ways consistent with this expensive preservative procedure.[54]

In fact, this third change imposed on the representation of the dead by the war coincided nicely with another change that does not seem related to the war, but to a concerted effort by funeral professionals to promote a new aesthetic of death, one that privileged "beautiful" corpses and equally beautiful surroundings. In this emergent aesthetic a central part came to be played by the newly named "casket," which replaced the coffin as the normal receptacle for housing the dead body.[55]

Caskets, unlike the more traditional coffin, were generally rectangular rather than shaped to the body. They were also made of more different materials. There were cast iron caskets, bronze caskets, cement caskets, cloth covered caskets, even rubber and wicker caskets, as well as caskets made of all sorts of different woods . What distinguished the casket from the coffin was that whereas the latter had been a simple convenience—a container in which the dead body could be laid out and carried to the grave—the former was designed to display the body, to render it more beautiful by providing it with a beautiful setting.

226

Even the name "casket" suggested that the dead body was a precious object, a jewel, perhaps, that required an elaborate container in which it could be safely held but also displayed.[56] With the introduction of the casket it was almost as if the body, having entered the commercial nexus created by funeral professionals, had now been transformed into a commodity, to be displayed to the public like something for sale in a shop window or showroom. As Habenstein and Lamers state, "There was an imminent desire on the part of the late nineteenth century burying public not only to display a body in its physical entirety, but to place it in a handsome setting, part of which is comprised by the casket."[57]

The embalmed body and the casket were connected. Before the war the body would be placed in a simple casket, so narrow that the arms of the corpse were most often tied together with a strip of cloth so the body could fit into the container. When it was photographed, it was rarely photographed in the casket, because such a depiction located the body on the other side of a divide between the living and the dead. Once the dead body was imbedded in the coffin, it had left the land of the living and entered a different geography.

The sentimental dead body was, rather, depicted among ordinary domestic scenes, perched on everyday furniture, wearing everyday clothes. It was not encumbered by its setting, but free within it. The new postwar dead were increasingly photographed lying as if asleep in their large, elaborate caskets, their bodies half-hidden, their eyes closed, positioned not to "look" into the camera as if sitting for a portrait, but faced nowhere in particular.

These photographs were not portraits because the dead person was not exactly their subject. Their subject was the funeral scene as a whole, of which the body made up the principal part. In these later pictures the surroundings all had references to death, and implicitly to the difference between the dead body and the bodies of the living. The deep casket in which the body was imbedded; the special funeral clothing; the arrangements of flowers, the very room itself, now no longer an ordinary room in an ordinary house but a room specifically designed for the display of death—all these artifacts captured the body in a chain of signifiers. Its meaning now developed from its relationship to the elements of the funerary scene, not with reference to the living.

It is also the case that photographers, like the family, had surrendered a great deal of their power to control the conditions of representation of the dead. It was now no longer the conventions and aesthetics of portraiture that controlled how the dead were represented even in photographs. Rather, what the photographer was doing was merely recording a scene already composed, according to a new aesthetic and a new convention, by the funeral professional, who had become the new director of the scene of death.

In this scene the dead body itself had been replaced by a transformed, embalmed, and cosmeticized version of itself. The body represented in prewar photographs was a vulnerable and awkward body, subject to the distortions of rigor mortis, the signs of which are evident in many post-mortem portraits. The embalmed body was composed, laid out carefully, in a canonical pose. It was recumbent, as if asleep, hands folded modestly across the lower abdomen. Prewar bodies, however conventional the poses they were permitted to assume, have a greater variety of looks and dispositions. The embalmed body had a single pose, just as the military cemetery had a single sort of headstone. In both cases the dead grew more remote by being cast into a single mold that always symbolizes death.

The embalmed body was also made "beautiful" by the application of specially produced postmortem cosmetics. Daguerreotypes were often lightly painted to reduce the harshness of their high contrast black and white textures. But the embalmed body itself is painted: it becomes auto iconic, a representation of itself, rendering post mortem portraits unnecessary.

Thus, the embalmed, cosmeticized body constituted by the funeral professional reinscribes in itself many of the motifs through which the prewar domestic body was represented. The body itself has become a kind of portrait of itself, though not one that stares back at any camera. It has also assumed, in public, its cemetery pose of sleeping. We need not any longer imagine the dead asleep in their rural cemeteries; they are asleep in the funeral parlor, asleep in their caskets. And this sleep is no longer an interval between wakings. It is permanent.

The new dead resemble the dead represented in consolation literature, in two ways. The embalmed and cosmeticized dead are more beautiful, with more durable, albeit more immobile, bodies than they ever had on earth. The embalmed dead, like the dead of consolation literature, are "improved." And the new dead have what might be characterized as a new career, as do the dead in consolation literature. Their career is very different: it is their job to be dead, and to remain unchanged in their deaths for as long as possible. The embalmed dead learn no languages and visit no bereaved families. Encased in their rigid bodies, filled with chemicals, imbedded in heavy caskets in concrete-vaulted graves, the new dead are imprisoned beneath the earth, their job to stay there, out of contact with the living.

In the postwar world, in which the control of bodies by funeral professionals altered the ways in which the dead appeared, a new form of the denial of death was taking hold in the culture, one that seems to have continued into our times. Now death is denied by being hidden from view. Even the embalmed body made for display hides the fact that the person represented has died. The dead person is hidden behind the makeup, hidden inside the enclosing casket, and under the minimalist monuments of the memorial park, no longer a dormitory, but a field of memories in which those who are sleeping are not expected to wake up again. If the earlier period annexed heaven and described the dead as if they were still alive, the later period has arranged for death itself to die, banishing the dead to special rooms in special homes, enclosing them in huge boxes, hiding them in parks.

The final phase of this dying of death was the passing of control from funeral professionals to health professionals. Today the dying disappear into hospitals and die hidden behind banks of medical equipment, their features erased by masks and catheters, their bodies overwhelmed by machinery. But that is another story. We have accompanied the dead on their journey from being colonized by the living to being banished from the scene of life. That is far enough for now.

NOTES

1. Charles Sloane, *The Last Great Necessity* (Baltimore: The Johns Hopkins University Press, 1991), p. 145.
2. Charles O. Jackson, "Death in American Life", Charles O. Jackson, ed., *Passing* (Westport: The Greenwood Press, 1977), p. 229.
3. Anonymous, "The Annexation of Heaven," *Atlantic Monthly*, New York, Vol. LIII, 1884.
4. Anonymous, "The Dying of Death," *Review of Reviews*, London, Volume 20, Sept., 1899.
5. Habenstein and Lamers, "Late Nineteenth Century Funerals," cited in Charles O. Jackson (ed.) *Passing*, p. 101.
6. Karen Halttunen, *Confidence Men and Painted Women* (New Haven: Yale University Press, 1977), p. 35.
7. Leroy Bowman, "The Effects of City Civilization," in Charles O. Jackson, *Passing*, p. 154.
8. Karen Halttunen, p. 58.
9. Halttunen, p. 58. The first citation is from Nancy F. Cott, *The Bonds of Womanhood* (New Haven: Yale University Press, 1977), p. 65. The second citation is Charles Burroughs, *An Address On Female Education*, delivered in Portsmouth, New Hampshire, October 26, 1827, quoted in Cott.
10. Halttunen, p. 59.
11. Richard Brilliant, *Portraiture* (n.a.: Reaktion Books, 1991).
12. Barbara McCandless, "The Portrait Studio and Celebrity," from Martha Sandweiss, ed., *Photography in Nineteenth Century America* (New York: Harry N. Abrams, 1991), p. 55.
13. McCandless, p. 55.
14. Trachtenberg, "Photography: The Emergence of a Key Word," from *Sandweiss*, p. 24.

15. Cited in Trachtenberg, p. 24.
16. Cited in Trachtenberg, p. 22.
17. Ellen Marie Snyder, "Innocents in A Worldly World: Victorian Children's Gravemarkers," in Richard E. Meyer, ed., *Cemeteries and Gravemarkers: Voices of American Culture* (Ann Arbor: University of Michigan Press, 1989), p. 13.
18. Charles David Sloane, *The Last Great Necessity* (Baltimore: The Johns Hopkins University Press, 1991), p. 7.
19. James J. Farrell, *Inventing the American Way of Death* (Philadelphia: Temple University Press, 1980), p. 106.
20. Sloane, p. 95.
21. Farrell, p. 120.
22. Farrell, p. 32.
23. Farrell, p. 106.
24. Blanche Linden-Ward, "Strange But Genteel Pleasure Grounds: Tourist and Leisure Uses of the Nineteenth Century Rural Cemetery," Meyer, p. 300.
25. Linden-Ward, p. 300.
26. Sloane, p. 12.
27. Sloane, p. 46.
28. Ann Douglas, "Heaven Our Home," in David E. Stannard, ed., *Death in America* (Philadelphia: Pennsylvania University Press, 1975), p. 61.
29. Cited in Farrell, p. 109.
30. Linden-Ward, p. 270.
31. Cited in Linden-Ward, p. 297.
32. David E. Stannard, "Sex, Death and Daguerreotypes: Toward An Understanding of Image as Elegy," in David E. Stannard, ed., *America and the Daguerreotype* (Iowa City: University of Iowa Press, 1991), p. 93.
33. Snyder, p. 13.
34. Snyder, p. 16.
35. Douglas, p. 61.
36. Douglas, p. 61.
37. Cited in Linden-Ward, p. 306.
38. Douglas, pp. 49–50.
39. Elizabeth Stuart Phelps, *The Gates Ajar* (Boston: Houghton and Mifflin, 1883).
40. *The Gates Ajar*, p. 87.
41. *The Gates Ajar*, p. 53.
42. *Beyond the Gates*, p. 126.
43. *Beyond the Gates*, p. 42.
44. *Beyond the Gates*, p. 44; *The Gates Ajar*, p. 122; *Beyond the Gates*, p. 181.
45. G.W.F. Hegel, *Aesthetics: Lectures on Fine Art* (Oxford: Oxford University Press, 1991, trans. by Knox), Volume One, pp. 502 ff.
46. Cited in Farrell, p. 199, quoting Howard Ward.
47. Cited in Farrell, pp. 116–117.
48. Farrell, p. 118.
49. Farrell, p. 119.
50. Sloane, pp. 107 and 120.

51. Farrell, p. 130.

52. See Roy Meredith, *Mr. Lincoln's Cameraman: Mathew Brady* (New York: Dover Publications, 1974), p. 194, Plate 20.

53. Robert Habenstein and William M. Lamers, *The History of American Funeral Directing* (Milwaukee: Bulfin Printers, 1962). See Chapter Seven.

54. Leroy Bowman, "The Effects of City Civilization," *Passing*, Charles O. Jackson, ed.

55. Habenstein and Lamers provide an account of the development of the casket from the coffin in Chapter Eight of their book.

56. Habenstein and Lamers, p. 270; Farrell, pp. 169, 170.

57. Habenstein and Lamers, p. 285.

TWELVE

THE PRESERVATION AND OWNERSHIP OF THE BODY

THOMAS F. TIERNEY

PART I: INTRODUCTION

In this essay I will examine the changing historical relationship between two fundamentally modern concepts: self-preservation and self-ownership. These two concepts have served a dual function in modernity. On the one hand, they are crucial parts of the theoretical underpinning of liberalism: the natural law of self-preservation is the foundation of the rational inclination to form civil society (e.g., Hobbes); and self-ownership provides the foundation for the liberal (i.e., Lockean) notion of private property. But on the other hand, these two concepts serve much more than a theoretical purpose; they also perform a duty in what I would like to call, borrowing Foucault's phrase, a modern technology of the self. At this level, the concepts of self-ownership and self-preservation shape individuals to follow certain routines in their behavior, to treat their bodies in specific ways, to organize their time in a particular fashion. In performing these routines, individuals participate in the collection and dissemination of that knowledge of individual bodies and groups of bodies which, as Foucault and Arendt in their different ways revealed, is endemic to modernity.

I am concerned here with both of these concepts in both of these functions, and their shifting interrelationship; for the practical activity of gathering, organizing, and using knowledge about bodies, especially in medicine and closely related disciplines, has recently caused disruptions in the juridical foundations of liberalism. Some recent challenges to medical authority, such as the right to die movement, are being made on the basis of self-ownership and/or self-preservation, concepts which I will argue once served an important role in making people amenable to the discipline of medicine. The legal response to these challenges, however, often throws those concepts into relief, opening them up to political contestation and, perhaps, creating the space for new techniques of the self to emerge.

In order to reveal some of the dimensions and implications of this late-modern disruption, this essay focuses primarily on the early-modern period, and covers a variety of discursive fields. I begin with a sketch of the way in which the content and function of self-preservation began to change in the religious context of seventeenth-century Puritanism. By using this lens of religious reformation, the difference between the traditional and modern conceptions of self-preservation is highlighted, and certain transformations which were occurring in the realms of medicine and political theory also become visible. After examining the role of self-preservation in Puritanism, I turn to seventeenth-century political thought, in which the preservation and ownership of the body were conceptually linked to form the juridical foundation of civil society. Then, in the third part of the essay, I briefly examine the role that self-ownership and self-preservation played in the popular medical literature of the seventeenth and eighteenth centuries, and suggest that here these concepts were deployed as a uniquely modern technique of the self. In the conclusion, I discuss the confusion which has emerged recently around this traditional relationship between self-ownership and self-preservation. After sketching the role that these two concepts play in the configurations of power in modernity, the implications of the recent wave of "bioethical" dilemmas, as well as the attendant possibilities, should become more apparent.

PART II:
THE REVALUATION OF SELF-PRESERVATION IN MODERNITY

The idea that a person could rank his or her own earthly existence at the very top of the moral scale is a modern phenomenon. In the premodern moral tradition, truly virtuous people had to be willing to give up their lives in certain circumstances, and I am referring here to nonmilitary circumstances. Even those moral philosophies that gave a prominent place to self-preservation, such as Aristotelianism and Stoicism, still held that good individuals should be willing to give up their lives in order to preserve their virtue. If I may be allowed one sweeping generalization at the outset, one could say that from Socrates to Thomas More, the most extreme manifestation of virtue in the West had always been a form of martyrdom for some ideal. This is no longer the case today, except in the case of military duty, but even this notion of duty has waned recently in the West. The individual that is fit for modernity was, and certainly still is, expected and encouraged to embrace its corporeal existence, and to be overwhelmingly concerned with the highly differentiated economy of earthly temporality. While earlier ethical systems and codes may have encouraged an intense concern about how one organized one's earthly time, the techniques of the self which have emerged in modernity, such as those associated with the standards of fitness, are unique in that they point toward no other benefit than a prolonged and pleasant earthly existence.[1]

This shift in the evaluation of earthly life did not occur in a flash. Rather, the revaluation of worldly existence began as early as the thirteenth century, with Aquinas, who reintroduced self-preservation as a universal good that all beings pursue:

> every substance seeks the preservation of its own being, according to its nature. And by reason of this inclination, whatever is a means of preserving human life and of warding off its obstacles belongs to the natural law (Aquinas, 222).[2]

For Aquinas, of course, the life which ultimately was to be preserved was that of the immortal soul. But while Aquinas clearly remained within the traditional framework that had contained the notion of self-preservation, it would not be too long before the ancient idea of self-preservation slipped these bonds and helped shape a new ethos that was fundamentally distinct from both Aristotelianism and Christianity.

By the sixteenth century, Calvin noticed a shift in the traditional relationship between earthly life and death. He was surprised and deeply disturbed that "many who boast of being Christians, instead of thus longing for death, are so afraid of it that they tremble at the very mention of it as a thing ominous and dreadful" (Calvin, II, 290). But while Calvin feared that Christians were clinging a little too tightly to earthly life, the Puritans of the seventeenth century had no difficulty embracing an ever-increasing attention toward earthly temporality. And the Puritans were concerned not only with the rational organization of earthly life for the glory of God, as Weber described in *The Protestant Ethic*; they were also greatly interested in preserving and ameliorating their earthly lives through the use of medicine.

In *The Great Instauration*, Charles Webster argues that many Puritan reformers viewed medical attempts to prolong life in light of their millennial eschatology.[3] They anticipated a utopian existence emerging after the apocalypse, and embraced developments in medical knowledge as harbingers of the eventual recovery of an immortal bodily existence which was lost through the Fall (Webster, 246–47). Francis Bacon provides an early example of this medicalization of the idea of self-preservation. Bacon praised Christ as "a Physician both of Soul and Body" (quoted in Webster, 247), and saw physicians as fulfilling a divinely sanctioned office. In the introduction to *The History of Life and Death* (1626), Bacon expresses the hope that inspires this publication:

that it may redound to the good of many; and that noble Physicians raising their minds, may not be wholly imployed in incleane cures, nor honoured only for necessity, but become also the Steward of Divine Omnipotency and Clemency, in prolonging and renewing the life of Man, especially since it may be done by safe, convenient, civill, but untryed new waies and meanes (Bacon, unnumbered).[4]

According to Webster, the Puritans linked "the conservation of health and prolongation of life" with the saving grace of God, and "came to regard a medical restoration as a corollary of their spiritual regeneration" (247). This use of physical health and illness as signs of one's religious status complements Weber's argument in *The Protestant Ethic*, that the Puritans ultimately came to view earthly success as a sign of one's election to salvation. The preservation of the flesh, not its mortification, became the symbol of one's piety. Again, Francis Bacon's introduction to *The History of Life and Death* exemplifies this link between health and salvation: "For while wee Christians aspire and labour to come to the Land of Promise; it will be a signe of Divine favour, if our shoos and the garments of our frail bodies, be here little worne in our journey in the worlds wildernesse" (Bacon, unnumbered; see also Wear, 71–73).

While this fleshy emphasis in the notion of self-preservation ultimately helped to undermine religious authority (as the concept came to serve as an important point of penetration for the discipline of medicine, which I will discuss later), it nevertheless began as a ministerial tool. For alongside the appreciation and spiritualization of the work of physicians, the seventeenth century also saw an intensification of the medical dimension of ministering both to oneself and others.[5] An interesting example of this is Richard Baxter (1615–1691), the prototypical Calvinist minister of *The Protestant Ethic*. In Weber's eyes, Baxter epitomized that Puritan anxiety about earthly entanglement, and encouraged a heightened concern with the economy of time as a technique for avoiding the seductions of leisure and wealth. But Baxter, like many Puritan ministers, was also an untrained practitioner of "physick" who offered medical advice to his flock (Baxter, 78; also see Webster, 255; Wear, 69). For the purposes of this essay, however, what is most interesting about Baxter is not the medical work he did among his parishioners, but rather the medical attention he directed at himself. For in Baxter's posthumously published autobiography, *Reliquiae Baxterianae* (begun 1664, pub. 1696), one can glimpse a personal account of an early manifestation of a uniquely modern technique of the self.

Early in his autobiography, Baxter noted that he suffered from physical problems throughout his life. "To recite a catalogue of my symptoms and pains, from head to feet," he wrote, "would be a tedious interruption to the reader. I shall therefore only say this, that the symptoms and effects of my general indisposition were very terrible" (Baxter, 11). And while Baxter did recognize his afflictions as being justly inflicted by a merciful God, he nevertheless took an active, experimental role in relieving his own suffering, and went into some detail describing the various attempts he made to promote and preserve his health. In particular, Baxter emphasized the benefits of following a specific regimen that allowed him to "study, and preach and walk almost as well as if [he] had been free" from the "daily and almost continual" pains he suffered:

1. Temperance as to quantity and quality of food. . . .
2. Exercise till I sweat. . . .
3. A constant extrinsic heat by a great fire, which may keep me still near to a sweat, if not in it (for I am seldom well at ease but in a sweat).
4. Beer as hot as my throat will endure, drunk all at once, to make me sweat (Baxter, 12).

Such regimens were among the most popular of the vernacular medical books that emerged early in modernity, and I will examine them more closely later on. Here, I simply want to indicate that the attention Baxter gave to his diet, exercise, and immediate environment is indicative of a regimental responsibility that would become more fully deployed later in modernity.

Aside from preserving his health through the regimentation of his behavior, Baxter also was quite eager to try new remedies and cures. For instance, he experimented with his regimen and found that replacing the hops in his beer with sage had a beneficial effect, and brewed his beer in this manner for many years (Wear, 96–97). He also sought medical treatment from a variety of physicians, upon "whose order [he] use'd drugs without number almost" (quoted in Wear, 92). However, the cures offered by physicians were generally unsuccessful, and Baxter ultimately found himself searching for new ways to relieve his physical misery.

What is most interesting about Baxter is that while he actively sought medical relief for his sundry afflictions, he never abandoned the view that illness and suffering were ultimately determined by God. Indeed, Baxter thought that the many remedies he unsuccessfully tried had failed precisely because "God thought not fit to make successful for a cure" (quoted in Wear, 92). And in his attempts to improve and preserve his health Baxter combined this eager pursuit of new treatments and remedies with the traditional practices of prayer and religious exercise, as the following description of his ministry in Kidderminster attests:

Once when I had continued weak three weeks, and was unable to go abroad, the very day that they prayed for me, being Good Friday, I recovered and was able to preach and administer the sacrament the next Lord's-day, and was better after it . . . when I had (after preaching) administered that sacrament to many hundred people I was much revived and eased of my infirmities. . . .

Another time, having read in Dr. Gerhard the admirable effects of the swallowing of a gold bullet upon his own father in a case like mine, I got a gold bullet and swallowed it (between twenty and thirty shillings' weight); and having taken it, I knew not how to be delivered of it again. I took clysters and purges for about three weeks, but nothing stirred it. But at last my neighbors set a day apart to fast and pray for me, and I was freed from my danger in the beginning of that day . . . (Baxter, 76).

This ambivalence in Baxter between a providential view of illness as a justly inflicted punishment that could be alleviated through prayer, and a revived medical view that saw illness as something to be understood and overcome by reason (Wear, 90–99), places him on the cusp of modernity. Admittedly, this ambivalence takes an extreme form in Baxter. On occasion he could claim that when his physical suffering was at its very worst he found "it much easier to repent and hate my sin and loathe myself, and contemn the world, and submit to the sentence of death with willingness, than otherwise it was ever like to have been" (Baxter, 252); nevertheless, on many other occasions Baxter still pestered so many physicians for a confirmation of his self-diagnosis of kidney stones that he ultimately was diagnosed with "hypochondriack melancholy" (Wear, 94–95; Baxter, 237–38). But it is precisely in the extremity of Baxter's ambivalence, I want to suggest, that one can glimpse the birth of a new technique of the modern self.

This new technique is grounded in a transformation which occurred in the role of self-preservation. Whereas self-preservation in the pre-Reformation Christian tradition had always been subsumed under an ultimate concern with the afterlife, with Baxter the effort to prolong earthly life almost, but not quite yet, had taken on a life of its own. For Baxter was preaching and writing in a period in which it was becoming increasingly difficult to follow Calvin's dictum that Christians should "ardently long for death, and constantly meditate upon it" (II, 290). And although Baxter's autobiography contains many traditional confessional elements—like Augustine, he even regrets robbing a fruit orchard (Baxter, 7)—it also indicates that when Baxter meditated about death he did so not solely out of a longing for death, but also out of a desire for deferring or postponing it. As indicated in the above passages, Baxter was a Christian minister who devoted a good deal of time and attention to preserving his health, and ordered his earthly time in a manner which would extend it. When he discusses these eager attempts at self-preservation in his autobiography, he does so not from a sense of guilt, but almost from a sense of duty.

This medical approach to self-preservation is not yet a juridical responsibility for Baxter, but he stands on the threshold of an age which, according to Charles Webster, "envisaged that the individual would assume greater responsibility for himself and become as effective a guardian of his health as of his legal rights" (259). I will eventually return to the medical dimensions of this responsibility that was being placed upon individuals early in modernity, but in order to get a better sense of its juridical dimensions, I will now turn to certain developments in seventeenth-century political thought. For as the function of self-preservation was shifting from a concern with the afterlife toward a concern with health and regimen, it was also assuming a central role in liberal political philosophy, where it would become linked with a proprietary view of the body.

PART III:
SELF-PRESERVATION AND SELF-OWNERSHIP
IN LIBERAL POLITICAL THOUGHT

By the middle of the seventeenth century, self-preservation had become central to political thought; indeed, it forms the cornerstone of Hobbes's *Leviathan* (1651). I do not want to focus on Hobbes in this essay, however, even though his writing reveals more clearly than anyone else's the relation between this concept and that abject fear of death which lies close to the heart of the modern subject.[6] Rather, I am concerned here with the relationship between self-preservation and self-ownership, and will focus on two other seventeenth-century theorists—Hugo Grotius and John Locke—both of whom were crucial in forging this conceptual link.

Grotius (who, incidentally, had a profound impact on Richard Baxter[7]) harkens back to the natural law tradition of Stoicism, particularly Cicero, when he discusses self-preservation. What Grotius finds in Cicero is really nothing more than the natural inclination and attendant obligation towards self-preservation that Aquinas had revived over four hundred years earlier.[8] Where Grotius becomes interesting, however, is in his development of the proprietary dimension of the self that natural law required one to preserve. Here, too, Grotius follows Aquinas,[9] but he develops the concept of self-ownership more explicitly than his predecessor, and in so doing helps to lay the foundation for the classic Lockean conception of property rights.[10]

Aquinas introduced the idea of self-ownership only in passing, when, in his defense of the necessity of human law, he claimed: "We observe that man is helped by industry in his necessities, for instance, in food and clothing. Certain beginnings of these he has from nature, that is, his reason and *his hands*" (Aquinas, Q. 95, 226, emphasis added). This implication that one has a natural right to certain necessities through the use of one's hands is explicated and elaborated by Grotius. Prior to the establishment of private property, Grotius claims, "the free use of life and limbs was so much the right of every one, that it could not be infringed or attacked without injustice. So the use of the common productions of nature was the right of the first occupier, and for any one to rob him of that was manifest injustice" (1901: Ch. II, Sec. 1, 33). The claim that one owned "the free use of life and limbs" was grounded, for Grotius, in the natural law obligation of self-preservation. For as James Tully has recently noted, these two concepts are so closely linked in Grotius's theory that he actually described "the principle of self-preservation in the terms of self-ownership (*suum*)" (1993: 82).

According to Grotius's conception of natural law, that which must be preserved is the *suum*, and it is comprised of that which can be claimed as one's own prior to the creation of political and legal rights to property. This "set of essential possessions" is ultimately derived from the body, and "is understood by Grotius to be—at least—life, limbs, and liberty" (Buckle, 29). So it is in order to preserve the integrity and liberty of this essential property—the body—that an individual has a right to use those things which were given in common to humanity by God. For Grotius, it is because of the possession of the body that we have a right to possess and use anything else.

John Locke takes up this juridical configuration of Grotius's and expatiates upon its religious foundation:

> For the desire, strong desire of Preserving his Life and Being having been Planted in him, as a Principle of Action by God himself, Reason, *which was the Voice of God in him*, could not but teach him and assure him, that pursuing that natural Inclination he had to preserve his Being, he followed the Will of his Maker, and therefore had a right to make use of those Creatures, which by his Reason or Senses he could discover would be serviceable thereunto (1960: Treatise I, Sec. 86, p. 205; see also II, 6, 270–71; II, 23, 284; and II, 25, 285).

Despite the traditional tone of Locke's justification for a use-right, he nevertheless makes an important contribution to this modern line of thought in his emphasis on the exclusivity of the claim that an individual can make on nature. And in refining and more rigorously specifying the right to use nature, Locke begins by making some rather exclusive claims about those primal possessions—the *suum*.

This exclusive dimension of self-ownership comes out clearly in one of the most closely attended passages in *The Second Treatise*:

> Every Man has a *Property* in his own *Person*. This no Body has any Right to but himself. The *Labour* of his Body, and the *Work* of his Hands, we may say, are properly his (1960: II, 27, 287–88; see also II, 44, 298).

Here Locke succinctly and emphatically forges the classical conceptual triumvirate of self-ownership, labor, and property. While it is the link between labor and property that has drawn the most attention to this famous passage, I want to focus on Locke's contribution to the Thomist-Grotian notion of self-ownership. For Locke goes beyond his predecessors in claiming not only that an individual has a property right in the *suum*, but that no one else has a legitimate claim to these primal possessions; in Locke's political theory, one has an exclusive, if not ultimate, ownership claim to one's body.[11]

Alongside this exclusive notion of self-ownership there also developed in early modernity a more specific and refined responsibility for the body, intimations of which we already saw in Baxter. I will examine the health-oriented dimension of this particular responsibility, and Locke's contribution to it, in the following section. At this point, however, I want to focus on the most extreme dimension of this responsibility, where it served not as an inducement toward a certain organization of one's life and time, but as a juridical limitation on the right of self-ownership. Like all the rights of liberalism, the right to one's *suum* is not absolute, and neither Locke nor Grotius recognized an absolute right to do what one will with one's body. For both theorists, the proprietary claim on one's self was always constrained by the more traditional concept which served as its foundation—self-preservation. In the juridical terms of liberal political theory, the limitation which self-preservation imposed on self-ownership took the extreme form of the prohibition against suicide. For suicide was the point where the potential for conflict between the ownership and preservation of the body became most acute, and where, given the intensity of the discussion of this extreme limit, the stakes seemed highest.

For even though liberalism ultimately maintained the Christian tradition's animus towards self-destruction, there was a vibrant discussion of suicide in the seventeenth and eighteenth centuries, and some, like Hume, explicitly argued against the traditional prohibition.[12] While the early liberal arguments in favor of suicide are certainly relevant to today's contests over the right to die, for the purposes of this essay it is the prohibition itself, not the challenge to it, which is most revealing. For the terms of the prohibition shifted over the course of these centuries, and the changing nature of this prohibition illuminates the increasing importance, and fragility, of the modern link between self-preservation and self-ownership.

Grotius, who was one of the first to elaborate the idea of self-ownership, was also one of the earliest to discuss suicide in uniquely modern terms. Although he casts the prohibition in a religious context, he also anticipates the terms that the suicide debate would take in the more rational discussions of the eighteenth century:

> As regards the individual himself everybody is obliged to preserve as best he can his own life, safety and health. The Christian does not hesitate to contradict Cato on that long-debated issue raised by Plato, whether it is permitted to commit suicide. For it is natural to all living beings to protect themselves and man is not placed in this world by chance but by divine decree, and is thus not free to desert his post without being summoned (1988: sec. 75, p. 129).

In regard to the modern discussion of suicide, this passage holds a position equivalent to that held by Locke's self-ownership passage in later discussions of property; all the essential elements of the future debate are brought together in an uncluttered and undeveloped form. In the eighteenth century, participants in the suicide debate will rely primarily on ancient Greek and Roman sources as their authorities, and the suicide of Cato[13] will become the most-widely contested example (Crocker, 48). The idea expressed at the end of the quote, that people should act like good soldiers and wait for God's orders, is a Pythagorean position that became a standard followed by some later opponents of suicide (Crocker, 52, incl. note 13).

Even though the modern debate on suicide borrowed extensively from the ancients, there is one uniquely modern element that Grotius brought to the discussion—the emphasis on self-preservation. For self-preservation was not stressed in ancient condemnations of suicide or in earlier Christian rejections (Crocker, 60), but for Grotius this is the key to the prohibition. All beings, not just humans, are bound by this natural law obligation; it is truly universal. And even though humans have the unique capacity to violate this duty— a point that will be stressed by later critics of the prohibition—for Grotius, the obviousness of the divine authorship of natural law seals the suicide prohibition with unchallengeable authority.

With Locke, the religious dimension of the suicide prohibition is maintained, but that divine element is no longer described in terms of authorship and decrees, but rather in terms of ownership and property:

> For Men being all the Workmanship of one Omnipotent, and infinitely wise Maker, All the Servants of one Sovereign Master, sent into the world

by his order and about his business, *they are his Property*, whose Workmanship they are, made to last during his, not one anothers Pleasure (1960: II, 6, 271, emphasis added; see also II, 6, 270–21 and II, 135, 357).

In claiming that suicide is prohibited because people are ultimately God's property, Locke was following another ancient tradition that would loom large in the next century's discussion of suicide. This tradition began with Socrates's rejection of suicide in Plato's *Phaedo*, where he claims: "I too believe that the gods are our guardians, and that we are a possession of theirs" (Plato, 493; also see Crocker, 51). There is an important difference between Socrates and Locke in regard to this prohibition, however. For along with suicide, Socrates also rejected the body as a tempting distraction and a hindrance to knowledge, and as something which philosophers should be eager to abandon (495–500). This condemnation of the flesh introduced a particularly powerful tension in the debate concerning suicide—one was expected, at once, to both long for death but also refrain from taking one's life. However, this Platonic-Christian tension was eclipsed in the early modern period by the conceptual shifts I have been tracing here, and a new tension emerged around the issue of suicide.

To begin with, the increasingly corporeal perspective on self-preservation transformed the longing for death into a desire for its deferral—recall Baxter's ambivalence. While this development released some of the tension that surrounded the issue of self-destruction, shifts in the early-modern conception of self-ownership only served to introduce a new tension. This is revealed most clearly in Locke's simultaneous recognition of God's ultimate property claim upon the body, and his extension of the exclusivity of the claims that individuals have upon their bodies. This Lockean tension blossomed in the eighteenth century, as the reinvigorated suicide debate came to be cast primarily in terms of conflicting property claims. Indeed, Lester G. Crocker describes the conditions surrounding the eighteenth-century debate on suicide in the following terms:

> the eighteenth century became the greatest battleground since ancient times over the inherent meaning of the act of self-destruction. . . . The reason is evident. In the multiplicity of arguments that flooded from the presses, one issue unmistakably dominates all others, although at times submerged or disguised in the subtleties of dialectic. . . . Is man's life God's property? Or is his life his own? (50–51).

By the end of the eighteenth century, both Grotius's and Locke's arguments against suicide had been significantly challenged. God's property right in the body was challenged on the basis of self-ownership, and God's role as author of the natural law obligation of self-preservation had eroded to the point where the doctrine would have to stand on its own. Immanuel Kant reveals this last shift when he writes: "Leaving aside religious considerations . . . we may treat our body as we please, provided our motives are those of self-preservation" (Kant, 149). But while Kant may have felt compelled to claim that self-preservation could do without its traditional religious foundation, his rather excessive claims concerning suicide indicate that this dislodged natural obligation was in dire need of some other conceptual support. For beyond the simple, rational requirement that people preserve themselves, Kant rejects in almost hysterical terms the very thought of suicide:

> We shrink in horror from suicide because all nature seeks its own preservation; an injured tree, a living body, an animal does so; how then could man make of his freedom, which is the acme of life and constitutes its worth, a principle for his own destruction? Nothing more terrible can be imagined . . . (150–51).

Suicide is the most terrible thought for Kant not because it violates any claim of God's, but because it violates the very foundation of liberalism—the idea of self-preservation. But without God as an ultimate authority over the end(ing) of life, Kant had to turn to some other conceptual mechanism for enforcing this natural law obligation. Indicating how important the concept of self-ownership had become, Kant chose to ground the suicide prohibition precisely in this primal property claim; of any person who would attempt suicide, Kant claims that "we are free to treat him as a beast, as a thing, and to use him for our sport as we do a horse or a dog, for he is no longer a human being" (151). In other words, anyone who would violate this most fundamental law of nature forfeits their exclusive proprietary claims to their *suum*; they no longer own themselves, but become instead a "thing" which can be used by others.[14]

I will return to the issue of suicide in my conclusion, but now want to turn to the less extreme obligations that self-preservation placed upon the exercise of self-ownership. During the seventeenth and eighteenth centuries, as the close relation between self-preservation, self-ownership, and exclusive property rights was being formed, and as the suicide prohibition shifted from religious to proprietary terms, a new technique of the self emerged that helped to instill the obligations of self-preservation and self-ownership in individuals. For people had to be trained in the proper use of their primal property.

PART IV: THE DEPLOYMENT OF REGIMEN IN MODERNITY

As I intimated earlier, there was an increase in the publication of vernacular medical literature in early modernity. The dissemination of such literature began in the sixteenth century, expanded quite noticeably in the middle of the seventeenth,[15] and continued throughout the eighteenth century. And as was the case in the political thought of this period, self-preservation played an ordering role in this diverse discursive field,[16] particularly in the most popular genre, the health regimen. It was from this position in medical discourse, more so than from its position in juridical or religious writing, that the modern conception of self-preservation was deployed as a technique that required a particular ordering of the body and the behavior of the individual.

European medical science was divided during the early modern period into two distinct realms: cure and prevention (Smith, 249). The curing of illness was the primary responsibility of trained physicians, but "prevention was at the periphery of the physician's professional interests," and occupied an intermediate area in which individuals bore the primary responsibility (Smith, 254; see also Coleman, 402). This peripheral preventative space was filled, through both oral and printed discourse, in the terms of health regimens. So prevalent was this particular genre that one student of such literature, Ginnie Smith, claims that "it is arguable that by 1770 few sections of the population would have been untouched by some notion of regimen" (Smith, 254). Although she is referring here to English medical literature, the health regimen was also well-established by the end of the eighteenth century in France, where it was disseminated through vehicles like Diderot's *Encyclopedie* (see Coleman). For the purposes of this essay, however, the development of the health regimen in England is most interesting, because in early-modern England a dramatic shift in this particular technique occurred alongside those other shifts I have noted.

Although I will stress the uniquely modern dimensions of the regimen, I must point out that this body of discourse, like modern conceptions of natural law and the suicide prohibition, was largely traditional. Through the end of the eighteenth century, regimens were cast in the terms of classical Greek hygiene, which was grounded in the Galenic categories of the *naturals*, the *contra-naturals*, and the *non-naturals*. The seven *naturals* included "the elements, humors, temperaments, faculties, and other characteristics of the organism" which constituted "'the physical basis of our being'"; the three *contra-naturals* encompassed "diseases, their causes and symptoms," and were properly treated by a physician (Coleman, 402). Modern writers on regimen stressed neither of these Galenic categories, however, but instead focused on the six *non-naturals*, which encompassed certain unavoidable activities of the body: "air, diet, sleep, exercise, evacuations, and passions of the mind" (Smith, 257; also see Coleman, 400). What set the *non-naturals* apart from the other elements of humoral theory is that they were particularly susceptible to regulation and control by the individual.

To a late-modern ear the term *non-natural* may evoke a negative connotation, but the activities which fall under this category are non-natural not in the sense that they are divorced from nature, nor in the sense that they should be wrested from the control of nature; rather, these activities were *non-natural* in the sense that they could easily diverge from a harmonious, natural balance. The regimen offered advice on obtaining and maintaining the proper balance, as Ginnie Smith's description of the regimen's function attests:

> Therapeutic control related particularly to diet . . . to activity . . . and to control of temperature and moisture (through housing, clothing, bathing, food) according to age and condition. Whatever procedure might be prescribed for the six universals, they were brought into harmony for each individual case by the principle of constant regulation—the ordering of the non-naturals—throughout life (Smith, 257).

But even though the regimens used the traditional hygienic category of the *non-naturals* to order and regulate these mundane temporal activities, they also served, especially in England, to introduce new medical standards that were demanded by the modern conception of self-preservation.

Around the middle of the seventeenth century, during that period in which medical literature suddenly proliferated in England, there occurred "an internal therapeutic shift" in preventative discourse (Smith, 256–62). Prior to mid-century, the regimen followed by the English was a "hot" one which "gave overwhelming preference to the physiological behaviour of the bodily fluids, and their manipulation through diet (food and drink) and other substances perfected in Arabic drug lore. Hot regimen cleansed and purged inwardly, throwing out excreta, infections and all 'nastinesse', using food and other drugs to regulate the inner functions" (Smith, 258). Recall here Richard Baxter's emphasis on heat and sweat, his steaming beer, and the "purges and clysters" he took to pass the golden bullet that he had swallowed. In regard to his regimen, Baxter was largely on the far side of this particular modern rift.

On the near side of this transformation, however, there was a "growing dissatisfaction" among popular medical writers with "the simplistic humoral theory" of hot regimen (Smith, 258). As they headed toward the eighteenth century, these writers displayed a greater appreciation of the full range of non-naturals, and eventually revaluated the benefits of the hot regimen itself. From the middle of the seventeenth century, the emphasis of regimens shifted from exciting the purgative activities of the body through heat, exercise, and drugs, to regulating and controlling the processes of the body through cooling. The following description of the "cool regimen" reveals the extent of this shift in the practice of self-preservation:

> "Cool" regimen emphasised the care of the external solids calling for a "hardening" of the body on a "low" diet; it was characterised by the idea of process, or dynamics. The emergence of balneology as a subdivision of the therapy of exercise was directly related to this change. The cooling and hardening of the body in water was analogous to ventilating and cooling the body in cold air; the passions could be cooled as well as heated; cool vegetables were the antithesis to hot meats. Living according to nature in the cool British climate meant employing cool regimen to bring body and environment into harmony (Smith, 259).

This cool regimen was disseminated by a variety of popular medical writers in late seventeenth- and eighteenth-century England (Smith, 259), and many of these regimens were infused with a religious fervor, indicating that the ambivalence I detected in Baxter lingered on in the century after him. However, rather than examine the variety of regimens offered by these popular medical writers, I will turn instead to one particular proponent of cool regimen who also played a central role in establishing the theoretical link between the preservation and ownership of the body—John Locke. For Locke endorsed this new regimen in a series of letters he wrote in response to a friend's request for advice concerning his son's education, and disseminated it through the continual publication of this response throughout his life under the title *Some Thoughts Concerning Education* (originally published, 1692/3).

Locke begins the *Thoughts* by stressing how important a healthy body is to worldly success:

> A Sound Mind in a sound Body, is a short, but full Description of a happy State in this World. He that has these two, has little more to wish for; and he that wants of either of them, will be but little the better for any thing else. . . . He, whose Mind directs not wisely, will never take the right Way; and he, whose Body is crazy and feeble, will never be able to advance in it (Locke, 1899: 1).[17]

He then spends the first thirty sections of the work discussing what he calls at one point the "Government of Health" (1899: 13). One of the primary objectives of this regulation of the body is that it—the body—should become hardened through frequent exposure to both cold water and air.

Contrary to Baxter's practice of spending as much time as possible before the fire, Locke, in general, advises that a "thing that is of great Advantage to every one's Health, but especially Children's is to be much in the *open Air*, and as little as may be by the fire, even in winter" (1899: 6). More specifically, Locke advises that children should not be dressed too warmly, and the head in particular should be exposed as much as possible. They should not wear caps, either at play or while asleep, since "there being nothing that more exposes to Headachs, colds, Catarrhs, Coughs, and several other Diseases, than keeping the *head warm*" (1899: 2–3). And at the other extremity, Locke stresses that the feet should be washed in cold water every day, and shoes should be thin enough to let in water, "the great End being to harden those Parts by a frequent and familiar Use of cold Water, and thereby to prevent the Mischiefs that usually attend accidental taking Wet in the Feet in those who are bred otherwise" (1899: 4).

In regard to diet, Locke followed the cool regimens of this period in recommending the beneficial effects of a vegetarian diet. He advised against meat in the child's earliest years, and in general imputed "a great Part of our Diseases in *England*, to our eating too much *Flesh*, and too little *Bread*" (1899: 11). Locke recommended plain, dry bread as the bulk of a child's diet, but in all cases whatever was served to children, whether it be meat or bread, should be "plain, and without much Mixture, and very sparingly season'd with Sugar, or rather none at all; especially *all Spice*, and other things that may heat the Blood" (1899: 9–10). For Locke, the benefit of this rather bland, vegetarian diet was that it would allow the non-natural activity of eating to be guided by the requirements of nature; as Locke describes the benefits of this bread-based diet: "If he be hungry more than wanton, *Bread* alone will down; and if he be not hungry, 'tis not fit he should eat. By this . . . you will not teach him to eat more nor oftener than Nature requires" (1899: 10).

In regard to evacuations, Locke abandons the hot regimen emphasis on purging and cleansing, and follows the cool regimen emphasis on the benefits of regularity and order. For just as the feet could be hardened to cold water, Locke believed that the bowels could be trained to evacuate on a regular basis. He urged that children, and also irregular adults, make a trip to the "Necessary-House" immediately after breakfast every day; ultimately, he thought, the body would become used to this routine and disciplined in this non-natural function. Locke stressed the importance of regularity for self-preservation, as if the regular accumulation of property that would allow a young man to make his way in the world depended upon regular evacuation: "People that are very *loose*, have seldom strong Thoughts, or strong Bodies. . . . I cannot but say, that considering the many Evils that come from that Defect, of a requisite Esing of nature, I scarce know any thing more conducing to the Preservation of Health, than this is. Once in four and twenty Hours, I think is enough; and no body, I guess, will think it too much" (1899: 17–19).

In Locke's advice on education one can glimpse a new sense of personal responsibility that emerged alongside the liberal property rights that he helped to ground. For aside from the widely discussed and extreme responsibility for avoiding suicide, there also emerged in early modernity a more mundane and more pervasive responsibility for preserving one's body through the regulation of the non-naturals. Although individuals have been encouraged to view the decisions they make in regard to activities such as diet, exercise, and hygiene as sovereign consumer choices, the regulation of basic bodily activities and functions has become increasingly regimented throughout modernity. As Foucault's studies have shown, the modern order is characterized by a wide variety of specialized fields of knowledge that study these bodily functions, establish standards for various segments of the population, and develop therapies which allow, or require, individuals to preserve themselves most effectively and efficiently.

Although this increasing specialization and regimentation have occurred in a range of activities that greatly extend the simple categories of the non-naturals, one example will quickly illustrate my point. In regard to diet, current standards have become so highly refined that food is increasingly consumed in accordance with recommended levels of various substances such as sodium, cholesterol, and fat. In the United States, food producers are legally required to provide such information in a "nutritional panel" which indicates the amount of various substances that one serving of the food contains, and the contribution that a serving makes toward the "recommended daily allowance" of those substances. To facilitate this dietary regimentation, an ever-increasing variety of specialty foods now allows individuals to tailor their dietary intake to meet specific standards, and even fast-food franchises have begun to produce low-fat and low-sodium versions of their fare.

The point I want to make through this example is not just that regimentation has continued apace since the seventeenth century, but that the development of such specialized knowledge about diet was made possible by the modern responsibility for self-preservation that was originally deployed through the health regimen. As individuals came to be responsible for monitoring and regulating their bodily activities, they contributed to the formation of these new fields of knowledge and the ever-changing standards of self-preservation these fields establish and disseminate. By the end of the eighteenth century, this particular technology of the health regimen was well-established both in England and on the Continent,[18] and individuals had become better fit for the exercise of bio-power[19] in modernity.

PART V: CONCLUSION

The early-modern transformations I have traced in the relationships between self-preservation and self-ownership have played a central role in the juridical and personal foundations of power in modernity, but recent developments in late-modern culture seem to have thrown these relationships into disarray. In particular, controversies have emerged recently around advanced medical techniques that raise not just legal questions, but questions about the nature of the modern subject as well. In this conclusion, I will mention a few of these controversies and sketch the challenges they pose to the conceptual and regimental order I have outlined here. My concern, of course, is not to map out all the ethical nuances of these controversies and try to settle the debates; on the contrary, my aim is to present these controversies from a perspective that will broaden the historical and conceptual context and expand the terms of the debate.

The most obvious challenge to the traditional relationship between self-preservation and self-ownership is the increasingly popular "right to die" movement. The claims made on the basis of this recently asserted right range from the relatively uncontroversial use of "living wills" (which allow individuals to determine in advance the level of life-support technology they will be subject to if they become incapacitated) to the more widely contested claim for the assistance of a physician in the "performance" of suicide. Although there certainly are important differences between these claims, this late-modern emergence of legal and ethical debates concerning the right to die is based on an inversion of the traditional conceptual hierarchy of liberalism. In regard to the right to die, the ownership claims that individuals make about their bodies are not just exclusive, but ultimate as well. Whether it is through the use of a living will or a suicide machine, individuals in these cases are no longer choosing to preserve themselves (at least in a corporeal sense), and they are rejecting this natural law requirement on the basis that their right to do what they will with their bodies takes precedence over established medical and juridical authority. In the late-eighteenth century, Kant may have grounded the suicide prohibition in the threatened loss of self-ownership, but in the late-twentieth century, strong claims of self-ownership threaten the suicide prohibition itself.[20]

Another situation in which the trajectory of modernity seems to challenge its traditional foundation is the economics of organ transplantation. Due to the remarkable success of contemporary medicine in developing techniques for preserving and transplanting organs, medical authorities have recently announced an "organ shortage." The responses to this shortage range from encouraging individuals to donate their organs to "organ banks" upon their death, to the more extreme claims for market transactions in the economy of organs.[21] Again, there are important differences between the donation and the sale of organs, but at both ends of this spectrum the body is treated as an assemblage of parts which an individual owns and can alienate. But while it may thus extend the concept of self-ownership, the economy of organs also disrupts, to some extent, the primacy which modernity has always afforded self-preservation. Depending on whether it is approached from the perspective of the recipient/buyer or the donor/seller, this fundamental law of nature is either reinforced or challenged by the increasing transplantation of organs. For those who would receive or buy an organ, self-preservation seems to retain its traditional precedence over self-ownership, but for those who would donate or sell an organ while they are alive, as well as those who advocate the sale of organs, it seems that self-ownership has broken free from its foundation in self-preservation.[22] To either give or sell an essential duplicate organ, such as a kidney, would place an individual's own preservation at risk. One has to wonder what Locke would say about a person who decided to sell a kidney to help make his or her way in the world.[23]

The last example I will mention is the most extreme, but in some ways it is also the most revealing. For on the fringe of contemporary medical practice there has emerged the science of self-preservation par excellence—cryonics. This is the branch of medicine that has developed techniques for deep-freezing the body, or, as is more frequently the case, the head, in anticipation of the development of techniques for reanimating these bodies or parts. Although juridical and medical authorities have had little difficulty dealing with the cryonic suspension of individuals who have died, recently an individual unsuccessfully tried to have his head frozen before his death. Thomas Donaldson argued that his chances for reanimation would be greater if he had his head frozen before an inoperable brain tumor killed him, and sought an injunction from a California court that would prevent authorities from interfering with his "premortem cryonic suspension."[24] Donaldson's request was refused on the grounds that his choice amounted to suicide, but the cryonicists claim that such a procedure is hardly suicide, and is rather a choice for self-preservation that individuals should be allowed to make on the basis of self-ownership.

In all these extreme examples, it is precisely modernity's success in allowing/requiring individuals to better preserve themselves that has given rise to the current controversy. Nevertheless, the discussion of these bioethical dilemmas seems to be cast primarily in terms of self-ownership. Issues like the right to die and the shortage of organs often devolve to a question of the extent to which individuals can decide for themselves what they will do with their bodies. And it is quite likely that the limits of self-ownership will be increasingly contested as medicine relentlessly develops new techniques for preserving the body, such as: biotechnological commodities that are produced from human tissue;[25] gene therapies that will be spawned by the human genome project; and the development of ever-more extensive techniques for preserving life (or, as often seems to be the case, postponing death). But while it seems as though the more juridical concept of self-ownership is beginning to displace self-preservation as the primary thread of responsibility between the individual and medicine, perhaps we are approaching the point where these two fundamental elements of the medically responsible subject are giving way to new possibilities. For as such bioethical dilemmas multiply, it may become apparent that not only must self-ownership be reconsidered (and one would hope that this discussion will occur in more than juridical terms), but that the concept of self-preservation, which played such a crucial role in the theoretical and regimental foundations of modernity, must also be thought about once again.

At this point, I would like to reconsider some of the claims I made earlier regarding the early-modern shift in the conception of self-preservation. Given the direction and pace of recent developments in medicine, it is possible that I miscast certain dimensions of that shift when I claimed that self-preservation had broken free from the traditional concern with an immortal afterlife. For along with the increasing corporeality of the concept of self-preservation, there may also have been a corresponding transformation in the conception of immortality itself, a shift which is just beginning to become noticeable. While the claims of medicine are still couched in the usual terms of self-preservation (e.g., it is the physician's role as preserver of bodily life that has led medical organizations to "officially" reject the possibility of assisting in suicide), out on the edge there has appeared a worldly, corporeal vision of immortality, complete with a liquid-nitrogen limbo. When Thomas Donaldson, the eager cryonicist, claims "that everyone should be immortal" and that "[t]he purpose of medicine should be to bring about that immortality,"[26] one has to wonder whether we may be approaching the surprising fulfillment of the fusion of physician and priest that Bacon heralded early in the seventeenth century.

If the modern medical regimen is indeed grounded not just in a sense of individual responsibility for maintaining one's health, but also in a more difficultly discerned desire to attain through science and technology that which was traditionally promised by Christianity, we have arrived at a truly ironic moment. This irony lies not just in the fact that modern medical techniques have provoked such discordant responses as the right to physician-assisted suicide and the nonsuicidal right to "pre-mortem cryonic suspension." Setting rights aside, there is another dimension to the irony of this late-modern situation, a dimension which is more interesting and perhaps more fertile than the juridical conflicts surrounding rights. This irony appears when one glances back at the changing role that death, the shadow of self-preservation, has played in modernity.

Although I have only been able to allude to this point here, the fear of death served as a crucial support for the obligation of self-preservation in early modernity. Contrary to Calvin's expectations, reflection on death did not lead people to overcome their fear of it, and to abandon their earthly concerns in favor of an otherworldly promise. Rather, seventeenth-century theorists like Hobbes and Locke relied on the fear of premature death to convince their readers that the civil order offered by liberalism, with its attendant responsibility for following already changing standards of health and fitness, was required by the natural law of self-preservation. But in the first half of the twentieth century, the status of death shifted dramatically, as writers like Heidegger and Camus turned to death as a way of challenging the dangerous inertia of modernity. For such late-modern figures, reflections on the certainty and absurdity of death, or to use Heidegger's phrase, the experience of "anxiety in the face of death," were treated as one of the most potent techniques for rousing moderns from their existential somnolence.

At this late point in the twentieth century, however, there seems to be on the horizon another shift in the status of death. Contrary to what the early-moderns or the existentialists thought, it may be neither *fear* nor *anxiety* about *death* which causes people to reconsider what it is that is really worth preserving in their lives. Rather, such a revaluation might be triggered by a *fear* that medicine, in its attempt to defeat, or at least defer, death, will impose a prolonged and undignified *life*. Indeed, such a fear seems to be the motivation behind the increasing clamor for a right to die, and the right to have a physician assist in ordering this most personal choice (Kevorkian has already named the orderly, medical form of suicide "patholysis"). However, I think that the most heartening possibility that has emerged around recent trends in medicine is that it may be *neither fear nor anxiety* which most effectively spurs a revaluation of modern regimens of self-preservation, but rather an ironic laugh at the lengths to which medicine and the medically responsible subject have gone in the attempt to preserve the body.

The reason that I think a lighter, amused response to the ironies of late modernity is preferable to either anxiety about death or fear of uncontrolled medical intervention, is because this stance seems the one most likely to challenge the regimented everydayness of modern life, and stimulate the possibilities for new techniques of the self to emerge. At this late stage in the development of bio-power, those who remain anxious or fearful about death would appear to be particularly susceptible to the subliminal suggestion that medicine may be able to indefinitely postpone, and perhaps ultimately defeat, death. Such individuals would quite likely become increasingly enmeshed in the endlessly proliferating processes of medical regimentation. And for those late-moderns who no longer fear death as much as they fear falling prey to medicine's ability to impose a life that they may not want to live, the right to die may amount to nothing more than an unreflective, defensive reaction. For such fearful people, the potentially disruptive notion of the right to die may never get beyond a grasp for control of the manner of one's death. But if one can appreciate the irony in, and perhaps even laugh at, the techniques to which people subject themselves in the pursuit of health (or is it the pursuit of corporeal immortality?), then one may go beyond the mere assertion of new rights in response to medical developments, and actually begin to reflect on the way in which modernity has gone about preserving the body, and to think again of what it is that is worth preserving, and of the *ways* in which such preservation might be accomplished. Who knows? Such thoughts may even lead to techniques of the self which are not grounded at all in the obligation of preserving the self.

NOTES

1. Even though Epicurus claimed that pleasure was the proper end or purpose of a human life, he did not emphasize the prolongation of life, Cicero and Hegel's claims notwithstanding. For an explication of those Epicurean doctrines that give the lie to the critique of the "unhappy hedonist," see Stephen E. Rosenbaum, "Epicurus on Pleasure and the Complete Life," *The Monist*, 73, Jan. 1990, 21–41.
2. James Tully acknowledges Aquinas's role in placing self-preservation at the center of natural law theory. According to Tully, the foundational idea that people are rationally inclined to follow natural law "stems from Aquinas's original presentation and analysis of self-preservation as the first law of nature" (Tully, 1980: 47). See also Buckle, pp. 11–12.
3. For his general view that the millennial eschatology of Puritanism fit well with early-modern developments in science and technology, see Webster, pp. 1–31. In the chapter of *The Great Instauration* entitled "The Prolongation of Life" (pp. 246–323), Webster discusses Puritan enthusiasm for: Paracelsian chemistry and astrology; educational reforms that emphasized anatomy and clinical experience; liberalization of licensing for physicians; and the development of public hospitals that would minister to the bodies of the poor.
4. Of course, this endorsement of medical experimentation and innovation in the means to prolong life did not completely overshadow the Puritan concern with death. Andrew Wear has examined the use of medical language in seventeenth-

century religious writers, and found a genre in which death was a central theme. In the literature Wear examined, which was primarily the diaries and autobiographies of religious writers, life was often treated as a preparation for death, and death was presented as "a learnt procedure, part of the ceremonial of life" (p. 64). And as one would expect, there were also complaints by religious writers that people were not meditating sufficiently upon death (p. 67). While Wear acknowledges that this emphasis on death among Puritan writers may have been intended to bolster the "indispensability . . . and power of the Church in this world, it also served as the background for the Puritan writers' mingling together of religion and medicine" (p. 66).

5. Webster points out that some Puritan medical reformers saw a clearly medical role for the clergy. In Gabriel Plattes's utopian *Macaria* (1641), for example, "'the parson of every parish is a good physician'" (quoted in Webster, p. 259). See also Wear, pp. 61–63.

6. I have discussed this relation elsewhere; see Thomas F. Tierney, *The Value of Convenience: A Genealogy of Technical Culture* (Albany, NY: SUNY Press, 1993), pp. 167–81; and "Foucault, Hobbes, and the Right to Die" (article currently under review).

7. Baxter expressed his deep debt to Grotius in *The Grotian Religion Discovered* (1658), where he claimed that in regard to theology, statesmanship, and law, "I have learned more from *Grotius* than from almost any Writer in those subjects" (quoted in Baxter, 288–89, in the note for p. 96).

8. Compare the following discussion of Cicero from Grotius's *The Rights of War and Peace* (1625) with the quotation from Aquinas in Part II of this essay: "He (Cicero) calls the care, which every animal, from the moment of its birth, feels for itself and the preservation of its condition, its abhorrence of destruction, and of every thing that threatens death, a principle of nature. Hence, he says, it happens, that if left to his own choice, every man would prefer a sound and perfect to a mutilated and deformed body. So that preserving ourselves in a natural state, and holding to every thing conformable, and averting every thing repugnant to nature is the first duty" (Grotius, 1901: Ch. II, Sec. 1, p. 31).

9. The link which Aquinas establishes between self-preservation and self-ownership occurs in his discussion of natural and human law (Questions 94 and 95 of *Summa Theologica*). For Aquinas, the natural law obligation that individuals have to preserve themselves is the basis for a use-right all individuals have to commonly owned nature. He writes: "Because in man there is first of all an inclination to good in accordance with the nature which he has in common with all substances; that is, every substance seeks the preservation of its own being, according to its nature. And by reason of this inclination, whatever is a means of preserving human life and of warding off its obstacles belongs to the natural law" (Q. 94, p. 222).

Stephen Buckle cites Aquinas as an authoritative medieval source for this idea "that an original right to use at least parts of the natural world is a necessary part of natural law," and claims that this idea was virtually undisputed by the time Grotius wrote (Buckle, p. 12).

10. James Tully notes Grotius's role in establishing the juridical function which

self-ownership will serve in the seventeenth century: "The primary use of the concept of rights over the self in seventeenth century is in the constitution of government and the relation of subjection to it. The framework in which this is discussed by both Hobbes and Locke is laid down by Hugo Grotius in *The Rights of War and Peace* (1625)" (Tully, 1993: 82).

11. In his discussion of the Lockean conception of *person*, James Tully argues that when Locke claimed individuals had a property right in their person he was using person in a sense which went beyond the physical dimensions of the body, and meant by *person* a rational, self-conscious actor (1980: 104–116). I agree with Tully on this point, although I stress the physical, embodied dimension of self-ownership. However, in his attempt to stress the proprietary claim one has to one's intentional action, Tully seems to imply that Locke did not recognize a property claim in the body itself. As Tully interprets Locke, a person's "body and his limbs are God's property: the actions he uses them to make are his own. . . . Although man neither makes the world nor himself, and so has no exclusive rights at birth, he comes to have a natural and exclusive right in the actions he makes as a person" (1980: 109). Tully is certainly right about Locke's insistence that God ultimately owns the body (I will turn to this issue immediately below in the text), but I think Tully goes a little too far in implying that a person has an exclusive property right only in that person's actions. Without denying Tully's claims about action, or ignoring the issue of God's ultimate ownership of the body, what I want to stress about Locke's concept of self-ownership is that Locke, following Grotius, did recognize a corporeal, embodied dimension of the *suum*, and that Locke made more exclusive claims than Grotius about an individual's ownership of that dimension.

    In any event, several contemporary theorists who are engaged in the debates concerning property rights and economic redistribution have interpreted the Lockean idea of self-ownership to include a property right in the body itself. See, John Christman, "Self-Ownership, Equality, and the Structure of Property Rights," *Political Theory*, 19, no. 1 (February 1991): 28–46, esp. 28; Richard Arneson, "Lockean Self-Ownership: Towards a Demolition," *Political Studies*, 39 (1991): 36–54, esp. 36; and G. A. Cohen, "Self-Ownership, World Ownership, and Equality" two-parts: Part I is in Frank Lucash, ed., *Justice and Equality Here and Now* (Ithaca: Cornell University Press, 1986); Part II is in *Social Philosophy & Policy*, 3, no. 2 (Spring 1986): 77–96., esp. Part I, p. 109.

12. Hume's posthumously published essay "On Suicide" was written around 1755. For discussion of liberal attitudes toward suicide, see: Crocker; S.E. Sprott, *The English Debate on Suicide: From Donne to Hume* (LaSalle, Ill: Open Court, 1961); and Georgia Noon, "On Suicide," *The Journal of the History of Ideas*, 1978, 39, 371–86.

13. Plutarch recounts with admiration Cato's decision to take his own life, rather than allow Caesar the opportunity to increase his own reputation by sparing it. Aside from the issue of suicide, Cato also provides a good example of the claim I made earlier, that traditional moral schemes never held the preservation of life as the ultimate aim of a good life. In response to attempts by friends

to keep him from his sword, Cato chastises them as follows: "'And you, do you also think to keep a man of my age (48 years) alive by force, and to sit here and silently watch me? Or do you bring me some reasons to prove, that it will not be base and unworthy for Cato, when he can find his safety no other way, to seek it from his enemy? If so, adduce your arguments, and show cause why we should now unlearn what we formerly were taught, in order that rejecting all the convictions in which we lived, we may now by Caesar's help grow wiser, and be yet more obliged to him, *than for life only*'" [Plutarch, *Lives of Illustrious Men*, trans. A.H. Clough (Boston: Little, Brown, and Company, 1911), p. 567, emphasis and parentheses added].

14. That Kant was not the only eighteenth-century figure to hold such a view is indicated by the discussion of suicide in the popular British *Gentleman's Magazine*, which Roy Porter claims "offered a middle-of-the-road viewpoint, reflecting moderate, enlightened common sense" on a variety of issues (Porter 1985a: 141). The traditional secular deterrent against suicide in England was the disinheritance of the suicide's heirs, but the majority of commentators in the magazine favored a weakening of this law (Porter, 1985a: 161). Some, however, favored a gentler treatment of the heirs, but nevertheless endorsed a complete disinheritance of the body of the suicide:

> The extreme and evident cruelty of this [disinheritance] law has produced an almost constant evasion of it, though it can be no otherwise evaded by perjury; and the coroner's jury generally find the suicide a lunatic, though there is no other evidence of his lunacy than his crime. I therefore propose that the goods and chattels of the suicide belong to his legal representatives and that whether lunatic or not lunatic, the body be delivered for dissection, either to the surgeons company, or to such persons as read private lectures, who shall take such bodies by rotation, entering their names with the coroner of the country for that purpose (quoted in Porter, 1985a: 153; the original quote is from *Gentleman's Magazine*, 1754, 24: 506).

Porter also cites several other instances in which this viewpoint was expressed in the magazine.

15. There was a particularly noticeable increase in such literature in the middle of this period, which Charles Webster describes as "a great flood of medical literature which appeared between 1650 and 1660, produced in an atmosphere charged with enthusiasm for every aspect of medical speculation" (pp. 265–68 and 489; also see Slack, p. 241). There is a series of interesting developments that also occurred during or around this period, which is perhaps worth noting. To begin with, *Leviathan*, that great work on self-preservation, was spawned at the beginning of this deluge, and Baxter's *Autobiography*, with its heightened ambivalence toward self-preservation, was begun in 1664, slightly after it subsided. Another interesting coincidence is that, according to the Oxford English Dictionary, the word suicide emerged in English in 1651, the same year that *Leviathan* was published. In her article on suicide cited in note 12, Georgia Noon notes an earlier use of the word; see p. 372.

16. In his examination of popular medical literature published between 1486 and 1604, Paul Slack found that "explanatory textbooks and regimens" accounted for the greatest percentage of titles (21.6%) and editions (29.3%) (Slack, p. 243). For an extended discussion of the Puritan contribution to such medical literature, see Webster, pp. 246–323; for an examination of the regimens of the seventeenth century, see Smith; and for a discussion of middle-class medical literature of the eighteenth century, see Porter 1985a and 1985b, and Coleman.

17. According to Patrick Romanell, Locke seems to have been as obsessed with his health as Richard Baxter was: "In view of what we can easily learn about Locke's personality and his actual medical practice from his manuscript papers preserved in various collections and libraries, . . . Locke must have been a chronic hypochondriac. In his correspondence with friends he was forever complaining about his 'ill lungs'" [see Patrick Romanell, *John Locke and Medicine: A New Key to Locke* (Buffalo, NY: Prometheus Books, 1984), p. 30].

18. Referring to England, Ginnie Smith claims that "by the third quarter of the eighteenth century 'Modern Medicine' had sublimated a radical enthusiasm for cool regimen into a moderate or liberal hypothesis of hygienic treatment" (p. 262). William Coleman makes a similar point in regard to the role of regimen in France; about the *Encyclopedia's* article on "regime," Coleman claims that it represents the Western tradition of "hygienic propaganda . . . at its moment of greatest popular dissemination" (p. 412).

19. In *Volume 1* of *The History of Sexuality*, Foucault introduces the term "biopower" to describe a nonrepressive form of power which emerged between the Renaissance and modernity, during that period which Foucault calls "the classical age." Unlike more traditional forms of power, which were ultimately grounded in the sovereign's right to kill subjects, bio-power was grounded in the right of society to promote the lives of individuals. Foucault describes this shift in the following terms:

> The death that was based on the right of the sovereign is now manifested as simply the reverse of the right of the social body to ensure, maintain, or develop its life. . . . This formidable power of death . . . now presents itself as the counterpart of a power that exerts a positive influence on life, that endeavors to administer, optimize, and multiply it, subjecting it to precise controls and comprehensive regulations (1980: 136-37).

While the health regimens I am discussing here are a good example of this new form of power, what also needs to be examined is the role that death played in the changes in medical knowledge which occurred during the early modern period. In *The Birth of the Clinic*, Foucault discusses the role of death in modern medicine, but he identifies the crucial shift as occurring at the turn of the twentieth century. In a larger work, I plan on carrying Foucault's treatment of the changed status of death farther back than he did, and linking those Foucauldian themes with the developments traced in this essay.

20. Although proponents of the right to die, like Dr. Jack Kevorkian (a.k.a. Dr.

Death) and Derek Humphry (author of the best-selling *Final Exit*) do not make their claims in terms of self-ownership, but in terms of human dignity, the legal battles around the right to die are fought on the juridical claim. In an unsuccessful bid in 1995 to have his Michigan court case heard by the U.S. Supreme Court, Kevorkian's lawyer claimed: "It's our position no one has to give us permission to control our own bodies" (quoted in *Roanoke Times and World News*, April 25, 1995, A5).

21. Although liberal nations have legally accepted and encouraged the donation of organs, even in cases where a specific recipient is identified, they have generally prohibited the selling of organs, and there seems to be little public support for such sales. In India, however, the kidney shortage has led to a physician-controlled market in organs. For a discussion of this trade in kidneys in India, see Ronald Bailey, "Should I Be Allowed to Buy Your Kidney?," *Forbes*, May 28, 1990, 370.

22. Some of the claims made in the British debate over organ sales present this strong self-ownership position. Michael McNair Wilson, a conservative member of Parliament who happened to be in need of a kidney transplant, claimed: "While there is a shortage of kidneys, I do not see why it is wrong for you to do what you will with your body." Another Englishman, Royden Harrison, professor emeritus of social history at Warwick College, took account of the benefits that could accrue to the seller of an organ, as well as the recipient, in a letter that he wrote to the London Times. Harrison asks, "What possible objection can there be if one person, of their own free will and without duress, should sell their kidney to someone else? The seller is able to indulge in a few of the good things in life. The buyer may well be paying to survive." Both are quoted in Terry Trucco, "Sales of Kidneys Prompt New Laws and Debate," *New York Times*, August 1, 1989, III, 1:1, p. 6.

23. Although this scenario may seem far-fetched, Terry Trucco recounts the interesting case of one West German businessman, Count Rainer Rene Adelmann von Adelmannsfelden, who contacted bankrupt business executives throughout West Germany and offered to buy one of their kidneys for $44,000, and had six positive responses before he was stopped by West German authorities. The Count also tried to set up an organ brokerage firm in England before legislation prohibiting organ sales was passed. See Terry Trucco, "Sales of Kidneys Prompt New Laws and Debate," *New York Times*, August 1, 1989, III, 1:1.

24. For a libertarian account of the legal and medical obstacles faced by Thomas Donaldson in this attempt, see Jacob Sullum, "Cold Comfort," *reason*, April, 1991: 22–29.

25. An interesting example of this issue is the case of John Moore, a man whose spleen was removed as part of the prescribed treatment for the form of leukemia from which he suffered. Unbeknownst to Moore, his physician at the UCLA Medical Center noted the unique immunological properties—and economic potential—of some of Moore's white blood cells, and developed a "cell line" from the removed spleen. When UCLA obtained a patent and a pharmaceutical contract for the cell line, Moore sued, alleging in part that his property—i.e., spleen cells—had been converted by the physician, and that

Moore had a continuing property right in the cell line. The California Supreme Court rejected Moore's claim that he had a property right in either his excised spleen cells or the cell line, although it upheld other allegations concerning the physician's behavior in the case. See *Moore v. Regents of the University of California*, 271 Cal. Rptr. 146 (1990). For a discussion of the facts and legal aspects of the California Supreme Court's decision and opinions, see "Tort law—informed consent—California Supreme Court Recognizes Patient's Cause of Action for Physician's Nondisclosure of Excised Tissue's Commercial Value," *Harvard Law Review*, Jan. 1991, 104, 3, 808–815.

26. This quote is from an Associated Press article which was written when Donaldson originally filed suit, sometime in 1990. But this sentiment was expressed as early as 1964 by Robert Ettinger, the author of *The Prospect of Immortality* and the founder of the Cryonics Institute: "Most of us now breathing have a good chance of physical life after death—a sober, scientific probability of revival and rejuvenation of our frozen bodies" (quoted in Sullum, p. 24).

Zygmunt Bauman has noted in passing the similarity between the traditional Christian response to the death and decay of the body and the science of cryonics: "As the decay of the physical body of the dead were too evident and unexceptional to be refuted, the preservation of the body could not be entertained in any but a miraculous form (the idea is entertained again in our time, in the form of the miraculously potent science and technology—as 'cryonics'—the artificially induced hibernation 'until such time when the medicine for the now terminal disease will have been found')" [Zygmunt Bauman, *Mortality, Immortality and Other Life Strategies* (Stanford, CA: Stanford University Press, 1992), p. 26].

REFERENCES

Aquinas, Thomas. 1952. *The Summa Theologica*, vol. II (vol. 20 of *The Great Books of the Western World*). Rev. trans. Daniel J. Sullivan. Chicago: Encyclopedia Britannica, Inc.

Bacon, Francis. 1638. *The Historie of Life and Death, with Observations Naturall and Experimentall for the Prolonging of LIFE*. Amsterdam & New York: Theatrum Orbis Terrarum Ltd. and Da Capo Press, 1968.

Baxter, Richard. 1974. *The Autobiography of Richard Baxter*, abridged by J. M. Lloyd Thomas. London: J. M. Dent and Sons, Ltd.

Buckle, Stephen. 1991. *Natural Law and the Theory of Property: Grotius to Hume*. Clarendon: Oxford University Press.

Calvin, John (Jean). 1845. *Institutes of the Christian Religion*, 3 vols. Trans. Henry Beveridge. Edinburgh: Edinburgh Printing Company.

Coleman, William. 1974. "Health and Hygiene in the *Encyclopedia*: A Medical Doctrine for the Bourgeoisie." *Journal of the History of Medicine*. October 1974: 399–421.

Crocker, Lester G. 1952. "The Discussion of Suicide in the Eighteenth Century."

The Journal of the History of Ideas, 1952, 13, 47–72.

Foucault, Michel. 1973a. *The Birth of the Clinic: An Archaeology of Medical Perception.* Trans. A.M. Sheridan Smith. New York: Pantheon Books.

———. 1980. *The History of Sexuality: Volume 1: An Introduction.* Trans. Robert Hurley. NY: Vintage Books.

Grotius, Hugo. 1901. *The Rights of War and Peace.* Washington, DC: M. Walter Dunne, Publisher.

———. 1988. *Meletius, sive, De iis quae inter Christianos conveniunt epistola.* New York: Brill.

Kant, Immanuel. 1963. *Lectures on Ethics.* Trans. Louis Infield. New York: Harper & Row.

Locke, John. 1899. *Some Thoughts Concerning Education.* Ed. R.H. Quick. Cambridge: Cambridge University Press.

———. 1960. *Two Treatises of Government.* Ed. Peter Laslett. Cambridge: Cambridge University Press.

Plato. 1973. *The Republic and Other Works.* Trans. B. Jowett. New York: Doubleday.

Porter, Roy. 1985a. "Lay Medical Knowledge in the Eighteenth Century: The Evidence of the Gentleman's Magazine." *Medical History* 29: 138–68.

———. 1985b. "Laymen, Doctors and Medical Knowledge in the Eighteenth Century: The Evidence of the Gentleman's Magazine." Roy Porter, ed. *Patients and Practitioners: Lay Perceptions of Medicine in Pre-industrial Society.* Cambridge: Cambridge University Press. 283–314.

Slack, Paul. 1979. "Mirrors of Health and Treasures of Poor Men: The Uses of the Vernacular Medical Literature of Tudor England." Charles Webster, ed. *Health, Medicine and Mortality in the Sixteenth Century.* Cambridge: Cambridge University Press. 237–73.

Smith, Ginnie. 1979. "Prescribing the Rules of Health: Self-help and Advice in the Late Eighteenth Century." Roy Porter, ed. *Patients and Practitioners: Lay Perceptions of Medicine in Pre-industrial Society.* Cambridge: Cambridge University Press. 249–82.

Tully, James. 1980. *A Discourse on Property: John Locke and His Adversaries.* Cambridge: Cambridge University Press.

Tully, James. 1993. *An Approach to Political Philosophy: Locke in Contexts.* Cambridge: Cambridge University Press.

Wear, Andrew. 1985. "Puritan perceptions of illness in seventeenth century England." Roy Porter, ed. *Patients and Practitioners: Lay perceptions of medicine in pre-industrial society.* Cambridge: Cambridge University Press. 55–99.

Webster, Charles. 1975. *The Great Instauration: Science, Medicine and Reform 1626–1660.* London: Duckworth.

CONTRIBUTORS

Thomas J. Csordas is Professor of Anthropology at Case Western Reserve University. He is a co-editor of the journal *Ethos*, and President of the Anthropology of Religion Section of the American Anthropological Association. His publications include: *The Sacred Self: A Cultural Phenomenology of Charismatic Healing* (1994); *Language, Charisma, and Creativity: The Ritual Life of a Religious Movement* (1997); and the edited volume *Embodiment and Experience: The Existential Ground of Culture and Self* (1994).

Hubert L. Dreyfus is currently Professor of Philosophy in the Graduate School at the University of California, Berkeley. His publications include: (with Stuart Dreyfus) *Mind Over Machine: The Power of Human Intuition and Expertise in the Era of the Computer* (1986); *Being-in-The-World: A Commentary on Heidegger's Being & Time Division I* (1991); *Husserl, Intentionality, and Cognitive Science* (1982); and *What Computers Still Can't Do: A Critique of Artificial Reason* (1992).

Stuart E. Dreyfus is Professor Emeritus of Industrial Engineering and Operations Research at the University of California, Berkeley. His publications include: (with Hubert Dreyfus) *Mind Over Machine: The Power of Human Intuition and Expertise in the Era of the Computer* (1986), and *Dynamic Programming and The Calculus of Variations* (1965).

Tracy Fessenden holds degrees from Yale University and The University of Virginia, and currently teaches in the departments of Religious Studies, Women's Studies, and Humanities at Arizona State University. She has published articles in the fields of Theology, Cultural Studies, and American Literature and is now completing a book on secularization, race, and gender in the American novel.

Honi Fern Haber was Associate Professor of Philosophy at the University of Colorado, Denver. She is the author of several articles as well as *Beyond Postmodern Politics: Lyotard, Rorty, Foucault* (Routledge, 1994). Her final research centered on the notion of subversive bodies, that is, bodies that refused normalization in a Foucaultian sense. She was especially interested in examining body building for women as a strategy of political empowerment and she intended to write a feminist analysis of her own struggle with the disfigurement created by the aggressive treatment of cancer.

David Couzens Hoy is Professor and Chair of the Department of Philosophy at the University of California, Santa Cruz, where he also teaches in the History of Consciousness graduate program. Dr. Hoy has also taught at Yale, Princeton, University of California, Los Angeles, Barnard, Columbia, and Berkeley. In addition to more than fifty essays, he has authored *The Critical Circle* (1982), and (with Thomas McCarthy) *Critical Theory* (1994); edited *Foucault: A Critical Reader* (1988); and is currently completing a book entitled *Critical Resistance*.

Martin Jay is Sidney Hellman Ehrman Professor and Chair of the History Department at the University of California, Berkeley. Among his books are *The Dialectical Imagination* (1973 and 1996), *Adorno* (1984), *Marxism and Totality* (1984), *Permanent Exiles* (1985), *Fin-de-Siècle Socialism* (1989), *Force Fields* (1993), *Downcast Eyes* (1993), and *Cultural Semantics* (1998). He is currently writing a history of the discourse of experience in European and American thought.

Mark L. Johnson is Professor and Chair of the Department of Philosophy at the University of Oregon. He is the author of *The Body in The Mind* (1990), and *Moral Imagination* (1994), and co-author (with George Lakoff) of *Metaphors We Live By* (1983), and the forthcoming *Philosophy in The Flesh*.

Sean P. O'Connell is Associate Professor of Philosophy at Albertus Magnus College in New Haven, Connecticut. He has published essays in Contemporary Continental Philosophy and Queer Theory and is currently completing a book entitled *Outspeak: The Pleasures, Perils, and Promises of Speaking Sexual Identity*.

Kevin O'Neill is Professor of Philosophy at the University of Redlands in California. He is a founding member of the Johnston Center for Individualized Learning and has co-authored a book on that program and its relation to the history of experimental education. Dr. O'Neill is currently working on a book on the history of the dead.

John T. Sanders is Professor of Philosophy at the Rochester Institute of Technology. His work on topics related to metaphysical and epistemological issues has appeared in *The Monist, Man and World, Ecological Psychology*, and other journals. He is co-editor of *Debating the State of Philosophy: Habermas, Rorty, and Kolakowski* (1996).

Charles Shepherdson is a Member in the School of Social Science at the Institute for Advanced Study in Princeton. He teaches in the Graduate Institute of the Liberal Arts at Emory University, and is on the faculty of the Psychoanalytic Studies Program. He is the author of *Vital Signs* (Routledge, forthcoming), *The Epoch of The Body* (forthcoming), and is currently working on *Insinuations: Encounters Between Philosophy and Psychoanalysis*.

Thomas F. Tierney is an Associate Professor of Philosophy and Political Science at Concord College in Athens, West Virginia. He is the author of *The Value of Convenience: A Genealogy of Technical Culture* (1993), and is currently completing a study of the relation between death and medicine in modernity.

Gail Weiss is Associate Professor of Philosophy and the Graduate Program in the Human Sciences at The George Washington University. She is the author of *Body Images: Embodiment as Intercorporeality* (Routledge, 1999), co-editor of *Philosophies of Race and Gender* (forthcoming), and is currently working on a book entitled *Indeterminate Horizons: Figuring the Ground and Grounding the Figure*.

INDEX